Our Hearts Are Restless Till They Find Their Rest in Thee

Our Hearts Are Restless Till They Find Their Rest in Thee

Prophetic Wisdom in a Time of Anguish

Selected Writings and Sermons

COLEMAN B. BROWN

Edited by MICHAEL GRANZEN
and LISA A. MASOTTA

With Reflections from
Peter Ochs,
Chris Hedges,
and Joshua Brown

CASCADE *Books* • Eugene, Oregon

OUR HEARTS ARE RESTLESS TILL THEY FIND THEIR REST IN THEE
Prophetic Wisdom in a Time of Anguish
Selected Writings and Sermons

Copyright © 2020 Irene Brown. All rights reserved. Except for brief quotations in critical publications or reviews, no part of this book may be reproduced in any manner without prior written permission from the publisher. Write: Permissions, Wipf and Stock Publishers, 199 W. 8th Ave., Suite 3, Eugene, OR 97401.

Cascade Books
An Imprint of Wipf and Stock Publishers
199 W. 8th Ave., Suite 3
Eugene, OR 97401

www.wipfandstock.com

PAPERBACK ISBN: 978-1-5326-8516-3
HARDCOVER ISBN: 978-1-5326-8517-0
EBOOK ISBN: 978-1-5326-8518-7

Cataloguing-in-Publication data:

Names: Brown, Coleman B., author. | Granzen, Michael, editor. | Masotta, Lisa A., editor. | Ochs, Peter, 1950–, foreword. | Hedges, Chris, reflection. | Brown, Joshua, reflection.

Title: Our hearts are restless till they find their rest in thee : prophetic wisdom in a time of anguish ; selected writings and sermons / Coleman B. Brown ; edited by Michael Granzen and Lisa A. Masotta ; foreword by Peter Ochs ; reflections by Chris Hedges and Joshua Brown.

Description: Eugene, OR : Cascade Books, 2020 | Includes bibliographical references.

Identifiers: ISBN 978-1-5326-8516-3 (paperback) | ISBN 978-1-5326-8517-0 (hardcover) | ISBN 978-1-5326-8518-7 (ebook)

Subjects: LCSH: Presbyterian Church—Sermons. | Sermons, American.

Classification: BX9178.B74 B74 2020 (print) | BX9178.B74 B74 (ebook)

Manufactured in the U.S.A.   MAY 14, 2020

Scripture quotations are from Revised Standard Version of the Bible, copyright © 1946, 1952, and 1971 National Council of the Churches of Christ in the United States of America. Used by permission. All rights reserved worldwide.

Excerpts from pp. 66–68 of *Telling the Truth* by Frederick Buechner. Copyright © 1977 by Frederick Buechner. Used by permission of HarperCollins Publishers.

"Provide, Provide" by Robert Frost from the book THE POETRY OF ROBERT FROST edited by Edward Connery Lathem. Copyright © 1969 by Henry Holt and Company. Copyright © 1936 by Robert Frost, copyright © 1964 by Lesley Frost Ballantine. Reprinted by permission of Henry Holt and Company. All rights reserved.

Excerpts from *A Knock at Midnight* by Martin Luther King, Jr. reprinted by arrangement with The Heirs to the Estate of Martin Luther King Jr., c/o Writers House as agent for the proprietor New York, NY. Copyright: © 1963 Dr. Martin Luther King, Jr. © renewed 1991 Coretta Scott King.

Excerpt(s) from A RUMOR OF ANGELS: MODERN SOCIETY AND THE REDISCOVERY OF THE SUPERNATURAL by Peter L. Berger, copyright © 1969 by Peter L. Berger. Used by permission of Doubleday, an imprint of the Knopf Doubleday Publishing Group, a division of Penguin Random House LLC. All rights reserved.

Excerpt from "The Rum Tum Tugger" from OLD POSSUM'S BOOK OF PRACTICAL CATS by T.S. Eliot. Copyright © 1939 by T.S. Eliot, renewed 1967 by Esme Valerie Eliot. Reprinted by permission of Houghton Mifflin Harcourt Publishing Company. All rights reserved.

Dedicated to
Irene, Justin, Susan, Bradford, and Joshua

Contents

Foreword | ix
   —Peter Ochs
Introduction and Acknowledgments | xv
   —Michael Granzen and Lisa A. Masotta

1 Our Fear of Rejection, and a Yet Deeper Fear | 1
2 "Our Hearts Are Restless until They Find Their Rest in Thee" | 8
3 "Come to Me, All You Who Are Heavy Laden" | 15
4 For the Joy | 23
5 "All Things Are Yours" | 29
6 Begin Now to Live Your Real Life | 37
7 Both Tears and Mirth | 43
8 Hope | 49
9 You Have a Vocation | 55
10 The Last Enemy Is Death | 63
11 On Courage | 72
12 Who Then Is This? | 78
13 "I Am with You All the Days" | 84
14 Some Questions | 91
15 Our Anger | 97
16 You Can't Keep God Dead in Your Life | 103

17	Homecoming and Our True Home	111
18	Zacchaeus	119
19	A Spirit Which Affects Us for Ill—and Our Empty House	127
20	God Believes in You	133
21	"Weeping May Tarry for the Night, but Joy Comes with the Morning"	139
22	"I Desire Mercy..."	147
23	Strong at the Broken Places	154
24	He Looks Around on All That Can Be Seen	162
25	None of Us Have It Together and We Are the Salt of the Earth	170
26	An Ordination Sermon	179
27	Words of Welcome Offered at a Wedding Service	187
28	Coleman Brown on Student Development: The Importance of Humility, Mystery, and a Sense of Reverence	189
29	Prayer of Confession for the Colgate University Church	192
30	Blessing	193

My Teacher | 194
  —Chris Hedges

Remembering My Dad, Coleman Brown | 199
  —Joshua Brown

Bibliography | 207

"Each morning that I enter my office as Provost and Dean of the Faculty at Colgate University, I am greeted by a photo of my teacher, Coleman Brown, standing in front of a chalkboard illustrating the words, 'Audacity and Humility. How to hold them together?' With these words and his image, Coleman Brown lives in my daily life reminding me of the wisdom he embodied; the compassion he demonstrated; and the integrity that defined his true life and character. Coleman Brown's spirit endures through his writings and sermons and his words impart lessons to us always from a true intellectual and moral Ancestor."

—TRACEY E. HUCKS
Provost and Dean of the Faculty, Colgate University

"This perceptive book contains sermons and other writings by the late Coleman Brown that reveal his exemplary spirit, rhetorical wisdom, and extraordinary skills as a memorable teacher and mentor. Readers will discover here three of Coleman's former students along with his son and a colleague offering testimonies that they graciously pass on to others with the hope that they will discern and embrace many new insights pertaining to our common life."

—PETER J. PARIS
Princeton Theological Seminary

"Coleman Brown's thought and presence are incisive and restless, drilling down for signs of divine justice and the way to unmerited reconciliation. Be careful! His meditations are likely to lead you into a restless, ceaseless search for what is true and just, until you finally rest in the audacious humility of the fulfillment of God's love."

—JEFF MCARN
Hamilton College

"These sermons and writings summon the man—his humanity, his deep humility, his fierce yet gentle witness—no less than his wisdom into the inescapable struggles and possibilities of life. They make clear why I—and I dare say why so many others who heard his sermons or studied with him, believers and nonbelievers alike—will say without embarrassment or exaggeration, 'Coleman Brown saved my life.'"

—RALPH HAMILTON
Author of *Teaching a Man to Unstick His Tail*

Foreword

God Is Not Known if God Is Not Feared: Midrash (Homily) on Coleman's Homilies

PETER OCHS

1. He did not fear entering our stories. (On "Who Then Is This?")

"And Jonah went to the bottom of the boat and fell asleep" (Jonah 1:5).

REVEREND COLEMAN BROWN MUST have feared the storm just as much as the rest of us do; otherwise he would not understand us so well: the storm that brews within our souls as too many societal storms brew around us. But we did not see him fear entering the storm with us. He did not fear entering our stories, nor the story of our stories. In the sermon "Who Then Is This?" he preached, "We are each living a story" and "we are in other peoples' stories—and they are in ours":

> On that day, when evening had come, he said to them, "Let us go across to the other side." And leaving the crowd, they took him with them in the boat, just as he was. And other boats were with him. And a great storm of wind arose, and the waves beat into the boat, so that the boat was already filling. But he was in the stern, asleep on the cushion . . . (Mark 4:35–38a)

Coleman preached,

> Water is ultimately the image of new life. But first it is the image of chaos.... The boat is filling, heavy—even like our souls—heavy with water. It's not going to make it, our boat isn't.... We're going to go under—overwhelmed by the storm, the storm of cultural forces, overwhelming ideas, friendships that have failed, our family's disintegration, personal suffering; overwhelmed by the heavy waters of lost motivation, we can't bail out our little boat fast enough. We're trying. But we're being overwhelmed.

Then, "Evening has come to our civilization in important ways." We have left the previous time—the evening, it appears, of a Western socioeconomic order. Our personal evenings may echo the societal evening. But the next time is not yet come. Coleman was not afraid to inhabit with us this time between the times, a time, says the Talmud, that is neither day nor night: a dangerous time when we are tempted to turn to imagined panaceas that may seem to relieve us more quickly of the uncertainty of living in neither a troubled past nor the hoped-for future. We are both anxious to cross over into that future and fearful of what we may lose in the crossing. Coleman preached, "But when evening had come, [Jesus] said, 'Let us go across—to the other side.'" "They took him with them, just as he was." Coleman asks, But will we, in this day between the days, have the wisdom to take him with us?

Jonah rested, too, in the in-between. But he did not want to go to the other side. If the boat did not hold, he would rather go to the bottom of the sea. I imagine that Coleman preached to him, too, the words of Mark's Jesus: "Peace! Be still! Why are you afraid? Have you no faith?" If you would give up your story, then why not "give [yourself] up, open [yourself], to the story beyond our power to write, beyond our power to make happen, or to be"? "That is the question from the story that lays claim to your story, and mine, this morning and in the evening."

I first met Coleman when I arrived, young, to take up the job of counselor to Colgate's Jewish students and half-time professor in the department of philosophy and religion. I was trained to be a teacher, and I knew how to lead services, but I was not prepared to meet the spiritual and personal needs of students as chaplain. I was ready to hide in the bottom of the boat. Coleman saw and heard me, and I gradually realized that he was coming alongside me into what felt like my own evening of uncertainty between what I was and what I might need to become. He stood by and also asked questions that opened new futures for me. I recall a line of questioning that went something like this: "Do you think you have to challenge individual students, directly, to eliminate their demons? Do you feel they—and you—are ready to face what else may lurk behind those demons? To serve others, must you rely on your own vision and voice, alone?" I soon began to attend his sermons, to stay closer to his words. In his words, I also heard a voice other than his own. Like members of his student congregation, I felt as if his sermons were written for me. I, too, was a student, and my story, it seemed, was not just my own, but part of a story beyond my power to write. But where was I headed?

2. But he respected our fears.
(On "Our Fear of Rejection, and a Yet Deeper Fear")

> *And Isaac trembled very exceedingly* (Gen 27:33). Scripture states elsewhere in allusion to this verse: *One who trembles in fear before a human gets caught in a trap, but one who trusts in the Lord is raised high (Prov 29:25).*[1]

In the Genesis narrative, Jacob wraps his arm in animal fur so that his blind father would think "this is the arm of Esau" and bless him. Isaac trembles with fear when he realizes he was deceived. A rabbinic homily, or midrash, asks why Isaac would bless Jacob despite the deception.

> Because of the fear that Jacob brought upon Isaac, it would have been fitting for him to have cursed him. What compelled him to bless Jacob? *One who trusts in the Lord is raised high.*[2]

The midrash likens Isaac's fear to the trap of fearing humans rather than trusting God alone; it likens Isaac's blessing to trusting in the Lord in the face of fear.

Concluding his homily by blessing us in the name of faith in (and fear of) God, Coleman begins by standing with us in our fear of other humans: "I suppose if there is any fear—which each of us knows very deeply and intimately; . . . which each of us tries to hide from . . . it is this: We fear, each of us, that we shall be rejected. We fear rejection." And we do so with reason: to be rejected is potentially to have "the very shape and direction of our personalities . . . called into question." More than that, "we fear something else as much, or more. . . . We not only fear rejection. *We fear that we may not be able to take it.*" This, the preacher suggests, may be one of our deepest fears of all: fear that, ultimately, we may not stand.

1. *Midrash Tanchuma*, Toldot 13:1.
2. *Midrash Tanchuma*, Toldot 13:1.

There were many reasons why, as a member of Coleman's chaplains' staff, I increasingly opened my ears to his words and sought his counsel. Perhaps the greatest reason was the way his words integrated truth-telling and care. His voice and his counsel communicated ever-attentive care and an unfettered witness to what is really there, before us. His care was itself about the truth: acknowledging the fact of whatever fear or complaint we might have, the fact of this dimension of human experience as we report it, bearing witness to what we tend to win or suffer from such an experience, and witness to what Scripture reveals about the force and significance of God's presence with us in such an experience. The lesson is summarized at this point in his homily: that, however much we may seek to cover over our fear of rejection, that fear may veil the far greater fear that we cannot take it. And his caring reply? It is that we should gaze all the more attentively at what may lie on the other side of this fear of stark incapacity.

Here, Coleman's homily addresses our civilization once again: asking how we might have been socialized to rely on ourselves, alone, when facing that which makes us tremble most deeply inside. Is it that, for "the natural American man or woman . . . self-reliance is still our deepest *hope* . . . 'to get it all together' *by my own powers and on my own*"? Remembering what Coleman asked me about my own belief in self-reliance, I believe his homily first asks if our fear of rejection veils a deeper fear of failing to be self-reliant and then asks why we presume we are supposed to be self-reliant. But if we are not supposed to be, then how do we overcome the presumption? "*But one who trusts in the Lord is raised high.*"[3] It is in the face of our deepest fears that we are most not-alone. But, to acknowledge *that* God is there is not yet to know and trust God. Coleman cites the psalmist's words that are gospel: "*God, my God, why hast thou forsaken me?*"

3. And he walked us over toward the other side, to fear the Lord God. (On "Our Hearts Are Restless until They Find Their Rest in Thee")

A Jewish morning prayer: "The beginning of wisdom is the reverence/fear of the Lord." A Talmudic commentary: Everything is in the hands of Heaven, except for the fear of Heaven.[4]

Facing the worst human fear, we cry, "O Lord, why have you forsaken us?" Standing with us in the depth of our fear, Coleman readied us to walk

---

3. Proverbs 29:25.
4. *TB Berachot* 33a.

over to the other side, of which Mark's Jesus said, "Let us go across to the other side." That is why, in my Colgate years, I thought of him as Colgate's Protestant rebbe. Like the great eighteenth-century Rabbi Moshe Luzzatto, Coleman was teaching us to recognize two different kinds of fear. In R. Luzzatto's words,

> There are two types of fear (*yirah*). The first . . . is very easy to attain, the second is the most difficult. . . . The first is the fear of punishment (*yirat ha'onesh*), and the second is fear of Divine Majesty (*yirat ha'romemut*). . . . Fear of punishment . . . [is fear] of violating God's commands because of the punishment to body or soul which is meted out for transgressions. . . . Fear of Divine Majesty [is] withdrawing from sin because of the great honor of the Blessed One.[5]

To mark the difference, we may refer to the first as *fear*, the second as *reverence*. In these terms, Coleman enabled us to own the first fear and walk it over to the second. By owning the first, we would remain true to our actual experience and avoid the temptation of trying to maintain our trust in self-reliance by concealing the first. By walking it over, we would bring our actual flesh-and-blood emotions and dispositions over to love of God and avoid the temptation of trying to conceal our humanity by spiritualizing that love. In this way, our walk would affirm truth over deception as well as affirming reverence alongside fear: "alongside" because, relinquishing deception, we would remain true to our humanity with its attendant fears. For us, the walk is not once and for all but daily, *semper reformanda*.

In "Our Hearts Are Restless . . . ," Coleman cited Luke: "In that region there were shepherds out in the field, keeping watch over their flock by night. And an angel of the Lord appeared to them, and the glory of the Lord shone around them, and they were filled with fear. And the angel said to them, 'Be not afraid; for behold, I bring you good news'" (2:8–10a).

In the voice of Augustine, Coleman preached, "Our hearts are restless. These are restless days at Colgate . . . restless days in the world." Restless, we might say, because we have learned that there is more than fear, but we have not yet found a way to walk to the other side. Therefore, "if we could be near God it would be all right." But how? We find ourselves in fear. Fear, Coleman preaches, is the first step! That is the beginning of the good news: "So often healing and new life begin with a kind of fear." Fear is the beginning of fear of God, reverence: "God is not known if God is not feared." Coleman cites Rudolf Bultmann (it also sounds like John Dewey!): "He who

---

5. *Messilat Yesharim* 24.

abandons every form of security shall find the true security." But there is nothing automatic here; walking to the other side remains perilous: "There is danger if we are not warned . . . that this night our souls may be required of us." The details shall come in due time, in God's time. For now, Coleman invites us to recognize this small step as a gift from God to whom we turn: "When you have discovered the side of the good news which is that, in a vital sense, there are no saviors after all; when you have discovered that the other saviors do not save . . . *then* we shall begin to learn *how* to seek, and *how* to live—and *how* to die—and *how* to be near God. Until then let us pray, 'Our hearts are restless until they find their rest in thee.'"

> Not to us, Lord, not to us
> but to your name be the glory,
> because of your love and faithfulness. (Psalm 115)

Introduction and Acknowledgments

Michael Granzen and Lisa A. Masotta

It is an honor to introduce to a new generation of "believers, seekers and doubters" the sermons and writings of the Reverend Dr. Coleman B. Brown (1934–2014), with accompanying reflections by Peter Ochs, Chris Hedges, and Joshua Brown.

Except for Joshua all of us met Coleman at Colgate University, where he served as Professor of Philosophy and Religion and University Chaplain in various capacities from 1974 to 1999. Peter was a fellow faculty member in the Department of Philosophy and Religion; the rest of us were undergraduate students in Coleman's classes and sojourner-seekers in the University Church.

The impact of Coleman's teaching and ministry on our lives is perhaps impossible to capture directly, to the extent that, if some set of circumstances divine and human directed each of us to Colgate, it might well have been so that we might meet and learn from this most extraordinary man.

Why these writings now? In an age of profound historical anguish and transition, Coleman's words are living Christian midrash that stir up hope—but not on a surface level. You must dive deep, and then surface. As Anne Lamott tweeted, "I've heard that if it's your will, it gets easier at first, and then harder. If it's God's will, it gets harder at first, and then easier." So too, Coleman's word is demanding hope for this hour.

At the Fourth Presbyterian Church in South Boston, its walls still pocked with bullet holes, he declared,

> Whether we're pastors or church agency people, homemakers or homeless, steamfitters or unemployed, lawyers or computer programmers, students or teachers makes no difference; no difference whether we're women or men; lesbian, gay, or straight; married or single. The life of each one of us could be a novel—or a TV soap opera—if the story were disclosed and told right. The sins and sufferings of those of us gathered here right now... are enough to break the heart of God.
>
> And God's heart is broken—and God assures us that where sin and, yes, death abound, there life and grace, yes, and love the *more* abound.
>
> Our sins and our sorrows and the power of death are where either we break into despair or we break into Christ's new life. Our sins and our sorrows are where all our great gifts are hidden—above all, the gift of our compassion, the gift of our love. ("Ordination Sermon")

Coleman's word invites us to join the human conversation of flawed, wounded people searching for fragments of community and meaning in a time of uncertainty. At Colgate gatherings like "Skeptics and Others Seeking," Coleman offered a living faith refined in the fire of doubt, an affirmation beyond certainties. He would invite us to name our central questions and, in so doing, discover that we are not alone. Some identifying more with one—seeking, believing, or doubting—but in some measure acknowledging all three in each one of us, we would enter the conversation. Why is there evil? Who is God? How are the two connected, if at all? Where was Jesus when my father died? Religious or not, worthy and unworthy, sufferers and sinners, Coleman helped us unpack our existential questions, our real questions, which in dialogue with others could, strangely, bring clarity to our confusion. For those who have ears to hear—believers, seekers, and doubters—his invitation still resonates.

As Coleman wrote,

> In chapel, prayer may come last. But in the classroom, the world (and, often, in chapel too), *questions* contain strange benedictions. Certain questions—if we really live with them—can bring us to life. Kant's four great ones we do well to remember: *How can I know? For what can I hope? What ought I to do? What is it to be human?* Do we recognize the answers we are giving—to these next two?
>
> "*To whom or what am I responsible and in what community of interaction am I myself?*" (H. Richard Niebuhr). And always

this question, from the third chapter of Genesis, addressed to me, I know, and, I believe, to us all: *"Where are you?"*[1]

Coleman's word is a bright light in a time of profound anguish and restlessness. As he declared, "Evening has come to our civilization in important ways. The end of many of the ways of our civilization is a great blessing; the passing of its day, a relief. But it is not all blessing and relief" ("Who Then Is This?").

One recent night in Elizabeth, New Jersey, several Black and Latinx teenagers from a church youth group were viciously assaulted by the police. When their pastor (Michael) saw their bloodied faces, he wanted to go on his own to the police station and rage against the thick plate glass window. Instead he listened to the hard word of Coleman, challenging him "to be angry; but sin not." Moreover suffer, turn, and give up the anger to God . . .

> [For] anger, when transformed by the Spirit of God, turns compassion [and rage] from . . . mere feelings . . . into action. God will, in short, take [your] anger and give it back to [you] as courage. So *be* angry: *be* angry . . . but sin not. That is, do not let your anger separate you from any other, or from yourself, or God. For God's Spirit can transform [our] anger . . . into courage: courage in the service of love . . . so that we can begin to live freely and decisively [in the service of justice]; the victory over fear beginning to be accomplished . . . God's life by the Spirit of Christ— beginning to be the life we actually *live* . . . ("Our Anger")

Little by little the journey is made, out of isolating rage and into the more transforming relationships, even covenantal relationships, with other flawed human beings. It continues, unfinished, incomplete, fragmented, but moving forward nevertheless in the pursuit of actual justice. Discovering the deep truth that Coleman embodied and taught, you cannot do it alone— for "the dwelling of God is with people."[2]

As the demons of white racism and moral nihilism lift their ugly heads anew, Coleman's words direct us to rediscover the radical truth-love of Martin Luther King Jr.: "I can never be what I ought to be until you are what you ought to be. And you cannot be what you ought to be until I am what I ought to be."[3] They call us to the humility and courage of real relationship, reflection, prayer, action, forgiveness, and perseverance against greed, cruelty, hate, and self-hate, which still rage in our nation. They call us to

---

1. Brown, "Colgate Continuum," paras. 20–21.
2. Revelation 21:3a.
3. King, "Remaining Awake through a Great Revolution," para. 11.

harness and engage our anger to God in the service of common justice and uncommon Beloved Community.

"Morning by morning You awaken—awaken my ear to listen as those who are taught," says the prophet (Isa 50:4). Coleman's spoken word was rooted in deep listening. Sitting with him in his office surrounded by books, you could almost hear him listening. Then, out of the depths in him to the depths in you, he would speak. And, as you received his word with openness, you were changed. Coleman was a man of prophetic faith; amidst despair, he delivered many from dread and sickness unto death, including the both of us. He believed in us when we could not believe in ourselves. And his light was trembling truth and grace. Most of all grace.

If this preacher-teacher is so excellent, some may ask, how come I have never heard of him? Perhaps you did meet him, after all, indirectly—through the mentorship of Peter Ochs, or Chris Hedges's writing and teaching; perhaps in a classroom, religious sanctuary, or street ministry with one of his students leading. And sometimes one's significance is magnified only after one's life is ended. Never preoccupied with self-promotion, Coleman (along with other notable colleagues in the Department of Philosophy and Religion) practiced a kind of Socratic education that is rare in most universities in the United States today.

As Chris notes so vividly, and the sermons illustrate, Coleman read widely—not only in theology, philosophy, and ethics but also literature, history, and depth psychology. And he listened to music. Coleman could quote as readily from Ludwig Wittgenstein and Martin Luther King Jr. as Leonard Bernstein. He published no books in his lifetime, yet his sermons (including the one that gives this book its title) won accolades, and he remained a sought-after speaker long after retirement. As his former students, we read copies of essays he corrected, letters he wrote—and his powerful sermons. So we convey to you words that continue to challenge us daily.

The book you have before you grew out of an earlier project, designed by Lisa, to self-publish a selection of Coleman's writings. Coleman guided that initial endeavor along with his wife, Irene, in response to various individuals over the years offering their strong encouragement. "Especially compelling," Coleman wrote in 2003 in his Preface, were "those students who, independently of one another, have told me they keep their own collection of some of the sermons (which were [reproduced] individually shortly after being preached); and who have then gone on to tell me that these copies have become frayed over the years from frequent re-reading."[4]

---

4. Brown, *Our Hearts Are Restless*, iii.

Introduction and Acknowledgments xix

The sermons are arranged chronologically, as Coleman originally desired, so readers can more easily trace themes developed over time. And because they are dense and demanding, know that reading just one sermon at a time may be the better way to digest them.[5]

Coleman wrote that in preparing sermons he always had in mind "a mythical, but to me very real person, the person attending the worship service of the University Church for the first time (and maybe the last), a person not even necessarily clear why she or he was there." He also sought, as Helmut Thielicke advised preachers to do, "to keep in mind those persons who probably would never be there at all"[6] on a Sunday morning.

Coleman saw decisive significance in each moment, each person, every encounter. Time and again, as the postlude to worship sounded and before the coffee hour began, he would spring forth from behind the lectern and sprint across the platform where the worship service took place to shake hands with and greet by name any visitors to the University Church attempting to slip out the back unnoticed.

Following his example, we want to recognize and thank some of the many people who helped make this book possible. We offer our appreciation to Peter Ochs for contributing his powerful midrash on Coleman's homilies. Peter extends and expands an interfaith conversation that began more than three decades ago during his tenure at Colgate. His counsel in the development of this volume has been a blessing.

We extend special love and gratitude to Irene Brown for giving her support to this project, as well as her invaluable assistance to Lisa in verifying citations and fact-checking details about Coleman's life and work. Heartfelt thanks to Joshua Brown for contributing, with input from his siblings Justin, Susan, and Bradford, his beautiful essay on his father, as well as his helpful input to the overall book project. The Browns graciously welcomed Colgate students into their home for church-related meetings and class gatherings, and to offer support and guidance for many campus organizations. Joshua and his siblings participated in most of those gatherings. Now a professional staff writer at the University of Vermont, Joshua is uniquely qualified to present Coleman's life and work to those encountering him for the first time.

We thank our friend, the Pulitzer Prize–winning author, teacher, activist, and Presbyterian minister Chris Hedges, for contributing his reflection, "My Teacher." Chris speaks for many students who, like us, were transformed by our encounters with Coleman. He was not only a man of tremendous intelligence and compassion: Coleman was a man of holy fire.

5. Brown, *Our Hearts Are Restless*, iv.
6. Brown, *Our Hearts Are Restless*, iv.

We thank Karen Hernandez-Granzen, Mikaella Granzen, and Olivia Granzen for their love and encouragement. Our gratitude goes to Shawn J. Smith and Christian G. Gregory for their friendship and generous assistance in helping finalize the manuscript. We also thank our editors at Cascade, senior editor Charlie Collier and copy editor Jacob Martin, for their practical wisdom in preparing this book, and Amelia Pang for her skillful help with copyright permissions.

Coleman concluded his last class of "Religion in America" by reading aloud the W. H. Auden poem "September 1, 1939." It ends with prayer:

> Defenseless under the night
> Our world in stupor lies;
> Yet, dotted everywhere,
> Ironic points of light
> Flash out wherever the Just
> Exchange their messages:
> May I, composed like them
> Of Eros and of dust,
> Beleaguered by the same
> Negation and despair,
> Show an affirming flame.[7]

The sermons are a cry from the depths, a prophetic witness to the paradoxical Light of Jesus, the humanity of God. In the words of the old African-American spiritual, they too sing, "This little Light of mine, I'm gonna let it shine, let it shine, let it shine!"

Let it shine!

Michael Granzen, PhD, Princeton, New Jersey
Lisa A. Masotta, MDiv, Providence, Rhode Island
March 2020

---

7. Auden, "September 1, 1939," quoted in Brown, "Colgate Continuum," para. 19.

1

Our Fear of Rejection, and a Yet Deeper Fear

First Sermon as University Chaplain

ORIGINALLY PREACHED SEPTEMBER 8, 1974[1]

And they compelled a passer-by, Simon of Cyrene, who was coming in from the country, the father of Alexander and Rufus, to carry his cross. And they brought him to the place called Golgotha (which means the place of a skull). And they offered him wine mingled with myrrh; but he did not take it. And they crucified him, and divided his garments among them, casting lots for them, to decide what each should take. And it was the third hour, when they crucified him. And the inscription of the charge against him read, "The King of the Jews." And with him they crucified two robbers, one on his right and one on his left. And those who passed by derided him, wagging their heads, and saying, "Aha! You who would destroy the temple and build it in three days, save yourself, and come down from the cross!" So also the chief priests mocked him to one another with the scribes, saying, "He saved others; he cannot save himself. Let the Christ, the King of Israel, come down now from the cross, that we may see and believe." Those who were crucified with him also reviled him.

And when the sixth hour had come, there was darkness over the whole land until the ninth hour. And at the ninth hour Jesus

---

[1]. Also preached October 14, 1979. Extended excerpts were published in a "Special Holiday Issue" of the student newspaper *Colgate Maroon*, December 6, 1977.

> *cried with a loud voice, "E'loi, E'loi, la'ma sabach-tha'ni?" which means, "My God, my God, why hast thou forsaken me?" And some of the bystanders hearing it said, "Behold, he is calling Elijah." And one ran and, filling a sponge full of vinegar, put it on a reed and gave it to him to drink, saying, "Wait, let us see whether Elijah will come to take him down." And Jesus uttered a loud cry, and breathed his last. And the curtain of the temple was torn in two, from top to bottom. And when the centurion, who stood facing him, saw that he thus breathed his last, he said, "Truly this man was a son of God!"*
>
> —Mark 15:21-39 (RSV)
> See also Psalm 35:1a, 3b–5a, 6a, 7–9, 11–12, 19, 21a, 22–23

I SUPPOSE IF THERE is any fear that each of us knows very deeply and intimately; that each of us spends a great deal of time, consciously or unconsciously, trying to do something about; that each of us tries to hide from (indeed, tries to hide that he or she even has), it is this: we fear, each of us, that we shall be rejected.

We fear rejection.

We are united this morning by more than we realize. Among the things that unite us is this fear that each of us has—those who gather to worship frequently and those who are seldom; young and old, professor and student; male and female; quiet or outgoing—the fear of being rejected.

In those lines and conversations as freshmen move toward a meal in the Student Union; at a cocktail party, a luncheon—the unspoken drama and power of the fear of rejection often lies behind almost every laugh, and word, and gesture: in the encounter with roommates; as the professor enters Lawrence or Alumni or Olin to teach his course; during faculty sherry hour at Merrill House; with the first man—or woman—at Colgate whom you find somewhat special, different; when the married couple, in their fifties, lie down to bed together.

At any of these points—and for *you*, more precisely, more secretly, at some *other* point: the fear of rejection seeks to make itself clear to your consciousness, often struggles to be acknowledged in your body.

Coming to church—and lingering afterward for coffee, only to discover that one knows no one here . . .

Perhaps you'll say that these examples are trivial. But the fear of rejection is encountered in both the trivial and momentous events and meetings of our lives.

Of, perhaps, the trivial kind, I have given example. In the momentous kind the very shape and direction of our personalities is called into question. And we can only bear a little, only a very little reflection on our deeper fears.

Perhaps we cannot bear *this* thought at all: the thought of rejection—at least potential, and usually encountered at some time—rejection by our parents, by our children, by our dearest friends. Much of the time, perhaps all of the time, such rejection seems inconceivable. It must. For we "repress" things—put them out of mind—for *good* reason.

Fear of rejection is fear of loss of that which makes life human, makes life worthwhile, and good, and glad. (May I then just remark in passing how wondrous, how glorious and good it is to be accepted.)

Now I want at this point to notice something about the psalmist. We heard portions of the Thirty-fifth Psalm this morning. I want us to notice something *great* about the psalmist, something great, greatly human, profoundly courageous and faithful.

The writer of the Thirty-fifth Psalm dares to feel, to acknowledge, and to express his fear—his fear of rejection.

It's easy to fault the writers of the Psalms for being vindictive; to fault them for being inadequate in love, for their self-centeredness on not a few occasions, their tendency to articulate their praise, their prayer, their words to God from the limited perspective of their own condition, and wishes . . . and fears.

I wonder if that for which we may easily fault them is not also their greatness. The writers of the Psalms acknowledge *how it is with them.*

The person behind this Thirty-fifth Psalm dares to *feel* his fears. He dares to let his fears wash over him, to give words to his fears. He dares to let his fears *be—to let them be.*

May we dare to feel our fears and not deny and submerge and repress them. May we dare to let our fears wash over us; to give words, honest words, and not succumb to rationalizations ("I'm sure *that* couldn't be"); or phony piety ("I'm a Christian, so I'm not bothered"); or poisonous indifference ("What do I care about her rejection!"); or demonic self-deception ("*I* have no regrets"). May we dare to give honest words to our fears. May we dare to let our fear of rejection wash over us; dare to let such a fear simply *be, let it be.*

For in these days and years to do so is to taste our very humanness, our very selves, our very humanity. To do so is to become *open to that new power, new life even*, which, strangely, will come to us only, only as the one we *really* are: only to me as I really am, only to you as you really are. New strength, new life will *not* come *to* the unreal self we seek to be—the unreal self we seek to be in order to protect ourselves from the truth of what we *really* feel and *really* are. Only as we are enabled to allow that idealized self-image to fall, enabled to allow the idealized self-image to begin to die, to allow the unreal self, the lie in which we try to enclose ourselves, begin to die—only then will our real self, and strength, and truth, our real life be found.

And our *real* self, you and I fear rejection, even as the psalmist feared it: we sometimes fear those who "contend" with us, and sometimes fear that even those who do not appear to will "contend" with us. Some of us fear that careless or uncaring others will, "without cause," dig, as it were, "a pit" for us. We sometimes fear that others will speak untrue things about us, behind our backs, when we're not there, and that such words will lead still others—who otherwise would have accepted us—to reject us, if, oh, ever so subtly. We fear that *our* good will, our desire to enter into conversation, into relationship, even into friendship, even into love, will not be met by a similar good will but rather by distaste, or boredom, or by a joke at our expense, or by worse, real hostility . . . rejection. We fear, like the psalmist, those who would rather exclude us, those who even take delight in our misfortune. For we wonder if there might not be such. *After all*, we know ourselves capable of excluding others, and even of delight in the misfortune of others . . . although that we dismiss from mind quickly.

We fear those who do or might "wink the eye." We fear rejection.

And, like the honest psalmist, we would, if likewise honest, say, let them fail in their rejection! Let them come to nothing! Let them come to worse than that!

Or do we rather *so* fear such feelings, *so intensely* fear them, that we cannot bear to fear such anger toward those who reject us, or threaten to? Do we, instead, grow confused and quiet, frightened, and full of pious or superficial wishes—though often unaccountably angry too!—and finally possessed of a vague refusal either to acknowledge that we have tasted rejection from time to time, or even that we fear it, fear rejection?

We fear rejection. And we fear something else as much or more. Here we begin to probe another secret which we all share, I think, yet a secret which again we usually hide from.

We not only fear rejection. *We fear that we may not be able to take it.* We fear that, if rejection comes, perhaps (even probably) we shall not be able to take it.

Here the matter may suddenly seem obscure. Fear that we shall be able to take it? We don't quite recognize that one. We don't remember, many of us, ever feeling that fear—though *some* of us do remember it.

Yet I'm wondering this morning, *nevertheless*, if this may not be one of our *deepest* human fears, the fear which often motivates our religious search, our search for a philosophy of life, and the self-image we try to present *first* to ourselves and *then* to others: the fear that—regarding real rejection, perhaps we can't take it. I wonder, indeed, if this deeper fear—that we shall not be able to take it—does not underlie our frequent inability to face and feel our fear of rejection. I mean by this deeper fear—let me repeat—that if and when rejection comes, real rejection by someone we deeply care for (or at an important place in our life), we simply shall not be able to take it.

Against this fear we make—as individuals, as groups, as cultures and civilizations—enormous *efforts*.

When I was about sixteen, a preacher taught us to think, "I am bigger than anything that can happen to me." You remember the old saying: "Sticks and stones may break my bones, but names will never hurt me."

I don't believe that saying anymore. Names can hurt as much, or more, than sticks or stones. And *I*, at least, am *not* bigger than anything that can happen to me. No.

Do you know, or remember, Emerson's essay "Self-Reliance"? Notice something in the months ahead. Notice something in our American culture. Notice something probably in yourself, probably in your own upbringing, probably in your own moral code—whether you think you don't have a moral code, or have a very elaborate one; notice what I suspect may be your one, perhaps your only moral absolute: you've *got* to be able, you *must* be able to take it.

Some of us wonder if the preacher isn't rather morbid about this rejection bit; he overdoes it a little, some of us are thinking. After all, if rejection comes, you just *have* to be able to take it, we often say. "I *must* be able to take it," we say somewhere deep inside.

Our parents or old friends may well accept us if we are rejected by an unappreciative peer or teacher. But can they bear signs of inability on our part to take rejection?

Often parents are *un*perturbed when their children are rejected. Parental anxiety is tapped (and I know: I'm a parent) if it appears to parents that their children might not be able *to take* rejection. Can our parents accept us if we are unable to take some particular form of rejection? Do we not all often seem to imply that the last word, the last word about life, is this: "Of course you can take it; you've *got* to be able to take it."

Our lover, our husband, our wife, our friend may well accept us if our work is rejected, *even* if we fail in our role as friend, lover, husband, wife, or parent. But will they accept us if we can't *take* our failure?

"You *mustn't*, you *can't* despair": that is often our moral absolute.

(The natural man or woman, and especially the natural American man or woman, is likely, if not a Stoic in fact—for I doubt if anyone ever is in fact—then a would-be Stoic. That is, self-reliance is still our deepest *hope*, and perhaps nowhere more than in those under twenty-five.)

Our deepest concern often: "to get it all together" *by my own powers and on my own.*

That we shall maintain *mastery over our wills* whatever comes: that is our deepest hope. In whatever comes, that we shall be *imperturbable.*

Our religion, our morality, our psychology tend to meet there, at that deep hope—that, if the worst came, if we *are* rejected, we shall have the stuff *"to take it."*

For there is no help, we say, nor hope, if we can't "take it." After all, doesn't God help those who help themselves?

Well, God may, but the Bible doesn't seem to know much about that.

Faith is not *imperturbability.* Faith is *not* having it all together. Faith is *not* the assurance that whatever comes, I can acquit myself imperturbably. Faith is not that. The Psalms, again, come from persons often amazed, anticipating, delighted, jubilant, but no less angry, afraid, uncertain, broken.

We fear rejection, you and I. And *we fear rightly.* For rejection diminishes, and perverts, and destroys. It destroys you, and it destroys me. *You were not created for rejection, nor I.* What is one of the deepest longings, the deepest drives our varying hearts long and drive for? Is it not for appreciation, and recognition, and respect, and celebration of ourselves and our lives by our fellow human beings, by our brothers and sisters in the human community? *We die for loss of love.*

We fear rejection, *and we fear rightly.*

We are not condemned for fearing rejection. Rejection is the destruction of our lives.

Of course we are and shall be rejected, every one of us—even as every one of us shall die. For *much* of what we *do* and *say ought to* be rejected. I am often wrong or stupid; moreover, in my defense against and attack upon those who have rejected me or who, I fear, may reject me, I take advantage, I exploit, hoard, lie, betray. Rejection is a part of life, of every life and of all life. But our fundamental *fear* of it, of rejection, is right and true. For we are meant to be "created in the image of God"—do you remember? Our lives are meant for unity and acceptance and mutual love. For thus we become and are enabled to give of who we are.

We cannot become ourselves if rejection is too intense, too deep.

Rejection leads us into the land of lies, into delusion, where we pretend (to ourselves and to others) to be what we are not in order to be accepted.

We believe in our heart of hearts that we are meant to be. And rejection by others is denial of that utterly deep, utterly right faith.

We respond to rejection with lies, or with that defensiveness which destroys authentic human relationships, or with continual hostility to others, hostility we seem unable to help. We respond with anger—as well we should, however misplaced or inappropriate that anger. (And, of course, the most inappropriate and devastating placement of that anger is often with ourselves. Many of us are angry with ourselves for having been rejected. Strange, isn't it? Some of us—we're so nice, so damned nice . . . to everybody else. But how much anger we turn against ourselves!)

We fear rejection, you and I; and if we cannot bear our fear, cannot let it wash over us, cannot let it be, then we grow defensive or hostile. Or we withdraw into apathy—which is *both* hostility and a defense. Or we condemn *ourselves* steadily and ever and again, nice as we are.

We fear rejection, and rightly.

So finally—the offense of the gospel, the strange Good News takes this shape this morning: the Good News comes in acknowledgment that at our deepest levels *we cannot take it, we cannot take it—being rejected*. We cannot take it, and still love. The cost of love is vulnerability, grief at times, brokenness.

The deepest fear of all is, after all, the truth about us: It is true we cannot take it. Rejection—every taste of it—is the taste of death. And in too great a dosage, we die of it—into despair, paranoia, dedication to destruction. We cannot take it.

And so hear this: *It is all right to fear rejection, and it is all right to fear that you cannot take it . . . as I cannot. It is all right.*

It is all right. There is no condemnation for being human. Let the fear *be*—let it *be*. This, at least, is faith: that at that point where the worst comes to pass—and rejection and inability to take rejection is certainly part of the worst—there at the broken place, precisely there, new life may begin.

The "pioneer and perfecter" of faith could not face his task without great cries of anguish; he could not carry his own cross. And he cried out and let it be: "My God, my God, why have you forsaken me?"

It is all right to fear rejection. For rejection is a fearful thing. It is *all right* to fear you cannot take it. There is an obvious sense in which Jesus could not take it. He did not die imperturbably.

And in that death, which *he* could not take, we may begin to discover that which is simply given to you and to me: new life.

Let them be, even your deepest fears—your fear of rejection, your fear that you cannot take it. The Good News is this: the gifts of *life* and *joy* and *love* are even there, yes, precisely there, hidden deep in your deepest fears.

2

"Our Hearts Are Restless until They Find Their Rest in Thee"[1]

A Communion Sermon for the First Sunday of Advent

DECEMBER 2, 1979

> *And in that region there were shepherds out in the field, keeping watch over their flock by night. And an angel of the Lord appeared to them, and the glory of the Lord shone around them, and they were filled with fear.*
>
> *And the angel said to them, "Be not afraid; for behold, I bring you good news of a great joy which will come to all the people; for to you is born this day in the city of David a Savior, who is Christ the Lord. And this will be a sign for you: you will find a babe wrapped in swaddling cloths and lying in a manger." And suddenly there was with the angel a multitude of the heavenly host praising God and saying, "Glory to God in the highest, and on earth peace . . ."*
>
> —Luke 2:8–14a (RSV)

OUR HEARTS ARE RESTLESS. These are restless days at Colgate . . . restless days in the world.

---

1. This sermon was published in 1980 (as one of seven prize-winning sermons preached the previous year in an academic context) in *NICM Journal for Jews and Christians in Higher Education*.

And we have come to this service of worship this morning, seeking... seeking a presence, seeking a friend, seeking a perspective, seeking a feeling, seeking a community, seeking self-knowledge, seeking new energy, seeking peace... seeking...

More than *one* person has prayed, "Our hearts find no peace until they rest in you." "Our hearts are restless... our hearts are restless until they find their rest in Thee."[2]

If we could be near God it would be all right.

Wittgenstein, the philosopher, makes a bold claim: "Tell me *how* you seek and I will tell you *what* you are seeking."[3] Consider that: *how* you seek may disclose what you are seeking.

We seek true friends, a community, a true community. Yet we fear we will be smothered, overwhelmed by the others. Our self, our soul is often like a bird fluttering, unable to take wing, in fear of being caught in a net, or otherwise finished off. We long for one another and for community, and at the same time seek to fly away from others.

We are seeking. Our hearts are restless. We have not found peace.

About the shepherds we hear that "the glory of the Lord shone around them, and they were filled with fear."

So often healing and new life begin with a kind of fear. Have you ever sung "Amazing Grace"? Do you remember that one of the verses is, "'Twas grace that taught my heart to fear"? "The fear of the Lord is the beginning"—"the beginning of wisdom," say the Proverbs.[4] The one who shall come forth from the stump of Jesse —the Spirit that will rest even upon him includes "the fear of the Lord."[5] "The fear of the Lord is clean, enduring forever," the psalmist exulted.[6]

It must be said: God is not known if God is not feared.

According to the gospel, it is the merciful will of God that you and I become able to rely entirely on God, place our lives entirely in God's hands, trust God completely and simply in and for everything.

---

2. There are various translations of this line—in fact a prayer—from the opening sentences of the *Confessions* of Saint Augustine.

3. Wittgenstein, *Philosophical Grammar*, 370, quoted in Holmer, *Grammar of Faith*, 203.

4. See Proverbs 9:10.

5. See Isaiah 11:1–9.

6. See Psalm 19:9.

And when really we hear that and even begin to believe it, it threatens us profoundly and fills us with fear.

The fear of God is a many-splendored thing.

It is awe at the glory that can shine in a field at night or *even* where we are working; awe at the glory that *can* shine out from anything and everything, any*one* and every*one*—embarrassing us and silencing us.

And we shall be filled with fear when we apprehend that we are being *sought where we are*; that we are being *sought*; you are, and I am—and not just a part of us, not just a token part of us, a religious part, or something like that, but the whole of us is being sought. The whole person and the whole community is being sought, and yet so quietly, so indirectly, we may even say—as if it were, somehow, that only in life as we *really* live it, only in the discovery of who we *really* are, are we being sought.

I should add: in fear of the Lord, the fear we have of others and of the world begins to go, begins to be cast out.

When the glory of the Almighty God begins to shine—and we somehow begin to observe it, even a little bit—when it really begins to dawn on us that there is a word for us, personally and as a community, then we are, indeed, filled with fear.

For we have not been raised for *that*, or educated for *that*. Our plans are not about that. Our hopes are not about that.

We want some peace, yes. We want some "perspective," indeed—even some help, we may acknowledge.

But as Daniel Berrigan, that disturbing Christian, puts it: we are "afflicted with the wasting disease of normalcy." He describes *us* this way:

> Even as they declare for . . . peace, their hands reach out with an instructive spasm in the direction of their loved ones, in the direction of their comforts, their home, their security, their income, their future, their plans—that five-year plan of studies, that ten-year plan of professional status, that twenty-year plan of . . . growth and unity, that fifty-year plan of decent life and honorable natural demise. "Of course, let us have peace," we cry, "but at the same time let us have normalcy, let us lose nothing, let our lives stand intact, let us know neither prison nor ill repute nor disruption of ties." And because we must encompass this and protect that, and because at all costs—at all costs—our hopes must march on schedule, and because it is unheard of that in the name of peace a sword should fall, disjoining that fine and cunning web that our lives have woven, because it is unheard of that good men and women should suffer injustice or [have their

lives turned around] or good repute be lost—because of this we cry peace and cry peace [in our world, and in our college, and in our particular worrisome tasks], and there is no peace. There is no peace because there are no peacemakers.[7]

God is not known if God is not feared.

Then the word comes, the great cry of the gospel, the angelic word, the word from the terrible Almighty God: "Be not afraid, for behold I bring you good news of great joy."
The music of the Advent season seeks to express it.
It is meant for all people.
To you is born a savior is the message.
And then, of course, those wonderful, almost comic words, the surprise of which has gone for us because we've heard them so many times: this will be a sign for you—the sign of the Almighty God—you will find a babe wrapped in swaddling cloths and lying in a manger, a manger: a box or trough from which animals eat in a barn.

The good news will often feel like this—strange as this way of putting it may be for some of you—the good news that to you is born a Savior will often feel like: *there are no saviors after all.*

If we can recover the surprise, even the comedy of that sign—a baby in swaddling cloths in a manger—then we, too, may hear a multitude of the heavenly host praising God and saying,

"Glory to God in the highest,
and on earth, peace . . ."

We *want* invulnerable poise. Maybe we don't believe we'll ever find it; but that, we think, would save us—and so we seek it desperately at times if still with really only half a heart (knowing better in our heart of hearts). But, oh, invulnerable poise: always to be able to say the *right* thing at the *right* time in the *right* way (or as exams approach, to be able to *write* the right thing in the right *amount* of time, in the right *way*—by which we often mean the way we think the instructor wants it).

We *want* assured success—even if we doubt that there can be such assurance; still that is what we want and secretly (a secret even from ourselves at times) that is what, if again with half a heart, we are secretly *seeking.*

---

7. Berrigan, *No Bars to Manhood,* 49.

Or we want a cause—a cause in the world about which we can be *positive*.

Don't misunderstand me now: poise *in the service of our neighbor* is good; success *at something worthy of free men and women* may be good *if we have not sold our souls for it*; and the gospel *ought* to lead us to discover a social cause. (For a great deal of suffering and most injustice is only reduced when an organized social cause focuses our moral passion.)

Poise, success, and certainly the obligatory social cause—these are among the good gifts of life.

But in the words of an older and more severe piety than ours, "The Lord gives, the Lord takes away, blessed be the name of the Lord." The danger of good things—even the best (even the best *people* in our lives)—is that we shall cease, stop receiving them as gifts and turn them into ways by which, compulsively, we shall be saved; ways by which, compulsively, we shall save ourselves from oblivion, restlessness, anxiety, emptiness, save ourselves from a sense of joylessness.

Tell me how you seek and I will tell you what you are seeking.

Again: *this* will be a sign for you. You will find a babe wrapped in swaddling cloths and lying in a manger.

From a stump—which was once a tree but now is nothing but a stump—a shoot from that old stump, from that poor old stump shall grow the tree of eternal life.

Or in the words of a servant poem in Isaiah (a poem with probably the most terrible tension in all Hebrew poetry):

> *How beautiful upon the mountains*
> *are the feet of him who brings good tidings . . .*
> *Behold, my servant shall prosper,*
> *he shall be exalted and lifted up . . .*
> *As many were* astonished *at him—*
> *his appearance was so marred . . .*
> *He was despised and rejected . . .*
> *a man of sorrows, and acquainted with grief.*[8]

Or in the words reported in the New Testament of a Roman centurion looking up at the man upon the cross, "Truly this man was . . . Son of God."[9]

---

8. See Isaiah 52:7–53:12, esp. 52:7, 13–14; 53:3.
9. See Mark 15:39.

Or yet again: the stone which the builders rejected has become the cornerstone, the stone which holds the structure together.[10]

What is more helpless than a baby? More unpromising of becoming a great tree than a stump? More doubtful as the one from whom good news comes than a person of sorrows, acquainted with grief? More unlikely to be Son of God than a man hanging, crucified? More suspect as the chief stone in the construction than the stone the expert builders reject?

To rely on the comic claim that you will find the Savior wrapped in swaddling cloths, lying in a trough in a barn—why, that is like relying on nothing, really.

Yes, that is very much what it is like: like relying on nothing.

As one preacher of the gospel has put it, "He who abandons every form of security shall find the true security."[11]

If we could be near God, I say to you again, it would be all right: it would all be all right.

Unto *you* the Savior, the baby is born. It may be that that will even happen *in* you.

The bird takes wing and flies with other birds to its home.

The friendships are found; the community comes together as a sign of promise of true community.

There is danger—remembering that God is not known if God is not feared—there is danger if we are not warned: warned that this night our souls may be required of us.

That warning perhaps should be the end of the sermon. Yet I conclude the sermon *this* way instead of with that warning: When you have discovered the side of the good news which is that, in a vital sense, there are no saviors after all; when you have discovered that the other saviors do not save; when you have discovered that, in order to enjoy the good things of life—and in order to enter into committed and loving relationships—you are to receive all things and all loved ones as the gifts of God, relying at the last only on the Giver; when you have discovered that success does not succeed in setting life right, that *all* the securities cannot bring security—

then hear anew about the stump of Jesse from which a tree of eternal life;

---

10. See 1 Peter 2:7; Psalm 118:22.
11. Bultmann, *Jesus Christ and Mythology*, 84.

then hear anew about this "Savior" (perhaps we should say it with quotation marks around it), this "Savior" whose sign is a baby wrapped in cloths and lying in a manger;

then hear anew about the person of sorrows, acquainted with grief;

then hear anew about the bread and the wine, the blood, and the body broken for you; about true security found in abandoning every form of security; about the confidence and the joy which seem like relying on nothing.

Then we shall begin to learn *how* to seek, and *how* to live—and *how* to die—and *how* to be near God.

Until then let us pray: our hearts are restless until they find their rest in Thee. Our hearts find no peace until they rest in you.

Amen.

3

"Come to Me, All You Who Are Heavy Laden"

Sermon at a Unified Service of the University Church and the Roman Catholic Community at Colgate

ORIGINALLY PREACHED MARCH 23, 1980[1]

> *"Come to me, all you who labor and are heavy laden, and I will give you rest. Take my yoke upon you, and learn from me; for I am gentle and lowly in heart, and you will find rest for your souls. For my yoke is easy, and my burden is light."*
> —Matthew 11:28–30 (RSV)

> *And as he sat at table in his house, many tax collectors and sinners were sitting with Jesus and his disciples; for there were many who followed him. And the scribes of the Pharisees, when they saw that he was eating with sinners and tax collectors, said to his disciples, "Why does he eat with tax collectors and sinners?" And when Jesus heard it, he said to them, "Those who are well have no need of a physician, but those who are sick; I came not to call the righteous, but sinners."*
> —Mark 2:15–17 (RSV)

---

1. Also preached March 8, 1987.

THE GOSPEL IS FUNNY. It's not for everybody. It's just for sinners, for those who haven't got it together—personally, morally, religiously; for those who don't know how to live. It's for the sick, not the healthy, and for those who have no righteousness of their own. If you know yourself to be among the righteous, you have no need for this bread, for this wine. His body broken for you? His blood poured out for you? The acceptance of your brothers and sisters? The forgiveness and mercy of God? What need have we of all that if we stand among the righteous? The gospel of Jesus Christ is not for those who have it together, not for those who know how to live.

Our text this morning is from St. Matthew's Gospel, 11:28–30. From it we may hear Jesus Christ speak to us (for the one who was crucified has been raised from the dead): "Come to me, all you who labor and are heavy laden, and I will give you rest. Take my yoke upon you, and learn from me; for I am gentle and lowly in heart, and you will find rest for your souls. For my yoke is easy and my burden is light."

With what are *you* heavy laden?

You, in your *real* life? You, in your life as you live it out, as the one you are? With what are you heavy laden?

Some of us almost cannot bear to hear the question. The weight is so heavy that we spend our energy (indeed, try to train our consciousness) to *forget* the weight upon our minds and hearts.

With what are you heavy laden?

What comes immediately to mind? Perhaps the midterm coming up this week. The paper already due but not yet finished. The exam already taken but on which you don't yet know how you did.

Perhaps it is the thought of those who have been coming to you for help, whose burdens you are trying to understand.

Perhaps it is a roommate situation that is deteriorating, or a friendship that is growing too complicated, or one that has become mostly quarrels.

Fear of losing one's place on a team or in some other important group.

For *you*, as an individual, something else.

How can we go so quickly from being psyched up to being brought low? How come a grade on a paper affects us so? Or a phone call? Or a letter?

The way we have organized our life—indeed, our very self—seems often like some great heavy weight that we must bear, careful not to let others know, really, how it is with us, how heavy leaden, really, we are.

The gospel is mercy and peace. But it may come to us as a question and *feel* even like judgment.

Yokes are frames that fit around our neck and shoulders for carrying things.

"Come to Me, All You Who Are Heavy Laden"

What yoke do you wear?

One of the yokes that we wear so close upon us that we wonder how ever it could be lifted—indeed, it seems we've always worn it—is the yoke of accreditation: a diploma from high school, a degree from a good college, good scores on the SATs, and, for many seniors, now on the GREs. We must be properly accredited so that we may have some place in the world! The question is bred into us: what good are you if you do not succeed? We are under *compulsion* to succeed: that is the heavy yoke which some of us wear always—waking or sleeping. To paraphrase one writer: a whole generation of youth has been told that faith means the assurance of going to college, hope means the certainty of landing a good job, and love means that mother and father will lay down their lives to see that their child gets all these blessings. With "faith" like that, who needs faith?[2]

"Take my yoke upon you, and learn from me . . . my yoke is easy, and my burden is light."

We doubt it. Anyway, we'll keep our yoke of accreditation and success, thank you. After all, you have to be practical, we say.

And what have we, in our society, done? What have we done in our alleged practicality—hundreds and thousands of us? We experience the life of leisure (for, believe it or not, that is the life we are invited to live here at Colgate) as some great and continual anxiety, as some great and heavy weight. The life of leisure—study, thought, good conversation mingled with sports and other worthwhile fellowship—we turn into a grim and frantic thing. We turn into a grim and frantic thing time meant for self-knowledge, knowledge of others and the world. This life of the liberating arts and sciences—the life that in most ages could only be lived by a few with leisure enough for it—what has it become for us? A preview of the rat race that some of us have already heard our parents moan over. In some kind of reverse alchemy, we have turned gold into lead, turned liberation into imprisonment, and turned the pleasure of civilization into pain.

Don't misunderstand me. The cure is a radical cure. The cure is not a little positive thinking, a little more effort at relaxing, a little better perspective. That's not what I'm talking about. The yoke is on us. But we are being invited to give up the yokes which we hold so firmly—indeed (if someone tampers with them), the yokes we hold so *savagely* about ourselves: accreditation, success, our social place, our life! What keeps us going.

"Don't monkey with that, preacher!" we say somewhere inside. "At least, don't expect your monkeying to change much."

---

2. DeLamotte, "Can Blacks Escape the Mainstream?," 277.

"Take my yoke upon you, and learn from me. I am gentle and lowly in heart . . . my yoke is easy, and my burden is light." The words sound all right in church, but if we hear them deeply they begin to undermine us, threaten us, to threaten our very values, our lifestyles, our dreams and hopes.

We are heavy laden not a little by our unquestioned and unquestioning acceptance of the yoke of accreditation and success whereby we find spoiled or destroyed the very meaning of study, learning, reflection, and even life itself.

I propose to you quite directly that Jesus Christ offers us his yoke here at this place *in part* that we may discover the meaning and joy of the liberating arts and sciences.

But so long as we insist on the primacy of our yokes of accreditation and success, there is little likelihood that we shall find liberation except in our recurrent and often pathetic efforts to *get away* from the liberal arts and sciences.

Another yoke we insist on wearing is the yoke of boredom. Let me read you part of a poem by T. S. Eliot—not so demanding as many of his poems; it's called "The Rum Tum Tugger."

> The Rum Tum Tugger is a Curious Cat:
> If you offer him pheasant he would rather have grouse.
> If you put him in a house he would much prefer a flat,
> If you put him in a flat then he'd rather have a house.
> If you set him on a mouse then he only wants a rat,
> If you set him on a rat then he'd rather chase a mouse.
> Yes the Rum Tum Tugger is a Curious Cat . . .
>
> The Rum Tum Tugger is a terrible bore:
> When you let him in, then he wants to be out;
> He's always on the wrong side of every door,
> And as soon as he's at home, then he'd like to get about.
> He likes to lie in the bureau drawer,
> But he makes such a fuss if he can't get out.
> Yes the Rum Tum Tugger is a Curious Cat.[3]

We are bored because we think that happiness comes with what we *have* or what we *experience*: the great god of our time—"Experiences" with

---

3. Eliot, "Rum Tum Tugger," 153–54.

a capital E; the more the better. And so, like the Rum Tum Tugger, we are always moving on—our outlook often a whine, as one thing after another disappoints us: full of self-pity, full of complaint, whatever we have inadequate, not really "it."

"Take my yoke upon you and learn from me . . . and you will find rest for your souls."

We are so restless, so compulsively self-centered, that often we turn every experience, every relationship, into something to evaluate like the ice cream flavors at a Baskin-Robbins. And because of our emptiness, our hunger that cannot be satisfied, our thirst that cannot be quenched, we judge and reject our brothers and sisters and the various mixed blessings of this life—bored with them, disappointed with them, let down by them, full of complaint. If we were cats, perhaps it would be amusing. But we are not cats, but men and women, and our restless dissatisfaction erodes and threatens to destroy our very capacity for love, our very capacity to become human.

We are heavy laden with the yoke of accreditation and success.

We are heavy laden with the burden of boredom.

We are heavy laden with hard and thankless hearts.

We do not have thankful hearts. Oh, we *want* them, I know. But not as much as we want all those other things that we are spending our lives for—thinking about, resenting that we don't have, worrying over, and planning. We do not have thankful hearts. And heavy laden are the hearts and minds we have instead.

A thankful heart flows in part from the willingness to imagine frequently the day we die—to imagine the day we die and how it will be, looking back . . . to these days. How shall we remember our sisters and brothers that day—sisters and brothers in our actual families, and sisters and brothers beyond our family—how shall we remember on that day our sisters and brothers, our mother and father, and friend and foe? A thankful heart flows from willingness to imagine fully and without reservation the day we die: from the perspective of that day, what do you think of the way you're living this day, these days?

The smell of breakfast. The trip to pick up the laundry. The chance to learn, the chance to wonder. The walk with your friend. Someday they will be taken away. But in the meantime they are yours. Can you treasure them for what they are?[4]

Imagine the day you die. When that will be, no one knows. But imagine yourself looking back to these days. How, *then*, will you have wanted to

---

4. Buechner, "All's Lost, All's Found," 283.

have lived them? From the perspective of that last day, can your heart be broken, broken down into thanksgiving, for the eyes and smiles and tears and laughter, the flesh and blood, the miracle of fellow men and women like yourself in the strange grace of living together these very days? Who can give us faith to stand in imagination at the last day and think about these days?

"Come to me, all you who labor and are heavy laden, and I will give you rest. Take my yoke upon you."

But our tragedy the Bible well knows. For the Bible is the history of God reaching out in this way and that for a people whom God loves—but a people who vainly feel and believe that *there must be some other way than by surrender to God.*

The Bible understands us.

There must be some other way (we say hiddenly), some other way than to come to the crucified one. We haven't exactly found it yet, but we're going to keep on trying. Our *real* hope is that there *must* be a way, *our* way. "I did it my way," we want to sing with Sinatra. There must be a way whereby we can beat the system, get it all together, and not only *pursue* happiness but also *be* happy, a way whereby we get over being heavy laden. There must be some other way than to come to God. We haven't found it yet, but our *honest* hope, our *real* hope—often—is that we will.

Now we've come to a dangerous point. Is God the answer? Turn over our lives to God and no more heavy ladenness? Is that it? Turn over our lives to God and then we'll have it together? Is that it? No more heartache? No more sin?

It was Pascal who said that it is equally dangerous for a person to know God without knowing his or her own wretchedness and to know his or her own wretchedness without knowing God.[5] We know something of our own wretchedness without God. But let us be careful.

We turn away in the depths of ourselves from those who come to us as if they have it made, those who have it together; we turn away from those who are going to tell us the answer as to how *we* are to live *our* life. Those who are condescending, those who possess, however faintly, a subtle sense of their own superiority: we turn away from those—often religious folk—who would convey to us that, somehow, they are not like other men and women, that they have overcome the heavy ladenness of life.

Jesus is saying: give up your pretensions, your tragic dreams, your delusions and delusional hopes. *Join the human race.* I am gentle and lowly in heart. I know this life you live. I came not to call the righteous but sinners.

---

5. Pascal, *Pensées*, 162 (no. 585).

Those who have it made have no use for me. I do not have it made. For my way is the way of a cross, the way of forsakenness and suffering and death. Come to me, all you who labor and are heavy laden, and I will give you rest.

For, says Jesus, my yoke is easy and my burden is light. My yoke is the yoke of becoming human, my burden is the burden of love. Hard, yes, and easy. Terrible, yes, and light. When you come to the last day will your accreditation and your success console you? Your gadgets and your compulsive habit of affluence: will they make it all worthwhile? When you come to that last day—and you must cross over the dark Jordan—will your many experiences sustain you then? Will you look back on all your complaining efforts to get beyond boredom and be glad? On your last day will you want to be heavy laden with that thankless heart, so very heavy, that you bear?

Our God is a God of love and comfort, a God who fills the soul and the heart. Therefore, our God makes us conscious of our sin, our brokenness, that we may receive the mercy, the humility, the joy, the trust, the love that is given us.

The One crucified and alive for us says to you and me: there is joy when you begin to see the truth, to feel the weight and the folly of the yokes you hold on to so tightly. There is joy for those who are beginning to see that they don't know how to live. There is joy for those who have tried the other ways, the many other ways—

increase pleasure; diminish pain;
more will power;
positive thinking;
get accredited; succeed;
beat boredom; you know, try something else;
watch out for "number one";
et cetera, et cetera, et cetera.

There is joy for those who have tried to save themselves and have begun to doubt, even to despair, that they can do that.

"Come unto me," says Jesus, "all you who labor and are heavy laden." But if you flee your neighbor, if you flee the human condition—keep hoping you can beat the system, keep hoping you can become independent of your fellow man and fellow woman, keep hoping you can work it out on your own, get it together on your own, work up your psychological or moral or religious solution—then, says the Lord, I go my way, you need me not. My death is in vain, my life of no account to you. I go my way and leave you to your devices—leave you to keep lying, to keep hiding your human condition from others and from yourself, leave you to keep blaming others for your troubles, leave you to keep building your little dreams, whether national or suburban or personal, in which you postpone the truth about living and dying—keep building your little dreams until they suck your life from you and leave you with ashes and despair.

    Yet again he says to us in the simplicity of love: come to me, with your sister and brother, and let us eat and drink together, let the yokes be removed which drive you on your foolish frantic ways; let the self-centered effort to end boredom stop and let boredom lift; and be thankful for breakfast smells, the trip to pick up the laundry, the chance to learn, the chance to wonder, the walk with your friend. Begin to be restored to your humanity. For I am come from God to show the way to be truly human. It will cost your life to be human. It will cost your life not to be human. Take my yoke upon you and learn from me. I am gentle and lowly in heart. My yoke is easy and my burden is light. Come to me, all you who labor and are heavy laden.

4

For the Joy

Sermon at a Unified Service of the University Church and the Roman Catholic Community at Colgate

FEBRUARY 15, 1981

> *Therefore, since we are surrounded by so great a cloud of witnesses, let us also lay aside every weight and sin which clings so closely, and let us run with perseverance the race that is set before us, looking to Jesus the pioneer and perfecter of our faith, who for the joy that was set before him endured the cross, despising the shame, and is seated at the right hand of the throne of God.*
> —Hebrews 12:1–2 (RSV)

SO YOU'LL KNOW WHAT I'm about, let me tell you I'm going to talk about joy; and my hope is that the way may be opened for joy to reach you. At the heart of what I'm going to try to say are these three claims:

First, joy is the joy of discovering powers in ourselves and in our communities that we have not yet even begun to tap.

Second, joy is the joy of being reunited with the persons from whom we've been estranged.

And third, joy is the joy of believing again in the happy ending.

I find myself giving thanks for each of us this morning: I am thankful that each of us is who we are.

And I am thankful for our vocation. Our vocation is nothing less than that a new age begin in us—right here at Colgate, right in these days.

Jesus inaugurates the new age beginning in us—if we will let that be, if we will let that happen.

The tradition reminds us, of course, that Jesus is a person of sorrows and acquainted with grief. And if we are to find and have what we most deeply want, we, too, will know sorrow and grief.

Sorrow is expression of love. And love—whatever its sorrow, whatever its grief—is the *way*, the only way to joy.

We heard this morning that Jesus endured the cross, despising the shame, for the joy that was set before him.

You and I long for joy—although many of us have almost given up hope for it. Whatever of joy we find in sexual liberation or success, in mellow music or in bright and golden skies, opens our heart to what we fear may be too good to be true: that we may simply enter joy itself.

If we understand a little the joy that was set before Jesus, it will help us enter the joy which is prepared for us.

First, that joy is the joy of discovering powers in ourselves and in our communities that we have not yet even begun to tap. Do you know that together—not any one of us alone, but together—we can begin to transform this college into a vastly more honest, forgiving, hopeful place? We shall not transform it by sitting around judging and condemning those who do what we disapprove of (especially if we do most of our talking behind their backs). We shall not transform it much by telling people to be better or to be less apathetic.

We shall transform Colgate by taking up the specific crosses that we shall find here every day—despising the shame of those crosses, for the joy that is set before us: the joy of a renewed college where mercy and trust and communion become increasingly the real spirit of the place.

What are the specific crosses before you—or, better, before us together?

There is a cross—for one of us and for more than one of us—of some inward anger, some suffering which you are called to learn how to share and be healed of: even as Conrad was in the recent movie *Ordinary People*.

There is a cross of speaking up—not as a judge but as an ordinary person—against a particular cruelty that's going on in your dorm or fraternity or apartment or organization. The cruelty may be racist, sexist, or it may take quite some other form. For you to resist it will involve your being laughed at, put down, or even ostracized by some. (Breaking down racial barriers, by the way, is something we must work at week after week, month after month, year after year. We can't say, "Gee, we tried that a couple of times in September, but we didn't get anywhere.")

There is a cross of breaking down barriers, and there is a cross of speaking up against a particular cruelty.

There is a cross that involves beginning to struggle to learn how to forgive someone that presently you can't even imagine how you can forgive.

There is a cross that means rethinking career values in the presence of the body and blood of Christ and the suffering in the world. Do you really need to make so much money as you intend to assure yourself of your worth?

Together we can begin to transform this college—and, yes, allow a new age to begin in us—by taking up painful crosses that we'll find before this week is out, indeed, perhaps before we go to sleep tonight; by taking up a cross, despising the shame that *each* of us feels when we suffer misunderstanding or vulnerability or the consequences of refusing to go along. It is, precisely, shame that we feel when we so suffer; but learn to despise that shame—to say grimly or cheerfully as we can, "To hell with it!" for the joy that is set before us: the joy of a place with mercy and trust and communion becoming increasingly real.

Of course, we cannot do it alone. Will we sustain one another? Will we receive one another? Will we turn to another—and not just a comfortable friend—and seek, against all the embarrassment, to continue communion?

There's no cheap grace: we must turn *toward* the cross we find in our daily life, *toward* it, not away from it. You sense where that cross is, as I do. Turn toward it, take it up, despising—like proud men and women—the shame of it, for the joy that is set before us.

The joy that is set before us is, first, the joy of discovering powers in ourselves and in our communities that we have not yet even begun to tap—powers that will transform us individually and transform this college.

Second, the joy is the joy of being reunited with those from whom we are estranged. Some of those from whom we are estranged we love so much our breath catches when we feel the grief of the estrangement and the depth of our love.

I've mentioned already the film *Ordinary People.* In that film there are two remarkable scenes of reunion. After many meetings, Conrad asks of Berger the psychiatrist, in effect, why Berger should care what happens to *him*, to Conrad. Berger answers, "Because I'm your friend." "You're my friend," Conrad discovers: he believes at last. All the fierce, anguished conversation brings forth its joy—and Conrad, with tears of sorrow and joy, embraces his friend. Estrangement from himself, from both the living and the dead, is being overcome. Later, Conrad will be able to say to his father, the man he always thought had it made, the man who understood and yet did not understand his son, "I love you, Dad." And again, as father and son embrace each other, estrangement is overcome, and hope, hope is restored.

Conrad has a cross that he has to take up—his memory, his grief, his guilt, his anger, his rejection, his estrangement. He *does* take it up—despising, finally, the shame of it. He does take it up in some indomitable hope that he is not alone. And his hope is not disappointed, however often he doubts it. And, of course, he does doubt it every step of the way, as do you and I.

Let me tell you a true story. I heard it from William Sloane Coffin. It happened some years ago. A man was riding on a train in a mountainous region of Tennessee, the train curling through gorgeous scenery. Sitting next to him was a man lost in thought, thoughts obviously not pleasant but apprehensive; in fact, the man next to him was restless and becoming more and more agitated. Finally, the first man asked him what was wrong. The second man told him that he had been in the penitentiary for the last ten years, that he had just been released and was heading toward his home. Because he was practically illiterate, there had been little correspondence between him and his family over the course of the ten years. With the help of a fellow inmate, however, he had written a letter saying that he was going to be released, that he was headed home, but that he would understand if they didn't want him back. If they *did* want him back, they were to tie a white ribbon around the lowest bough of the last apple tree in the family orchard, the one nearest the railroad tracks. He would see it before the train came into the station. If there was no ribbon, he would just go right on through, and they wouldn't hear from him again. As the train approached the town, the former inmate was getting so nervous that the first man offered to watch for him. Suddenly, he saw the tree, and he cried, "Hey, look, look." The second man did. The whole tree was white with ribbons.[1]

What is the joy that was set before Jesus? It is, third, the joy of believing again in the happy ending—the happy ending of which we're afraid because it seems too good to be true.

Oh, don't get me wrong: when someone tells me that he or she is *absolutely certain* of the happy ending to the troubles of the world and that I *must* believe in this or that version of the happy ending if I am to be saved, that person usually discloses hidden despair. Claims to *absolute certainty* about the happy ending—because "the Bible says so," or because one has had this or that "experience"—usually become *un*happy, desperate, even

---

1. Coffin, "Righteousness of Faith," 5.

fanatic. Fanaticism is rigid defense against despair—despair which, if we'll give up the phony protection in the delusion of absolute certainty, may be transformed into faith and hope and love.

It is all right to doubt, to be uncertain. It is all right to grieve. It is all right to be unhappy. It is all right to be in despair.

The joy that was set before Jesus is a joy which gave him the freedom to cry out to the One he knew more intimately than any other, "My God, my God, why hast Thou forsaken me?" And it is a joy which may allow you or me to cry on the shoulder of one whom we trust: "I don't believe"; "I don't feel it"; "I don't care anymore." The beginning of the happy ending, then, is *not* to have someone reply, "Oh, really you do," or "You must!" or "Get yourself together!" No, the beginning of the happy ending is to hear in response, "You're my friend. We're together in this—and others with us."

The joy that was set before him, the joy of the happy ending that often seems too good to be true, is the joy of finding acceptance and communion as doubters and sufferers and sinners, as men and women of the late twentieth century whose civilization doesn't appear to have a happy ending. (I don't think our *civilization* will have a happy ending.)

Do you remember a song from the musical *West Side Story*?

> There's a place for us,
>   somewhere a place for us. . . .
> Hold my hand and we're halfway there:
>   hold my hand and I'll take you there,
> somehow, someday, somewhere.[2]

The joy that was set before Jesus is the joy of believing again—in order to be faithful to ourselves, to our unquenchable hopes, and to our deepest love—of believing again that there is a place for us, a time for us; that there is a new way of living and caring; that we *will* find a way of forgiving; that if in the meaning of the symbol you hold my hand, then we *are* halfway there; that if in the meaning of the symbol we begin to take *each other's* hands, we do begin to take each other there.

These matters take the power of God to achieve, the power of God to bring us out of our despair and to keep us from delusions which are but masks for despair.

We must be able to learn that we shall die; perhaps, indeed, we may even learn from Jesus how to lay down our lives, every day, for the joy that is set before us. We must learn how to grieve, and, in grief, how to give up

---

2. Bernstein and Sondheim, "Somewhere."

those who have died and to grieve for them because they are dead. But we must recognize the contrary movement of God's power—a movement of the cross itself. Jesus does not teach us to say, "It will soon be over with me, I will shortly be dead." Neither does Jesus teach us to say of those who have died, "They have become nothing." Rather, Jesus teaches us—as he taught Bonhoeffer, the German martyr, when he came to die, to say to his fellow prisoners: "This is the end. For me the beginning of life."[3]

Seek God's kingdom, says Jesus, and the things you need shall be yours as well. Your God knows what you need. Provide yourselves with a treasure that does not fail, where no thief approaches and no moth destroys. For where your treasure is, there will your heart be also.[4]

So finally we speak the mystery, even the mystery of the Sacrifice of Christ which we celebrate and partake of. Finally the joy that was set before Jesus—for which he endured the cross, despising the shame of it—is that everything that joy *is* should come to pass for you and me, for us, and for all humanity together: the discovery of our powers; the overcoming of estrangement; reunion; the power to believe again in the happy ending beyond the pain and the darkness.

However we understand the consciousness of Jesus, the joy that was set before him is that you and I might come into our own, our sin and despair overcome at last, our freedom secured for the beginning of a new life, the new age of forgiveness and love.

For us, he endured the cross, despising the shame. The mystery is that you and I, all of us together, are part of the joy that was set before him.

Amen.

---

3. Bethge, "Editor's Foreword," 11–12, quoting Best, *Venlo Incident*.
4. Luke 12:33–34.

5

"All Things Are Yours"

A Sunday in which an offering of Sacred Dance was made by Vanessa Ochs and Pat Dutcher[1]

MARCH 15, 1981

> *Let no one deceive himself. If any one among you thinks that he is wise in this age, let him become a fool that he may become wise. For the wisdom of this world is folly with God. For it is written, "He catches the wise in their craftiness," and again, "The Lord knows that the thoughts of the wise are futile." So let no one boast of men. For all things are yours, whether Paul or Apollos or Cephas or the world or life or death or the present or the future, all are yours; and you are Christ's; and Christ is God's.*
> —*1 Corinthians 3:18-23* (RSV)

I WANT TO POINT out at the outset that this passage from Paul's letter to the Corinthians is ecstatic. Not often in the University Church have we heard preaching from one of the ecstatic passages of Scripture. But it is well that we do so—and that we do so this morning. Furthermore, I want no one to take what I say this morning as calling us to ethical quietism. If any one thinks she or he hears me doing that, let me say immediately that this is a

---

1. Vanessa Ochs served as Senior Lecturer in English and Writing at Colgate from 1980 to 1986; Patricia "Pat" Dutcher was Assistant Chaplain.

misunderstanding. I hope you will know me better—or, better, that you will know the Bible better—than to hear ethical quietism now in this preaching.

We belong to God: to Christ if you are Christian, and thereby to God; to the people Israel if you are Jewish, and thereby to God. We belong to God. That is Paul's faith. And that is the basis of all that I try to say this morning: you and I belong to God—unreal though that may seem, puzzled as we may be to find meaning in that.

At least, of course, it means we belong to no other. You do not belong to your grade point average, your pension plan, your "analysis" of things (no matter how much you have put into that analysis).

We do not belong to our parents. We shall be, as long as we live, whether our parents are alive or dead, the children of our parents. Professor Hartshorne has said from this pulpit what I must say: "In spite of my being a parent, in spite of my being no longer young, I, too, have been and remain a child of parents." We are to honor our parents . . . and to forgive them. But we do not belong to our parents.[2]

We do not belong to our friends, nor to our husband, wife, or lover.

We belong not to the world, or the flesh, or the devil, not finally.

Of course, if we do not believe and trust that we belong to God, we shall find ourselves inevitably believing—whether consciously or unconsciously—that we belong to or are possessed by *some* person or power: parents, friends, spouse, lover, society. Indeed, that is precisely the way we feel much of the time: it is to "society" that, really, we "belong," it often seems, and we feel compelled by social "pressures," as we say, driven by a need to succeed that we can't help, brought down by anxiety over failure that we can't overcome. Or we feel *possessed* by appetites or *controlled* by needs: we seem, often, to live life in the service of our needs—as if we *belonged* to our needs, as if all we *were* is our needs.

Sometimes we try to find our way out by insisting that we belong only to ourselves. To belong to myself is finally one of the grimmest of all slaveries. It is based on the fiction that *I* have created my life, on the illusion that I can liberate myself from self-preoccupation: and we all know that self-preoccupation is one of the greatest of all miseries. To think I belong to myself is to think that I am the judge of life and of myself; and this leads me into simple ambitious selfishness and exploitation of others or into self-condemnation from which I can find no rest.

---

2. Hartshorne, "Honor Thy Father and Thy Mother."

No—you do not belong to yourself or to any other person or power. You belong to Israel or Christ. And Israel and Christ are God's. You belong to God.

To discover that we belong to God is to discover that we are *free* men and women.

And to begin to know that we belong to God is to begin to discover a transformation of *everything*; to begin to know that we belong to God is to begin to see all things, everything, transformed.

Discouraged by petitions and quarrels and jealousy among his friends and those who have learned from him, Paul nevertheless rediscovers a joy—an ecstatic joy—right in the midst of his discouragement: all things are yours, he exults, whether Paul or Apollos or Cephas (Apollos and Cephas were other leaders and teachers of the community of faith whom many at Corinth preferred to Paul), all things are yours, whether Paul or Apollos or Cephas—or the world! or life! or death! or the present! or the future! all are yours!

Everything, everybody is, though not our possession, yet a *gift*. While we possess no one or *anything* that's able to make life worth living, yet everything and everyone is a gift of God to you: everything and everyone is ours.

Do we begin to understand? Did we begin to understand as Vanessa Ochs and Pat Dutcher, through dance, led us in prayer?

> O Lord, my God,
> I pray that these things never end:
> The sand and the sea,
> The rush of the waters,
> The lightning of the heavens,
> The prayer of the heart.[3]

Do we possess the sand and the sea, the rush of the waters, the lightning of the heavens? Do we possess this beautiful morning? Do we possess the prayers of all the burdened, hoping human hearts? Do we possess even the prayers of our own hearts? Are not even the prayers of our own hearts *given* to us, surging up out of our longing to be reunited with one another, out of our longing to be ourselves at last? Are not the deepest prayers of our hearts as if we were being given the passion and the hope and the love to call out to God for what God alone can do and be?

---

3. Hannah Senesh wrote these words in 1941—a Jewish girl, twenty years old, who died three years later in a Budapest prison, a hero of the Jewish resistance against the Nazis. See Marder, "Meaning of Life."

"All things are yours." What does this mean? There are ten thousand ways of saying it. Emilie Griffin tells us this about herself:

> Oddly enough, it was the writers and filmmakers who were most distant from God who began to surround me [as I matured] with a sense of his reality. Many of the plays which were current then were of the absurdist school. They asserted, as an act of faith, that the world did not make sense and could not be put together in any coherent order. Perhaps the most striking of these plays was Samuel Beckett's *Waiting for Godot*. The two men were waiting forever in a senseless universe, completely bleak and without consolation, for a god who never came. *Endgame* was another example; there were dozens of others.
>
> Somehow I felt that God was right there on the stage with them, but that through some quirk of vision—rather like a stage convention—they were ignoring the fact that he was there! I was rather like children in theaters who want to stand up and shout at the actors, "Look out, he's right behind you!" I could see God in the artistic brilliance which they were using to invent their empty universes; I could see him in their compassion for the sufferings of others; I could see him even in their denial of him. God was like the hidden pattern drawn into a picture of something else, the puzzle one finds in children's magazines. I would be looking at a play or a film which said how empty it all was, and I would see God even there.[4]

What does it mean to learn that "all things are yours"? Doesn't Thomas Merton tell us something about it?

> In *The Seven Storey Mountain*, Merton had described how much the city of Louisville, Kentucky, had seemed to him symbolic of the ugliness and emptiness and false values of the world which he was leaving behind. Four years after its publication . . . Merton was required to accompany the Vicar General of the Trappists [the monastic order to which Merton belonged], who spoke French but no English, into Louisville as an interpreter. Merton's journal [describes] this experience: "I met the world and found it no longer so wicked after all. Perhaps the things I resented about the world when I left it were defects of my own that I had projected upon it. Now, on the contrary, everything stirred me with a deep and mute sense of compassion. . . . I went through the city, realizing for the first time in my life how good

---

4. Griffin, *Turning*, 105.

are all the people in the world and how much value they have in the sight of God."[5]

All things are yours: you don't have to do it alone anymore, just you walking and thinking about it, maybe even praying—but praying in anguish, alone. There is help. God often helps much more powerfully through the gift to you of concrete real persons; God often helps much more powerfully that way than by *isolated* prayer. All things are yours, yes, counselors and doctors are yours, listeners, people able to listen and to support. You *can* have a new imagination: the sense of the impossible can come to an end; the vicious circle can be broken. Will you receive what is yours? Human help, the gift of God.

All things are yours: those from whom you have become estranged, the living and, yes, the dead. You ask me how? I say *begin*; begin to look for the gifts in dreams and memories and tears . . . where and how in your daily life you may be in touch with those from whom you are estranged, living and dead. All things are yours.

Any experience may minister the goal of God for us: that is, your freedom and mine, the ending of our loneliness, the ending of our compulsions and binds, the ending of our sense of impossibility, the beginning of our freedom to believe and to hope and to love.

All things are yours; everything is a gift of God.

Even my sufferings? we ask bitterly.

"Let no one deceive himself," Paul says. "If any one among you thinks he is wise in this age, let him become a fool that he may become wise."

Suffering confounds wisdom. There is no wisdom sufficient to explain suffering. There are, finally, only various ways of receiving it: in despair, bitterness, self-pity, resigned agnosticism: suffering compounding suffering. Or in compassion, trust, and *hope*. For all things, including suffering, are yours.

Death even. Even death is ours. Death is not the devil's instrument but God's. We do not belong to death but to life, what the Bible calls eternal life, to the life of God.

All things are yours: the world or life or death or the present or the future. *Whoever* has led you to trust and helped sustain you in trust. And every one of us is yours, the community is yours, coming together to acknowledge anxiety and sin, to recover faith and hope and love—the community is yours; dance is yours, and songs; all exchanges of peace are yours; simply

---

5. Griffin, *Turning*, 162–63.

being together is yours. Will you receive what is yours? The way of faith is a way *together*; it is a way of life. It is yours. All things are yours.

The difference between all things being yours and your giving a *part* of yourself to *this* and a *part* of yourself to *that*—and thus being torn apart and exhausted—begins to become clearer with this question: Can we let things and persons be themselves? Can we let people be themselves when we come together? Can we let peace be peace and songs be songs and dance be dance? Can we let sin be sin, and anxiety be anxiety, and suffering be suffering, and death be death? Can we let hope be hope, and faith be faith, and love be love? Can we let each other begin to be who we are? And can we begin to let ourselves be ourselves? Can we let Torah be Torah? Can we let Christ be Christ? Can we let God be God?

Only what we give up is ever truly ours.

And we are called to give up trying to make things be other than they are: when we begin to do that, we shall begin to receive them, as gifts—even the gifts of God from whom comes every gift.

Do you love the sand and the sea? The rush of the waters? The lightning of the heavens?

And the prayer of the heart: can we pray, "O Lord, my God" that the prayer of the heart be one of those things that never end? The prayer of your own heart, the prayer of your loved one's heart, of your neighbor's heart, and of your enemy's heart, the deepest prayers of all human hearts? Can you trust God that much? So much that you can believe that, at last, the deepest prayers of all human hearts are to know God and to be empowered to love God and all God's creation? Can we pray that the prayer of the human heart never ends? That it be, eternal, forever with God?

While we *possess* no one or anything, yet everything and everyone is a gift.

Wordsworth once wrote this:

> Vain is the glory of the sky,
> The beauty vain of field and grove,
> Unless, while with admiring eye
> We gaze, we also learn to love.[6]

Learn to love—the sand and the sea, the rush of the waters, the lightning of the heavens. (Then shall we find strength to battle for their

---

6. Wordsworth, "Poems of the Fancy, XX," 130.

preservation.) And learn to love the prayer of the heart—your heart and my heart, the human heart, the human heart *become* human again—a heart of flesh and no longer a heart of stone: can you sense the prayers of human hearts this morning, here and everywhere, hearts like yours? Can you feel and hear the prayer of the human heart?

O Lord, my God, I pray that these things never end.

That is, we pray that that which we love and those whom we love you will take care of forever, that our love will not perish, and that, indeed, we may begin to live from our love and no longer from our dumb, numb defenses, our hates and binds and fears.

We know, I think, what the prayer of the human heart is. It is so simple, but it takes countless forms; it is so vulnerable.

It is embedded in the Lord's Prayer. Give us our daily bread. Relieve us of the burdens of all that we have done and been: forgive us, that is. Lead us not into temptation, but deliver us from evil.

The prayer of the human heart is a gift of the Spirit. Let us reason together. Make us one. Let us love one another. Bring her to life again.

In the words of Gardner Taylor, one of the great Black preachers of our age:

> A few more days shall roll and a few more seasons come and in them . . . "we must . . . serve on, must forgive on." We must go sometimes when we do not feel like going, trying when nobody seems to care. Our work is ours to do. . . .
>
> And then, please God, we shall be able to say, "I've done what you told me. It is finished, not cut off, but finished. Father, take me into thy hands." Put a light in the window. Let some old friends stand in the doorway to welcome us home—"Father, into thy hands . . ." And then with a shout we may cross over. "Cares all past, home at last, heaven to rejoice."[7]

Give us peace.

The prayer of the heart, the human heart: it takes countless forms, I say. It *is* so vulnerable—is it not? *We* are so vulnerable, so vulnerable.

But nothing, you see, that we have not, in love, given up to be itself will ever really be ours.

Give up, to be themselves, all those and all things you love. Then all things are yours.

O Lord, our God,

---

7. Taylor, "At Calvary," 148.

we give up to you the prayer of the heart.
May that prayer never end but
be with you forever.
And hear us as we pray, "Our Father . . ."

6

Begin Now to Live Your Real Life

A Communion Sermon

MAY 3, 1981

For you have died, and your life is hid with Christ in God.
—*Colossians 3:3* (RSV)

For where your treasure is, there will your heart be also.
—*Matthew 6:21* (RSV)

WE'VE LOST OUR PERSPECTIVE.

We're tired . . . tense . . . puzzled . . . guilt-ridden . . . worried . . . regretful . . . preoccupied. It's "one damn thing after another." (And it's not the work that wracks us—not really. It's precisely the worry, the resentment, the lack of self-knowledge, the awareness that we have given up our freedom, and our grace.)

But—we say—"I'll think about it later. I'll do something about it . . . later."

Like Augustine we say, "Give me faith, but not now—later . . . not yet—later."

"Right now my hands are full. Later."

"In June [or October], when I can relax, then I'll try to get my perspective . . . after the term is over . . . after I'm graduated . . . after things have settled down."

We comfort ourselves these days with the new intentions we don't really have now but wish we might have—someday.

We try to get through *these* days with the *delusion* that "in a while," "after the pressures are off," *then* I'll learn how to live, *then* I'll get control over my life, *then* I'll get my act together.

But the gospel is both more compassionate and more severe than our ruminations: *now*—*now* is the time of salvation: not someday, but now.

Grace is grace under pressure.

Our *deeper* hope—and our *real* responsibility—is to become transformed: to let God *begin*—begin to have God's way with us.

To put it in very homely fashion: our deeper hope and our real responsibility is to return to our friends, our families, our tasks and troubles, as transformed persons.

This may not happen; but let's not lose clarity about what God is about:

God is trying to break down your sense of isolation, your sense of being so alone.

God is trying to overcome your self-condemnation, your fear of failure, and your fear of other people.

God is trying to set you free to find the courage to be yourself and to find the power to love other people and yourself.

I saw this cartoon the other day: this very timid minister is preaching in a very wealthy church. The pews are filled with very haughty and luxurious people, and he says, "Now if I've said anything that suggests you ought to change your lifestyle, please disregard it. I didn't mean to do that."

We may smile. But what about Colgate, and *our* lifestyle at the end of terms: resentful, frantic, guilt-ridden, worried, regretful, "one damn thing after another."

No, I can't be that timid minister. The Word of God comes after—homes in on—our lifestyle.

This is *not* a service primarily and simply to help us *get through* these days—whether we're freshmen, seniors, in our thirties, or in our seventies.

This is a service which—in order to give God the glory—is meant to help us become what we ought to be or, better, to help us become our true selves, the ones that deep down we want to be and, by the grace of God, *will* to be and *can* begin to be.

But it's *we* who will be changed, not our situations. Indeed, if the situation is to be changed, it is only through *our* transformation that it will be.

For this transformation, we need a new capacity for honesty—and courage for it: we need to discover what and where our treasure is.

"Where your treasure is, there will your heart be also," Jesus says to us, with that terrible power of his to lay bare our hearts—albeit with complete love for us: where your treasure is, there will your heart be also.

The condition of our hearts reveals our treasure.

What *are* you worrying about?

Where—where is your heart this morning?

For the honesty we need and for the transformation God wills in you and me, take this standpoint, experimentally: "You have died, and your life is hid with Christ in God."

Often when we hear the term "imagination," we think of something "fantastical." But there are other kinds of imagination. Why, sometimes we even say to someone when he or she doesn't "get" something quite obvious, "Hey, use your imagination."

There is something we can call the imagination of the *real*. The imagination of the real *can* be a way to new life.

Anchored in that which we know does come to pass, each of us is asked by St. Paul to imagine that "you have died." Then this imaginative act reaches out to new possibilities which trust and hope and love open up to us: "And your life is hid with Christ in God." But notice the tenses. It is not someday but already and now. *Already* you have died, and *now* your life is hid with Christ in God. You have died; you are not alone; you are secured in love. Those whom you care for, you begin to see, are loved—loved with a love you had forgotten.

Now from *that* standpoint, what is important?

Consider what is important to you, where your treasure is . . . as if you looked back from death on to these days. Not as if this day were the last day of your life but as if you looked back from death on to your life, or looked back *from* your last day on to *these* days. Are you living these days as you would want to remember *having* lived them, looking back on them from the last day of your life?

A free and thankful heart flows from willingness to imagine fully and without reservation the day we die: from the perspective of that day, what do you think of the way you're living this day, these days?

How, *then*, will you have wanted to have lived them? From the perspective of that last day, can your heart be broken, broken down into thanksgiving for the eyes and smiles and tears and laughter, the flesh and blood, the miracle of fellow men and women like yourself in the strange grace of living together *these* very days?

Look around. This "beautiful" morning. Consider the beauty of the world.

Think on loved ones, the dead and the living, friends; people in need.

Consider the memories that are already important to you. Are you living out of those memories? Keeping them before you?

Are you keeping before yourself your *real* hopes? The commitments that *really* matter?

Are you keeping before yourself your *vocation*—that is, your real "calling"—in *these* days and for the days to come?

You have died, and your life is hid with Christ in God.

Begin to *practice* that standpoint—even as you would practice a new dance, or a new language, or a new batting swing. Begin to practice that standpoint as the imagination of the *real*. Begin to consider your life, your treasure (your "values"), begin to consider your life, every day, from that standpoint: I have died, and my life is hid with Christ in God.

How then will I live today? How will I live my *new* life?

I propose that from that standpoint, freedom and glory and joy begin to come into your life and mine. Then morning has, indeed, "broken." Then, *truly*, you will begin a "joy to the world!" For "the Lord *is* come."

You have died, and your life is hid with Christ in God.

There's a wrench to it, of course, even a terrific wrench. We had intended to live life on our own terms—and now that's over, as we know when we imagine ourselves at the last day and look back. From that vantage, it's love and friendship and responsibility and sacrifice. (When you have died, what have you to lose? Your life is hid with Christ in God.)

From that vantage, it's sacrifice and responsibility and friendship and love. It's the world's beauty and—and the persons. Oh, yes, the persons—those from whom we are estranged and long for, and those with whom we are in touch and with whom it's OK—it's the *persons* that mean so much.

As Karl Barth, the great theologian, suggests, the action of God in Jesus Christ has made *persons* the measure of things. From the standpoint of persons, think on politics, economics, knowledge, careers, success, how you *are* and *will be spending* your life.

When, through Christ, we learn to make persons the measure of things, we, too, with St. Paul, will learn how to rejoice—whether we are brought down or raised up. In any and all circumstances we shall learn the secret of facing abundance and want. We shall learn to do all things in Christ who strengthens us.

You have died, and your life—your new life, your real life—is hid with Christ in God.

Now you can begin to live.

Now you can begin to give up that shell of isolation.

Now you can begin to give up that fierce pride. (Of course that pride may wear a kind and even humble smile.) Now you can begin to give up that fierce pride that you give so many justifications to, and which keeps you from ever *really* being *with* others, or *for* them.

Now you can begin to give up that self-condemnation that is so important to you. Maybe you can even begin to face why it is so important to you, begin to discover how deeply you have been hurt, even long ago, by someone you loved so deeply.

Now you can begin to give up insistence on control over your life—that control which is so important to you but which leads (you dimly sense) time and again to anger and despair. You can begin to give up your insistence on control. You have died . . . and your life is hid with Christ in God.

From *that* standpoint what is important? What do you want? Where and what is your treasure?

There *will* be a last day.
How would you then look back on these days?
The imagination can imagine the real: you have died.
Then go on: your life is hid with Christ.
Begin to practice that standpoint even now.
And you may begin to hear God speak to you.

From that standpoint, we may hear God speak thus:

It is not a spirit of timidity and anxiety and regret and guilt, not one of defeat and "one damn thing after another" to which I call you.

It is, rather, to a spirit of power and love and joy.

God wills to give us a spirit of power and love and joy.

God knows how inclined we are to feel overwhelmed.

We need not be defeated and we won't be defeated if, instead of cooperating with our fears, we begin to discover the courage of our conviction that God has more love for us than we will ever have hearts ready to receive.

This is the choice—every day, almost every hour, and in almost every decision: will we cooperate with the fears that tell us "we have no choice," that we are condemned? Or will we cooperate with our conviction (hard as it may be to believe) that we are loved with an absolutely overwhelming love?

On the cross Christ laid bare the heart of God for all to see.

The Word of God to us?

This is my body broken for you.

This is my blood, poured out for you—for each and every one of you, because whether you *believe* it or not, my love for you is greater than any telling of it.

We eat this bread and drink this cup to proclaim the Lord's death till he comes . . . till he comes to us, and we begin to die to ourselves, and to live for one another and the world—even as Christ does.

God would have us receive *the death of Christ* as our *treasure*. For in Christ's death *we* have *died*. And, dying to ourselves, we begin to *live* and enjoy and trust and hope and love . . . and come together.

Your real life *is* hid with Christ in God.

Begin *now* to *live* your real life in the world. Begin now to be free. Don't wait. Begin now to live.

To that glorious purpose, the table of Jesus Christ is spread before us.

7

Both Tears and Mirth

Sermon at a Unified Service of the University Church and the Roman Catholic Community at Colgate

SEPTEMBER 6, 1981

And he said, "There was a man who had two sons; and the younger of them said to his father, 'Father, give me the share of property that falls to me.' And he divided his living between them. Not many days later, the younger son gathered all he had and took his journey into a far country, and there he squandered his property in loose living. And when he had spent everything, a great famine arose in that country, and he began to be in want. So he went and joined himself to one of the citizens of that country, who sent him into his fields to feed swine. And he would gladly have fed on the pods that the swine ate; and no one gave him anything. But when he came to himself he said, 'How many of my father's hired servants have bread enough and to spare, but I perish here with hunger! I will arise and go to my father, and I will say to him, "Father, I have sinned against heaven and before you; I am no longer worthy to be called your son; treat me as one of your hired servants."' And he arose and came to his father. But while he was yet at a distance, his father saw him and had compassion, and ran and embraced him and kissed him. And the son said to him, 'Father, I have sinned against heaven and before you; I am no longer worthy to be called your son.' But the father said to his servants, 'Bring quickly the best robe, and put it on him; and put

> *a ring on his hand, and shoes on his feet; and bring the fatted calf and kill it, and let us eat and make merry; for this my son was dead, and is alive again; he was lost, and is found.' And they began to make merry."*
>
> —Luke 15:11-24 (RSV)
> See also Luke 14:15-24

THERE ARE TIMES—RIGHT NOW, for many of us—when you wonder each hour what you're going to meet *next*—and what it's going to be like.

One has an inner focus: "What's happening inside me? Who *am* I in all of this?"

And we have an outer focus: "Who do you be with here? Who do you stay away from?"

"What is *she* like?"; "What is *he* like?"

We are in a great variety of conditions this morning.

Some feel, half-consciously, that they have been pressured into coming to college. "This is what my parents wanted, or the guidance counselor. But have *I* really chosen this?" some ask themselves.

For some, Colgate feels like liberation: it's great.

For some, it feels like incarceration.

Some feel well matched to things and happy to be here; some are asking, deep down, "Will I survive? Will I find friends?"

Some of us are homesick.

Some of us are feeling virtually nothing.

Basically, the question is, *Who tells you who you are here at Colgate*?

And don't say, "I tell myself who I am." For we see ourselves as those whose acceptance is important to us see us.

"So I ask you, who is going to tell you who you are?" William Sloane Coffin expands that question this way: "Is it going to be some institution? Or is it going to be God?"[1]

> If it's God who tells you who you are, you don't have to *prove* yourself at all. All that is taken care of. You are precious, you are unprecedented, you are irrepeatable, and in the divine dispensation, you are indispensable. So you don't have to prove yourself again. All you have to do is *express* yourself. What a world of difference there is between proving oneself and expressing oneself. What a different world it would be if all we felt called on to do

---

1. Coffin, "Baccalaureate Sermon."

was to express the beautiful selves that we are made and meant to be by God.²

To express the real selves we are made and meant to be by God: that means, among other things, that we begin to discover our capacity for *mirth* and for *tears*.

Some of us have not cried since we were in sixth grade—and we are dry and taut because we have not.

Some of us cried yesterday—or even this morning.

As for mirth. Mirth is a rejoicing, a spontaneous happiness that may issue briefly in laughter but is there before we laugh, and it continues after we have laughed.

Let me tell you a true story I got from the same Bill Coffin, a story I told a considerably different Colgate congregation last spring.

> A man was riding on a train in a mountainous region of Tennessee, the train curling through gorgeous scenery. Sitting next to him was a man lost in thought, thoughts obviously anxious and apprehensive. Finally the first man asked the man full of apprehension what was wrong. And he learned that the second man had been in the penitentiary for the last ten years, that he had just been released and was heading toward his home. Because he was practically illiterate there had been little correspondence between him and his family over the course of the ten years. With the help of a fellow inmate, however, he had written a letter saying that he was going to be released, that he was headed home, but that he would understand if they didn't want him back. If they *did* want him back, they were to tie a white ribbon around the lowest bough of the last apple tree in the family orchard, the tree right next to the railroad tracks. He would see the tree before the train came into the station. If there was no ribbon, he would just go right on through and they wouldn't hear from him again. As the train approached the town the former inmate became so nervous that the first man offered to watch for him. Suddenly he saw the tree, and he cried, "Hey, look, look." The former inmate did. The whole tree was white with ribbons.³

Mirth: a rejoicing, and joy, deep down.

The gospel is a gospel of cross and resurrection. It seeks to unite in us our capacity for tears and our capacity for joy, for mirth: to unite them. If it

2. Coffin, "Baccalaureate Sermon" (emphasis added).
3. Coffin, "Righteousness of Faith," 5.

is God who tells you who you are, you can begin to discover that capacity both for tears and for mirth.

Fred Buechner helps us draw out the gospel in those parables of Jesus we heard this morning—the parables read by Father Leonard and Marie Lindhorst.[4]

> God is the eccentric host who, when the country-club crowd all turn out to have other things more important to do than come live it up with him, goes out into the skid rows and soup kitchens and charity wards and he brings home . . . the man with no legs who sells shoelaces at the corner. The old woman in the moth-eaten fur coat who makes her daily rounds of the garbage cans. The wino with his pint in a brown paper bag. The pusher, the whore, the village idiot who stands at the blinker light waving his hands as the cars go by. They are seated at the damask-laid table in the great hall. The candles are all lit and the champagne glasses filled. At a sign from the host, the musicians in their gallery strike up "Amazing Grace." If you have to explain it, don't bother.
>
> And then of course there is that Prodigal Son who goes off with his inheritance and blows the whole pile . . . on what? . . . on liquor and sex and fancy clothes? Anyway on whatever he blows it on, until he doesn't have two dollars left. He gets a job . . . and keeps at it long enough to observe that the pigs are getting a better deal than he is, and then he decides to go home. We can't be sure at all that he realizes he's made an ass of himself and broken his old man's heart. . . . He decides to go home for the basic reason apparently that he knows he always got three square meals a day there and a comfortable room. He sets out on the return trip and on the way rehearses a speech he hopes will soften his dad's heart enough to let him in. And just about the time he thinks he has it down, the old man spots him coming around the corner of the yard and starts sprinting wildly down the drive. Before the boy has time to get so much as the first word out, his father throws his arms around him, his whiskers, his tears, his joyous mirth all mingled in his embrace of his son.
>
> The boy is back, that's all that matters. Who cares why he's back? And the old man doesn't do what almost any other father under heaven would have been inclined to do. He doesn't say he hopes he has learned his lesson or I told you so. He doesn't say he hopes he is finally ready to settle down for a while and find

---

4. Fr. Leonard Kotzbauer served as Chaplain to Colgate's Catholic community; Marie Lindhorst was Assistant Chaplain in the University Church.

some way to make it up to his mother. He just says, "Bring him something to eat ... Bring him some warm clothes." ...

And when the boy finally manages to slip his prepared remarks in edgewise, his father seems hardly to hear him. All he can say is the boy was dead and is alive again. And then, as Jesus, the teller of the parable, says, "They began to make merry."[5]

The elder brother we must leave for another day. But the truth, of course, is that his father loves him, too; he has always loved him and will always love him, only the elder brother never notices it because he is too busy trying to get his due, too busy trying cheerlessly to earn things.

"The blind receive their sight, the lame walk, the deaf hear, the dead are raised up," even as the prodigal son himself was raised up. "And," says Jesus, "blessed is he who takes no offense at me."[6]

Everything human must have in it both joy and sorrow. Tears and sorrow are a fundamental element in all true life and love, mine and yours. But mirth and joy are also fundamental, can be fundamental, that is, if the One who tells us who we are is the One who spangles the Tree of Life till it is white with ribbons, is the eccentric host of the candlelit banquet, is the One who when we come back into view after "losing it," losing it all, sprints down the drive—and before our words are out—throws arms, even everlasting arms around us and says, this my grown child was dead and is alive again, was lost and is found.

At this time and in the days ahead, do not hide from any failure, any suffering, any grief, any sin, any loss. Bring them up to consciousness; have the courage to come to yourself; trust in the compassion at the heart of God. Do not condemn yourself when you are not happy (it is all right not to be happy), when you are soul-sick or sin-sick, bewildered or lonely or afraid. Do not condemn yourself—instead remember the gospel.

The one who fills the gospel is Jesus the Christ, the truly human being and the second person of God: his pathos is natural, almost casual. He does not always smile certainly. No, no. And his sign is not the three little monkeys who see no evil, hear no evil, speak no evil. No, his sign is a cross—on which the prince of glory died. As G. K. Chesterton observes, the Stoics conceal their tears. Jesus does not conceal his tears. He shows them plainly on his open face—at daily sights, and most certainly at a friend's death—though he brought again to life his friend, even as he can bring us to life. His heart goes out to the crowds, harassed and bewildered. And his

---

5. For the development of Luke 15:11–32; 14:15–24 here, a quotation from (and adaptation of) Buechner, *Telling the Truth*, 66–68.

6. See Matthew 11:2–6.

tears are intense and powerful as he looks on what we have done to our civilization. He does not conceal his tears; yet, as Chesterton remarks, he conceals something. Solemn men of power are proud of restraining their anger. He does not always restrain his anger. He flings furniture down the front steps of the temple and asks the self-confident (perhaps especially the religiously self-confident) how they expect to escape damnation. Yet he restrains something, something in that shattering personality—is it a kind of shyness? There is something that he hides from people when he goes off to pray, to pray for us. There is something he covers by abrupt silences.[7]

There is some one thing too great for God to show us until we have begun to come to ourselves; until we have begun to overcome letting anyone or anything (power, money, institution, even peers or parents), anything or anyone but God tell us who we are; until we have returned from our journeys into far countries of delusion and emptiness; until *with* God we walk through the dangers, toils and snares of our own life and generation—bearing the cross that is ours to bear (its gift *hidden* in it); until we have entered truly into the new life that we are given through God's sacrifice.

It awaits us, it surrounds us, even now it is at hand—in the midst of our tears, our dryness, and, yes, when we feel nothing at all. It is the surprising accompaniment of an unbreakable love. There is some one thing too great for God to show us until—until we are ready. And that *is*: God's mirth; we may say the deep-down merry-heartedness, yes, the *joy* of God as God beholds us, individually and together, and even now—leaving that unapproachable light and mystery in which God dwells—fully human and bearing the marks of His brokenness, He comes to meet us in the actual life we are living.

---

[7]. For several insights and sentences here and in the following paragraphs, see Chesterton, *Orthodoxy*, 294–99.

8

Hope

A Communion Sermon

FEBRUARY 7, 1982

> *Jesus our Lord . . . was put to death for our trespasses and raised for our justification. Therefore, since we are justified by faith, we have peace with God through our Lord Jesus Christ. Through him we have obtained access to this grace in which we stand, and we rejoice in our hope of sharing the glory of God. More than that, we rejoice in our sufferings, knowing that suffering produces endurance, and endurance produces character, and character produces hope, and hope does not disappoint us, because God's love has been poured into our hearts through the Holy Spirit which has been given to us.*
> —Romans 4:24b—5:5 (RSV)

PAUL THE APOSTLE OFTEN puts things—how should we say?—"compactly." And I want to spend a few minutes trying to break open those verses from Romans we have just heard read:

"Jesus our Lord . . . was put to death for our trespasses"—

for our false steps, Paul means;

because we have missed the mark with our lives;

because together, we human beings have cut ourselves off from the *source* and *fulfillment* of our real life;

and cut ourselves off from others,

and from ourselves.

Jesus "was put to death for our trespasses and raised for our justification": God finds glory in making all things new for us.

Jesus has been raised to establish, without qualification and without hindrance, our right to be. Jesus has been raised to establish

our acceptability;

to establish our freedom to be ourselves—without apology or self-condemnation;

Jesus has been raised to establish in our heart of hearts—and in the presence of all the world—enduring knowledge of our own worth;

an enduring sense of self-worth;

and thereby establish in us, even as for the first time, the power to worship—to declare, in our words and in our lives, the worth of God; to begin to forget ourselves, to begin to lay ourselves aside, and to love the One who sets us free; the One who establishes us in the face of the world, the flesh and the devil, who gives us a place and a life that cannot be taken away.

"Therefore," Paul continues, "since we are justified by faith, we have peace with God through our Lord Jesus Christ. Through him we have obtained access to this grace in which we stand."

It is as though there were—as often there is according to our perceptions or our feelings—an angry crowd of accusers who say, "You can't come forward to this table, or come forward to anything else. You are to be ashamed of who you are. You are worthless. You should go off. You should go off and hide yourself. Indeed, if really you knew you should go off—and die." It is as though—indeed, it is the *fact* that Christ rebukes our accusers, those within and without, whether they speak truly or falsely and then opens a way through them, takes away the power and authority of those who condemn us (the voices without and the voices within, conscious and subconscious), clears the way, makes room, gives us a place to stand, to be, and lets us rejoice—rejoice in our hope: rejoice in our hope of sharing the glory of God.

"More than that," Paul goes on, "*now* we rejoice" even "in our sufferings," knowing that suffering—

suffering produces endurance when our lives have been justified;

suffering produces endurance when our worth has been established;

suffering produces endurance when a place has been opened for us and a place given us to stand; and such "endurance produces character," and such "character"—in us, and before others—"produces hope." That is, character, which comes when we suffer and endure no longer ashamed of ourselves, no longer believing ourselves worthless, no longer having to answer to our accusers—within or without, no matter how right they may be;

but, instead, confident that we are meant to be, confident that we have right to be: such character participates in producing hope. For God is its source.

And this hope—this "hope does not disappoint us." Because something has happened. Something has happened. "God's love has been poured into our" dry hard "hearts."

To have God's love poured into our hearts is not to have some special feeling—though it may transform our feelings about everything. Paul uses the image of something being "poured" into us to make this point: something has happened which is not of our doing—any more than our being born is of our doing. Hope, which endures, which does not disappoint us, is not something we produce out of our own hearts. This gift, I should point out, often comes in unexpected ways. It may seem, for example, like an attack upon us. Something happens, and we lose confidence in our ability to control our lives, to have life on our own terms.

But then we may begin to understand Paul's image of God's love being "poured" into our hearts. It is an image for the help that is not of our own making, that comes to us through another.

To *feel* the image a little—let me play for a moment: think of your mouth on a hot summer day—if you can in this weather—dry and thirsty, your mouth and your whole body, and poured into it a cold beer or an iced lemonade;

or think of your mouth—better again, your whole body, on a cold, windy winter night when your feet hurt with it and your back shivers with it, after a long, unexpected walk—and poured into you, softly, gently, but fully, a hot cider or rum or chocolate.

The point is that it's not something we produce out of ourselves: any more than that beer or lemonade in the summer, that hot drink in the winter, comes out of ourselves. It comes into us. "God's love" is "poured into our hearts through the Holy Spirit"—not through *our* spirit but through the Spirit who helps us in our weakness, the Spirit who intercedes for us: the Spirit "which has been given to us"—simply given to us.

Because God's love has been poured into our hearts; because we have been given space, a place to stand; because Jesus died for us while we were isolated, cut off, and has been raised to establish our sense of our worth, to give us unity and real life, we begin to worship, to rejoice in our hope of sharing the glory of God. And that *hope* does not disappoint us.

As I say, in six verses of the Letter to the Romans, Paul the Apostle perhaps cries out the whole gospel of Christ: we are assured that there is hope that does not disappoint.

In an old-fashioned sense of the word "study," you and I have studied *much less* the Good News of hope than we have studied disappointment.

The hope that does *not* disappoint sounds strange, remote, incredible, too good to be true. We find ourselves asking, "What is that all about?" even as, deep down, we find ourselves hoping—hoping against hope—that we might come to know it;

that however *little* we understand or believe it, such hope might, really, be true—and that we, too, might live daily in hope: even in hope that does not disappoint us.

But, as I have remarked, you and I have much more studied disappointment: about disappointment we can say much more. About disappointment *we* can be much more articulate. It's a subject we have "studied" much better. We know what disappointment is, every one of us.

What disappointments do you know? And where would you begin?

With your grades last term?

With your January program? Even the courses you have for this term? Or is it the fraternity system?

Is it disappointment with certain Colgate students? Or members of the administration or of the faculty? Or perhaps just Colgate in general?

Is your disappointment over not making a team—perhaps some time ago but the disappointment still rankling?

Or is it disappointment with some other decision made in regard to you?

Or with your job prospects?

Is it disappointment with political events and politicians? With the Reagan administration? With the world situation?

Is it over relations between women and men at this college and in this culture?

Is it with the selfishness or apathy of others?

Is it disappointment with one with whom you have, or had, fallen in love? Or with some other friend?

Or is it with a parent? Or both your parents? Or a brother or a sister?

Is it disappointment with religion and religious people? Or the church?

Is it disappointment with your failure to keep your own resolutions about something?

Is it with something you have done?

Is your disappointment with yourself?

Is your disappointment that deep-down disappointment of all human beings at some time that we cannot—alone or together—overcome the power of death?

The Bible, remarkably, has rather little to say, directly, about disappointment. Oh, in the book of Job, God warns Job, at last, that a person whose hope rests in human ability to master nature will be disappointed.

And Job recognizes, earlier, that no disappointment is probably more intense than the disappointment which comes when, in great need for them, our friends fail us.

When the Bible speaks of disappointment, its dominant word is about that which does *not* disappoint us. "To you, O my God," declares the psalmist, men and women have cried out in their disappointment. In You they trusted and were not disappointed. In the midst of their disappointments they trusted in You—they hoped in You—and in You they were not disappointed.

The gospel does not give a direct answer to our disappointments—to yours, or mine—much as we want it to: we want either to have things our way or not to feel disappointed.

But the gospel neither promises that things will go our way nor gives us a technique for not *feeling* our disappointments. Rather, we are told to cry out—to cry out!—to let your disappointments be known: to yourself and to God.

It is not a matter of being free from doubt.

It is not a matter of not being, really, disappointed. We *really* are disappointed—with all kinds of things, with others, with ourselves, yes, often with our lives as we have known them. We really are disappointed.

But hope is not destroyed when we doubt or are disappointed. There hope begins. Cry out your doubt and disappointment. Cry out, "O God." Then listen: *this* will *not* disappoint you . . . even in the midst of your disappointments.

There is hope that will not disappoint us.

It is that hope which is produced by character that has endured suffering and into which—amidst that very suffering—the love of God is poured.

The peace of God, for which we hope—and in which God would have us *live*—is not contradicted by tribulation or even calamity. It is not removed from us even when we disintegrate. Our struggles without and our fears within do not quench it. When we cry out, "O God!" the cry is heard, and then and there we are the children of God. We are always restless in our tribulations; we can never *accept* them. People of faith are full of longing. And they cry out if there is misery . . . like Jesus their Lord. But our hope does not have its nerve center in ourselves. Our hope is in the One—unto whom we cry out our disappointment, our grief, our loss, our heart; and that hope will not disappoint us.

The hope that will not disappoint us? It is the hope that God means what, through Christ, God says—

The broken-hearted are blessed; they have the special eye and compassion of God. Can you hope for that?

Those who are outcast and feel that they are worthless are to be brought forward. There is a place for them—now and forever—in the very presence of God. Can you hope for that?

There is a place for you—a place for you with all kinds of companions. Can you hope for that?

And for love for those companions? And for peace with God? And for the simple ecstasy of worship? When God will be everything to everyone—and *real* life will begin.

Can you hope for that?

You can. You do. Even against hope you hope for that. As do I.

The glory of God is the glory of being able to love—no matter what. Our hope is that we shall share the glory of God. Our hope is that we, too, shall be able to love—no matter what. Have you not heard that "love bears all things, believes all things, hopes all things"?

Even when we come to our last hour, when we feel life no longer, when our dreams dissolve and we are parted from those we love, when the songs are silenced and the sun on the dazzling snow is gone, then, even then, this hope—this love does not desert us. Then it gives reality to an old prayer: "When I depart, depart Thou not from me."

The Good News is that *Hope*, even the Spirit of God is given to us. It is not our poor spirits of which I speak: we don't have to prove ourselves anymore. It is not like feeling good about something good we have done. It is not a reward for being religious, God knows.

The person who lives in this hope no longer lives in despair over what time brings—*whatever* it brings, whatever our disappointments—but in the hope of God which does not disappoint us.

Christ has died: Christ has been raised. And by the cross and resurrection comes the Spirit, the Spirit of hope that does not disappoint us—hope for ourselves, hope for our world, hope for our real life together as children of God.

The way has been cleared. We have a place to stand in hope.

The bread and the wine are for us. For us the broken body, and Christ's blood poured out.

9

You Have a Vocation

February 14, 1982

Being asked by the Pharisees when the kingdom of God was coming, [Jesus] answered them, "The kingdom of God is not coming with signs to be observed, nor will they say, 'Lo, here it is!' or 'There!' for behold, the kingdom of God is in the midst of you."
—*Luke 17:20-21* (RSV)

SOME OF YOU MAY know the following reflection by Peter L. Berger from *A Rumor of Angels*:

> A child wakes up in the night, perhaps from a bad dream, and finds himself surrounded by darkness, alone, beset by nameless threats. At such a moment the contours of trusted reality are blurred or invisible, and in the terror of incipient chaos the child cries out for his mother. It is hardly an exaggeration to say that, at this moment, the mother is being invoked as a high priestess of protective order. It is she (and, in many cases, she alone) who has the power to banish the chaos and to restore the benign shape of the world. And, of course, any good mother will do just that. She will take the child and cradle him in the timeless gesture of the Magna Mater who became our Madonna. She will turn on a lamp, perhaps, which will encircle the scene with a warm glow of reassuring light. She will speak or sing to the child, and the content of this communication will invariably be the same—"Don't be afraid—everything is in order, everything

is all right." If all goes well, the child will be reassured, his trust in reality recovered, and in this trust he will return to sleep.

All this, of course, belongs to the most routine experiences of life and does not depend upon any religious preconceptions. Yet this common scene raises a far from ordinary question, which immediately introduces a religious dimension: Is the mother lying to the child? The answer, in the most profound sense, can be "no" only if there is some truth in the religious interpretation of human existence. Conversely, if the "natural" is the only reality there is, the mother is lying to the child—lying out of love, to be sure, and obviously not lying to the extent that her reassurance is grounded in the fact of this love—but, in the final analysis, lying all the same. Why? Because the reassurance, transcending the immediately present two individuals and their situation, implies a statement about reality as such. . . .

Every parent (or, at any rate, every parent who loves his child) takes upon himself the representation of a universe that is ultimately in order and ultimately trustworthy. This representation can be justified only within a religious . . . frame of reference. In this frame of reference the natural world within which we are born, love, and die is not the only world, but only the foreground of another world in which love is not annihilated in death, and in which, therefore, the trust in the power of love to banish chaos is justified.[1]

When Jesus is asked when the kingdom of God is coming, he answers, "The kingdom of God is not coming with signs to be observed; nor will they say, 'Hey, here it is' or 'There!' for behold, the kingdom of God is in the midst of you."

Not, notice, according to the most reliable reading, "within you" but "in the midst of you," in your midst.

Jesus never defines the kingdom of God. Rather, he tells parables about it, many parables, all with the message—the kingdom is at hand. It cannot be stopped. It cannot be overcome. It is not yet, you say? It will come, wait for it, hope for it, *live* for it. And although it is "not yet" in its glory, yet it is already here—in your midst: discover it, seek it out.

To make the reality of God present: this is the essential mystery of Jesus.

The reality of God's ethos, the environment of God, is not yet, according to Jesus, certainly not: look at the world, look at your life.

---

1. Berger, *Rumor of Angels*, 67–71.

You Have a Vocation

But it is dawning! And, against all our attempts to establish *another* ethos, *another* environment, *another* world (all of which attempts fail), the kingdom is already present. The person with ears to hear—let that person hear. The person with eyes to see—let that person see.

God's world, God's reality, God's ethos, God's environment is both revealed to us and hidden from us. But it is hidden in the everyday world of the present time, not in some far distant realm from which we are cut off.

We are to pray: "Thy kingdom come, thy will be done on earth as it is in heaven." And we are to hear the word that "the kingdom of God is in the midst of you."

Therefore, in the everyday world of the present time we are to seek and to disclose—to seek and to disclose in our world, in our lives, the ethos, the environment, the relationships and rule, yes, the kingdom of God.

Seniors are going for interviews, sending off applications in the everyday world of the present time at Colgate; they are trying to decide or figure out what they'll do after Colgate. They are called to believe that there is life after Colgate. And they are becoming "believers."

But the job situation is complex and difficult; and knowing oneself and where to head often seems more difficult still.

"Where am I going? Where am I? *Who* am I?" in the midst of the interviews and applications, many seniors ask. And not only seniors. Sophomores think about their major, their concentration, often with the same concern. First-year students think about the same questions and have already been asked—perhaps often—"and what are you preparing for at Colgate?" Juniors sense that the seniors' questions are racing toward them. And those of us who are older: we, too, wonder about our careers, our prospects, our selves, our lives. We *all* wonder about our *vocation*.

The word "vocation" is often used interchangeably with the word "career." We rather assume if we don't have a job we have no vocation. But let's pause on that word "vocation." It comes from the Latin *vocatio*, which means a call, a summons. To have a vocation is to have a call.

And here we begin to reach down into the depths: and many of us must confess, we seem to hear no call. A call for *me?* That would be nice. But there seems no call to us. Oh, if there would be, that would be great. Then I would not go round and round so. But all there seem to be are "options," "prospects," "chances," "possibilities," "limits," and "dead-ends." And *I?* I must sort them out, sort them *all* out somehow, decide (I guess)—at least that's what so many seem to be telling me: "Decide!" "*When* are you going to decide?" they ask. "*What* are you going to decide?"

Or more despairingly—and sometimes the voice wells up from within—"What's going to become of you?"; "What's going to become of me?" we echo in anxious depths that sometimes come to the surface to confound or even panic us.

We have walked on the old golf course or on back streets at home, in the hills or down Broad Street; we have sat at a desk and chewed on a pencil or lain on our beds—in the morning, or afternoon, or late at night—and we have heard only the sounds of silence or our own confusion, the voices of our own "socialization," as we put it. We have heard no call but only the condemning voice which says, "You haven't decided?! Not yet?! You *must* decide!" And then, perhaps, we have heard that cry of our own: "What will become of me—especially if I can't decide? How can I decide? My call? I hear none." Only the many voices of my culture, through parents, friends, my many wishes, my conflicting wishes—wishes that so often cancel each other out. "Where am I? Who am I? My call? I want to decide, but how can I? What will happen to me?"

You and I are anxious. We are anxious about many things. There seems no foundation for our lives, no fundamental security for us.

Anxiety is to be distinguished from fear—to be distinguished from fear of something in particular. Anxiety is our search for fundamental meaning and fundamental security for our lives. Anxiety is our search for fundamental security, our search for some way to hear—through all the many and conflicting voices—to hear our call, our vocation.

Some of us already realize that what Nietzsche says is true: A person can bear any *how* if a person has a *why*. If I have an answer to the why of my life, I can bear any *how*. *How* I shall live becomes clear, bearable, even joyous when I have the *why*, when I have my call, my vocation.

We are, however, anxious about our *why*. We are anxious because we seem to have heard no call. We are anxious about our place in the world; what will become of us; whether or not there is, for us, any call.

And precisely *here, here* Jesus addresses us—simply and straightforwardly, so simply and straightforwardly that we are distressed, even angered with his word: "Be not anxious." Be not anxious.

But those three words—"Be not anxious"—are not words of condemnation, however easily we may turn them into that. *Jesus does not say* (in condemning tones): Be not anxious or you'll get zapped, by God or something.

Jesus says (quietly and compassionately), "Be not anxious" because he knows we *are* anxious. Our call begins with this word to us: "Be not anxious."

Of course we resist our call. After all, we ask, how shall I be sustained? How shall I find sustenance, even some happiness for my life? How shall I gain some *recognition*?

And there it is—near the heart, perhaps the *very* heart of our anxiety: our need for *recognition*. Every one of us seeks a life that will assure us some recognition, a life that assures us that we count, a life that assures us that some significant others see us, or another sees us and values us.

We die for lack of recognition: an infant or small child, literally—all of us, psychologically and spiritually.

Why is making money so important? *In part* because we've trivialized ourselves and gotten hooked on consumption—I mean, really hooked on it (as much as someone can be hooked on heroin): we can't resist it.

But, more deeply, making money is so important to us because making money is the measure of *recognition* and the source of *recognition*. Money is power, yes, but above all, power to gain *recognition*.

Money doesn't bring happiness; yet often we can't imagine being happy without orienting our lives on making money. We feel *driven* to find careers that make good money. Even those of us who are thinking about other kinds of careers feel uneasy, *even guilty*, about *not* setting our lives on good incomes.

For money in our culture means recognition. Indeed, it often seems the only way to recognition. When parents speak of children who are "doing well," what do they mean? They so often mean, he or she is making good money, or is doing well in a graduate program with good prospects for good money.

It's not the money (as we say) —it's the things money will buy: the cars, the trips . . . and the recognition. With money, then we count; then we shall have to be reckoned with. And we *must* have recognition.

Indeed, I say again, we die for lack of recognition.

And so what does Jesus say? He says, Be not anxious. He says, But seek first the kingdom, and all that you need will be yours as well.

Our responses vary.

Some of us find what Jesus says—and the preacher repeating it—just silly. We may not say so, but that's how we find it—just silly. And those who find it silly may be closer to the kingdom than those who nod in agreement, earnestly and piously. For we who find it just silly have begun to hear. We who find it silly recognize that there must be another reality—another reality than the one that seems to prevail—if Jesus' words are to be heeded at all. (The claim of the gospel, of course, is that the word of Jesus actually begins to create and disclose another reality—by which we may live and die.)

Another response is that of the religiously sophisticated among us. They say it's an *inner* attitude, a *spiritual* matter.

But sometimes we must beware the religiously sophisticated. For, as common sense knows, the test of *inner* attitudes and *spiritual* matters is how people live.

The religion of Hamilton, New York—and perhaps of your hometown—is houses. When people get down, in Hamilton, to what they're really interested in, to what *real* life is all about, they talk of houses. Church people and non-church people alike seem to share in that religion. "Where your treasure is, there will your heart be also."

Others of us respond to Jesus with a variation of an Arab saying: "Trust God, but tie your camel."

(I am struck by how different the saying is when one says, Tie your camel . . . but trust God.)

Some of us respond with "God helps those who help themselves." God may even help them, I suppose, but that is neither the message of the Bible nor the gospel of Christ.

Let us hear Jesus again:

> No one can serve two masters; for either he will hate the one and love the other, or he will be devoted to the one and despise the other. You cannot serve God and mammon.
>
> Therefore I tell you, do not be anxious about your life, what you shall eat or what you shall drink, nor about your body, what you shall put on. Is not life more than food, and the body more than clothing? Look at the birds of the air: they neither sow nor reap nor gather into barns, and yet your heavenly Father feeds them. Are you not of more value than they? And which of you by being anxious can add one cubit to his span of life? And why are you anxious about clothing? Consider the lilies of the field, how they grow; they neither toil nor spin; yet I tell you, even Solomon in all his glory was not arrayed like one of these. But if God so clothes the grass of the field, which today is alive and tomorrow is thrown into the oven, will he not much more clothe you, O men of little faith? Therefore do not be anxious, saying, "What shall we eat?" or "What shall we wear?" For the Gentiles seek all these things; and your heavenly Father knows that you need them all. But seek first his kingdom and his righteousness, and all these things shall be yours as well.[2]

---

2. Matthew 6:24–33 (RSV).

Some who sense or have discovered the awful misuses of religion believe we hear Marx's "opiate" of the people when we hear that lesson.

The child without shoes and without food made proper answer to the cruel-minded person, a religious person, too, who asked the child, "But if God loved you wouldn't God send you food and shoes?" The child replied, "God told someone, but the one God told, forgot."

And those who may be wondering if the preacher forgot that he was preaching about vocation can be relieved. There it is again: your vocation and mine. God has told us about those in need of food and shoes, those in need of warmth and friendship and inclusion, those in need of justice and care.

God's care is not lowered from the sky but provided through hands and hearts that are moved—yes, broken—by the power of love.

You *have* a vocation. It is not that you are waiting to find your vocation or me mine. It's rather that our vocation is waiting for us—right now.

Will you accept your vocation, your calling? That is the only question.

The details you will work out and "with fear and trembling." Yet no longer in anxiety—not really; rather, with trust that your anxiety is being turned into the power to search out—those who *wait* for you!

You see, we are *recognized*. We are *recognized* in our anxiety. "Be not anxious" is the first word of recognition. You are *recognized* in your anxiety . . . in your search for what sustains . . . in your search for recognition . . . in your search for a "why."

The word of Jesus comes above and beneath the countless other voices throwing you this way and that. Jesus is at work—transforming your anxiety, transforming your search for recognition, your search for fundamental meaning, for fundamental security.

What does Jesus call his work? He calls it "the kingdom of God." Where is it? Where the blind are, and the lame, and the outcasts, the deaf, yes, and the dead—wherever there is hunger and thirst for a human, caring response and for recognition.

That is your vocation, your calling—and mine. Your vocation is to search out the kingdom now, to search it out in every ordinary thing—today and tomorrow—in everything and everyone you find in the midst of ordinary life.

Your longing has a goal. Do you not *long* when you go for those walks and sit at your desk and lie on your bed? You can kill that longing. But there is nothing else that will *meet* that longing.

And are you not—and I—those who have been told but have forgotten? You are. And so am I. You are needed. You are, desperately. You are *recognized*. You are *called*. The world is dying for lack of hope, for lack of those to feed the hungry and care for the broken—which, finally, is all of us.

If we do not accept our calling to be Christ-bearers, our lives are failures—that is the hard word. If we *do* accept our calling—no matter what happens—we shall succeed. That is the promise. We shall have the *why* to bear any *how* . . . even under conditions of the breakup of our world.

So your major, your concentration, is *given* you.

Seek it *first*. For as a great nineteenth-century preacher warned: Do not touch the gospel unless you are willing to seek the kingdom first. I promise you a miserable existence if you seek it second.[3]

You are recognized. You are recognized in your very anxiety.

Thus in compassion and acceptance Jesus says to us, "Be not anxious." You are recognized. Recognize that you have been recognized. Recognize my recognition of you.

And in your longing seek first now the kingdom of God. Let it concentrate your mind, and break and warm your heart. And whatever else you need will be provided. That is my promise.

Enter into the struggle—the new struggle—to follow your calling, your vocation. For you are recognized. You have a vocation. You are called even now.

Seek first, from now on, the kingdom of God.

For that kingdom—is in the midst of you.

---

3. Henry Drummond, no book reference; remark given during a theology class (date unknown).

10

The Last Enemy Is Death

An Easter Sermon

APRIL 11, 1982

Lo! I tell you a mystery. We shall not all sleep, but we shall all be changed, in a moment, in the twinkling of an eye, at the last trumpet. For the trumpet will sound, and the dead will be raised imperishable, and we shall be changed. For this perishable nature must put on the imperishable, and this mortal nature must put on immortality. When the perishable puts on the imperishable, and the mortal puts on immortality, then shall come to pass the saying that is written: "Death is swallowed up in victory." "O death, where is thy victory? O death, where is thy sting?" The sting of death is sin, and the power of sin is the law. But thanks be to God, who gives us the victory through our Lord Jesus Christ.
—*1 Corinthians 15:51–57* (RSV)
See also verses 1–8, 20, 23–27a, 28, 35, 50

When I was a child, I spoke like a child, I thought like a child, I reasoned like a child; when I became an adult, I gave up childish ways. For now we see in a mirror dimly, but then face to face. Now I know in part; then I shall understand fully, even as I have been fully understood. So faith, hope, love abide, these three; but the greatest of these is love.
—*1 Corinthians 13:11–13* (RSV)

FROM THIRTY-SEVEN YEARS AGO, we have report of a personal event in Germany. It concerns a man named Dietrich Bonhoeffer, whose writings since his death—thirty-seven years ago this past Friday—have had considerable influence both in and beyond the churches. Bonhoeffer had run an underground theological seminary under the Nazis and had then been implicated in a plot against Hitler's life. He had been put in a prison camp.

> Bonhoeffer's last weeks were spent with prisoners drawn from all over Europe. One who survived wrote this after the War: "Bonhoeffer always seemed to me to diffuse an atmosphere of happiness, of joy in every smallest event of life, and of deep gratitude for the mere fact that he was alive . . . He was one of the very few persons that I have ever met to whom his God was real and close to him. [On] Sunday, April 8, 1945, Bonhoeffer held a little service and spoke to us in a manner which reached the hearts of all, finding just the right words to express the spirit of our imprisonment and the thoughts and resolutions which it had brought. He had hardly finished his last prayer when the door opened and two evil-looking men in civilian clothes came in and said: 'Prisoner Bonhoeffer, get ready to come with us.' Those words—'come with us'—for all prisoners . . . had come to mean one thing only—[execution].
>
> "We bade him good-bye—he drew me aside—'This is the end,' he said, 'for me the beginning of life.'"[1]

So what do we make of this Easter business?

"I'm not very religious," some of us answer from inside ourselves, quietly, but simply and directly.

And those who respond, "I'm not very religious" speak not only for themselves—but for something in us all. For to say "I'm not very religious" means at least some very familiar things. It means *at least* something like this: "I don't claim to know just how to live. But I want to get on with living. There is so much to live. I want to do that. I want to be there. I don't want always to be looking over my shoulder. Sure, I'll make some mistakes. But I'm willing to take that risk. I want to get on with my life.

"When I'm called to bear losses, I'll bear them. When I'm called to die, then I'll die. When I've really done something bad, then I'll make up for it as best I can. But in the meantime—and with all respect—but as some poet put it, 'The strong are saying nothing till they see.' I want to live my life—to get on with living."[2]

---

1. Adapted from Bethge, "Editor's Foreword," 11–12, quoting Best, *Venlo Incident*.
2. Frost, "Strong Are Saying Nothing," 299–300.

Let those who are religious remember the words of Jesus: "Judge not, that you be not judged."[3]

And again the words of Jesus: "The children of this world are wiser in their own generation than the children of light."[4]

In fact, we can hear the words from the Old Testament, which I can imagine Jesus saying to some of us religious, perhaps to all of us religious: "Be not righteous overmuch, and do not make yourself overwise."[5]

The question remains: What do we make of this Easter business?

To find the claim that Jesus Christ has been raised from the dead too much to believe, or too much to know what to make of, or too good to be true, in short, simply, too much—and those who say they're not very religious often say things like that—is to be brought strangely, frighteningly closer to what Easter is about.

The meaning of Easter morning *is* beyond us—beyond the powers of most of us preachers certainly. I'm struck as I read Easter sermons that the preachers are seldom up to it.

There's something instructive in that.

Freud once wrote in effect that life as we find it is too much for us.[6]

A member of this faculty told Colgate seniors back in 1972: Life in the end will probably break your heart. May life fill your heart before it breaks it.[7]

What is this Easter business? It is at least to be addressed with questions like this: Will you let life break your heart? (The psalmist knew that "a broken and a contrite heart, O God, thou wilt not despise.")[8] Will you let life fill your heart even as it breaks it?

We are told by a great preacher of an earlier day that the gospel expresses itself often in what seem, at first, paradoxes to ordinary thinking. And so, he says, it is a paradox how we should in all things be sorrowful yet always rejoicing; in all things dying yet in all things living; always have nothing, really, yet possessing all things.[9]

Will you let life break your heart—in love? (For it is love that breaks it, is it not?) Will you let life fill your heart even as it breaks it?

3. Matthew 7:1 (RSV).
4. Luke 16:8.
5. Ecclesiastes 7:16 (RSV).
6. Freud, *Civilization and its Discontents*, 22.
7. See Kistler, "Unpublished Remarks."
8. Psalm 51:17 (RSV).
9. Newman, *Heart of Newman*, 339.

Can you afford to do that—with all you've got to do? With all your ambitions, and plans... and fears?

Is it not true that to hear of the resurrection of Jesus Christ suggests to us an unspeakable joy—if only for a moment in the music or as a hope we quickly repress—and at the same time (again, if only for a moment) to hear of it comes to us as something terribly fearful? Even as it was for the earliest who heard of it: terribly fearful.

For if it is true that Jesus Christ died for *our* sins—and what the hell does that mean anyway, more than a few of us ask (and for more than a few different reasons)—if it is true that Christ died for our sins, my sins and yours, and that he was buried, and then on the third day he was raised; if that is true, then it occurs to us in almost inaccessible places of our hearts and minds that this world and life—our life and the whole business of living—are different than we're going about it. And wonderful as that may sound once in a while to part of us, another part of us wants *not at all* to hear that life is different than we're going about it: for we're putting all we can—indeed, at times, all we *are*—into the way we're going about it. Don't tell us it's different than we think. We can't afford to believe it's different.

Anyway, we hardly know any other way to go about it than the way we're going about it. And besides, there are all the "expectations," and the pressures.

We sense the bind that the resurrection seems to put us in if we were to let it come in on us.

We all die, and everything and everyone we love dies. This is one of the simplest, most obvious truths there is. Some of us caught sight of it when we were five or six years old or younger—some of us in our teenage years—and we have been, in some sense, running from that sight ever since.

We all die, and all that we love dies.

And here some of us begin, down underneath, to feel some anger—some anger with the preacher. "You're trying to move us *now*, preacher. You're beginning to play with our emotions. That's the trouble with preachers—they play with the most precious and vulnerable of human emotions."

"Sure we caught sight"—some of us say back to the preacher—"sure we caught sight of death when we were five or six or younger, some of us in our teens. But we can never fully believe it, and that's probably best." And now, with that anger at the preacher that some of us are feeling, we say to ourselves, "We shouldn't really be confronted with it, a captive audience on Easter morning. We came to church because we thought we should—to sing some fine music, to get *some* hope for Spring. And we have a lot of work to do this afternoon. In order to do that work, indeed to get on with our lives as best we can and know how, we can't take any of this too seriously. We'll deal with those things when we have to."

With what things?

"With death and loss, preacher—with death; damn it, man, with death. We'll deal with it when we have to! Right now you're just a preacher standing there on Sunday morning—OK, Easter Sunday morning—but taking yourself too seriously, a preacher that I have to listen to for twenty minutes (if you're courteous—or thirty, as I'm beginning to fear). But then the service will be over. And we'll all ease or stumble back into our roles—you, too, preacher, you'll go around smiling at everybody and shaking hands. But you don't fool me, preacher, you've no more got this thing, death, under control than I do. When it comes to your death and the death of your kids or your wife, your parents and your friends, your causes and projects, your career and your loves, I bet you find it just as bewildering, as painful, as I do. You can't go around thinking about death all the time. And I bet, preacher, you say the same things inside that I say: when death comes, all right, I'll deal with it then. But now I want to live my life—to get on with living. And if you really want to know the truth, preacher, one reason I don't like to come to church is because I'm reminded at church of death. Thinking about God reminds me of death. And I don't want to be reminded—at least no more often than I have to. Do you understand me? Do you understand us, preacher?"

(And a few of you think you want to be a preacher?)

Sure, you're right, you whose words I've just reported. You're right about the preacher and about a lot of things.

As Paul the Apostle puts it: The last enemy—the last enemy is death.

And we here this morning live in a culture that beholds the last enemy and believes firmly—in the main—that death will prevail late or soon. Our culture—and we are part of the culture—finds not Paul or the Gospel of John but Bertrand Russell more congenial; as he says, "Brief and powerless is man's life; on him and all his race the slow, sure doom falls pitiless and dark."[10]

Less heroically and less eloquently we say, "You only go round once." "You only go round once" has become not only advertising simulation but the *dogma* of our time.

We don't need to be told that the last enemy is death. *In our own ways*, we all know that.

---

10. Russell, *Mysticism and Logic*, 56.

What fills us with wonder and dread and fear to be taken in—and, yes, hope against hope at the joy of it—is the news that the last enemy, death, will be destroyed: and that God will be everything to everyone.

Pat Dutcher spoke from this pulpit three weeks ago. Hear what she said to us: "Conviction that we must be involved in resisting the nuclear arms race is based on a new understanding of what true security is. It is based on a growing sense of a new and much more real security, and that is the love of God and the care of the Creator for this world." Pat did not *promise* us the arms race would be stopped or nuclear war be prevented; rather, she filled us with resolution and hope for that. She said, "While we can no longer trust our weapons, we can trust the One who created us." The absurdity and scandal of the gospel: we live in times, she was saying, in which the only security from which to choose life rather than death is security like that of the gospel. And then she let us hear again Christ's words: "Peace I leave with you; not as the world gives do I give to you. In the world you have tribulation, but do not let your hearts be troubled, I have overcome the world."[11]

It's *all* too much for us—death and life; our fears: our hopes. Our despair: the gospel. Too much. Too much for us. Do you see, in that, the new way?

We don't make good our earnest intentions to get on with our lives. For we don't trust for life enough—not really. Aware of death, including the social death of being neglected or rejected—for such neglect or rejection is to taste the very power of death—we live defensively. We live hiding our resentments, but resentfully. We live too earnestly or too superficially. Or we live it cool, unable after a while to respond to anything except with more cool. Or we live life in great desperation, trying not to miss anything before it's taken away (or we are); or trying to get it all *right*—or to do it all *perfectly*, lest something terrible fall on us.

Ernest Becker, in his important book *The Denial of Death*, has remarked that we Americans are drinking and drugging ourselves out of awareness (out of awareness of death and its different faces, he means); or we spend our time shopping—which is the same thing, he goes on to say; or working compulsively, we might add, which is also often the same thing. We die, fighting for life. And most of life's guilt and shame come from our fight to have our needs met (who would dare question our *needs*?) or from our fight to advance ourselves.[12]

---

11. See John 14:27; Dutcher, "Sojourners in Our Time."
12. Becker, *Denial of Death*, 284–85.

Easter at least is this: to be reminded that we don't know how to die or live.

Easter would teach us in all things to be sorrowful, yet always rejoicing; in all things dying, yet in all things coming to life; always having nothing really, yet possessing all things.

Would you begin to live your life each day and with all people as you would want to have lived it looking back from your own last day?

Can you begin to sense more easily the vulnerability of life, yours and all those with whom you deal, those you love and those you hate (there is much hate in the world, and much at Colgate), and those whom you neither love nor hate but to whom you have become indifferent? Can you begin to sense the vulnerability of our lives and the incredible power of sin—and yet, at the same time, begin to cry, "Where, O death, is now thy sting?"

You say you don't know how to do all that very well? Those whom Christ calls don't know how to do all that very well, but they hear that they are forgiven; and they are beginning to acknowledge that life *is* too much for us. And death is too much for us. The resurrection of Christ is too much for us. God is too much for us.

Oh to begin to learn to dwell in the presence of that One who overwhelms us, to begin to *cry out* something before we die.

"The strong are saying nothing till they see."

O God, have mercy on us in our strength, that we not die before we have cried out to one another and to Thee! That others and, yes, we ourselves may know that we have been present at our life together, and that we have heard the silent cry of others unto us: and that we have loved . . .

O God, you often seem the great Enemy of all our hopes and loves—as Woody Allen, that wonderful blasphemer, suggests, as our deliverer, O God, you seem—an underachiever. As the psalmist of old confessed, perhaps also with some hidden blasphemy, "By Thy wrath we are consumed." There is no protection against Thee.[13]

But to whom else may we turn?

For in our honest moments we know we are not God, nor are any of our causes worthy to be God. We know even that we seek . . . that we seek Thee, Lord.

And we have heard that Christ died for our sins, that he was buried, and that he was raised on the third day.

Sisters and brothers, may you—and I—discover that we do not know either how to live or how to die, and thereby become open, as even for the first time, to learning both—both how to die and, dying, how to live.

---

13. Statement by Woody Allen in the film *Love and Death*. The psalm is 90.

I began with a word about Dietrich Bonhoeffer. Let me conclude with something he wrote in that prison camp before he was hanged:

> Who am I? They often tell me
> I stepped from my cell's confinement
> Calmly, cheerfully, firmly,
> Like a squire from his country-house.
> Who am I? They often tell me
> I used to speak to my warders
> Freely and friendly and clearly,
> As though it were mine to command.
> Who am I? They also tell me
> I bore the days of misfortune
> Equably, smilingly, proudly,
> Like one accustomed to win.
>
> Am I then really all that which other men tell of?
> Or am I only what I myself know of myself?
> Restless and longing and sick, like a bird in a cage,
> Struggling for breath, as though hands were compressing my throat,
> Yearning for colours, for flowers, for the voices of birds,
> Thirsting for words of kindness, for neighbourliness,
> Tossing in expectation of great events,
> Powerlessly trembling for friends at an infinite distance,
> Weary and empty at praying, at thinking, at making,
> Faint, and ready to say farewell to it all?
>
> Who am I? This or the other?
> Am I one person to-day and to-morrow another?
> Am I both at once? A hypocrite before others,
> And before myself a contemptibly woebegone weakling?
> Or is something within me still like a beaten army,
> Fleeing in disorder from victory already achieved?
>
> Who am I? They mock me, these lonely questions of mine.
> Whoever I am, Thou knowest, O God, I am Thine![14]

---

14. Bonhoeffer, *Prisoner for God*, 165.

Now we see in a mirror dimly, but then face to face.

Now I know in part; then I shall understand fully, even as I have been fully understood.

That is the promise of the love of God in Jesus Christ our Lord.

Begin to pray again. And think on these things as you are working this afternoon and this week; as you are deciding, with fear and trembling, for what and for whom you are giving up *your* life; as you consider whether your dying and living are being shaped by our last enemy, death, or by the One who raised Christ from the dead, even the Enemy who would become your friend. Amen.

> *Reach out now*
> *to women and men like yourselves who will die,*
> *but unto whom Christ says,*
> *"Because I live you will live also."*
> *Reach out to friend and stranger alike, and say—*
> *"The peace of God be with you."*

11

On Courage

A Communion Sermon

SEPTEMBER 12, 1982

May the God of hope fill you with all joy and peace in believing, so that by the power of the Holy Spirit you may abound in hope.
—*Romans 15:13* (RSV)

DANTE IN THE *INFERNO* has just entered "the woeful city." "Here," he writes, "sighs, laments, and loud wailings were resounding through the starless sky, so that at first they made me weep. Strange tongues, horrible outcries, utterances of woe, accents of anger, voices shrill and faint, and the beating of hands among them, were making a tumult that swirls unceasingly in that dark and timeless air, like sand when a whirlwind blows."[1]

And he cries out, "What people are these who seem so overcome by pain?"

They are, it turns out, people neither bad nor good. Neither heaven nor deep hell will have them.

Overcome now by pain, they are the people who spent their lives trying to avoid pain.

They are the cowards.

They are—Dante especially notices—*envious* of every lot, *envious* of everybody else. (This seems, this envy, really, a deep source of their pain.)

---

1. See Dante Alighieri, *Divine Comedy*, 25, 27, 29.

They never really *lived*, Dante suggests. Of them, he writes, "I should never have believed death had undone so many." They are the cowards.

There is no abundant life, finally no lasting peace or hope or happiness or joy—without courage.

You and I do not often face it: but what we often want (or think we want) is the good life, the moral life, the religious life, a happy life—without having to bear pain; without having to be courageous. It *sounds* reasonable; yet life and experience alone disclose it to be unreasonable.

To want the good life, the moral life, the religious life, the happy life without having to be courageous—we do not immediately think of that as *cowardice*. (It just seems so natural.) But that is what it is: we want to have the good life—to be moral, religious, happy—without having to bear pain or, more to the point, as a coward.

Yet when it's brought into focus like that, we know that's not what we want. We don't want others to think us a coward. Finally, we don't want to be a coward. For, however dimly, we know what Dante knew—that to live, and certainly to live toward happiness and joy, takes courage.

We may well realize, as one person has put it, that "cowardice, alone of all the vices, is purely painful—horrible to anticipate, horrible to feel, horrible to remember."[2]

If, as the gospel has it, faith, hope, and love abide—but the greatest of these is love—the devil knows (and we do, too) that to break down our power to love, our courage must be defeated first.[3]

Wherever we cast our lot, *wherever* we live, *whatever* we do, *whatever* the circumstances—if our life is to know any lasting peace, any real hope, any real happiness or joy—we are called to courage.

Let me be clear: courage does not *guarantee* happiness and joy. But there is no happiness or joy without it. As one person has said, where courage is not, no other excellence, no other virtue can survive except by accident.[4]

Now courage is not pure absence of fear. Indeed, courage is knowing the right things to fear and how to fear them. That is no easy matter—for you or me. Courage is, in part, to fear cowardice; in part to *fear* that I shall live life trying only to avoid pain and fear. "The fear of the Lord is the beginning of wisdom."[5]

---

2. Lewis, *Screwtape Letters*, 136.
3. Lewis, *Screwtape Letters*, 136.
4. Boswell, *Life of Samuel Johnson*, 109.
5. Proverbs 1:7; Psalm 111:10.

The coward fears the wrong things and in the wrong way.

If you are seeking above all a painless life, your life will be full of fear—and fear of littler and littler things—and your fear will deepen until you are afraid of everything . . . and envious of everyone . . . even as those whom Dante first met when he entered hell.

A life of happiness and joy will include much pain. Indeed, William James invites us to endure, every day, some unnecessary pain—in order to master it, put it in its place, and diminish our fear of it.[6]

A life of happiness and joy will be full of uncertainty and insecurity—real uncertainty, real insecurity (both of which, of course, are painful).

But the more we seek to avoid uncertainty and insecurity, the more afraid of every uncertainty and insecurity we become: indeed, we become cowards in our fear-driven effort to avoid uncertainty and insecurity. And cowards are miserable: always afraid—and, eventually, of almost everything.

Courage without wisdom, justice, and what is called temperance is insufficient. Courage does not guarantee us other excellences of personality. It does not guarantee justice or happiness or joy. But without courage—I say again—there is no justice or happiness or joy.

We all need to learn better how to love ourselves. But courage is recognition that you can love your life too much; can love your life and, yes, yourself too much—certainly in the wrong way. Those poor folk whom Dante tries in bold imagery to describe thought they were taking care of themselves, watching out for themselves in trying to avoid danger and pain. Yet in the end they had only anguished insecurity and pain.

If you and I can never give up our life and our self, you and I will suffer the torments of the cowards.

A wise modern writer has this to say:

> To the modern science of psychology, we owe the insight that the lack of courage to accept injury and the incapability of self-sacrifice belong to the deepest sources of psychic illness. All neuroses seem to have as a common symptom an egocentric anxiety, a tense and self-centered concern for security, the inability to "let go"; in short, that kind of love for one's own life that leads straight to the loss of life. It is a very significant and by no means accidental fact that modern psychology frequently quotes the scriptural words: "He who loves his life will lose it." Above and beyond their immediate religious significance they denote accurately the psychiatric-characterological diagnosis:

---

6. James, *Talks to Teachers on Psychology*, 62.

that "the ego will become involved in ever greater danger the more carefully one tries to protect it."[7]

"What do you mean?" we ask when we hear the words of the Christ: "Do not be anxious about your life."[8]

What do you mean, do not be resentful, do not be envious?

We all know so much anxiety, so much resentment, so much envy, these words strike as incomprehensible—strike as if our condition were not known to the One who addresses us.

"Abstain from accusing others even in your most secret thoughts: accusations only destroy our peace of mind, they serve no purpose at all."[9]

Be not envious . . . be not resentful . . . be not anxious may be unfolded for us in countless ways. But they are at least this: give up, begin at least to give up the pain and isolation of your cowardice. There is no joy or happiness in it—you already know that. Your envy brings you no good. You do not enjoy your resentment . . . or if you do, who wants to be restricted to such a sickening enjoyment?

And why do you cling so to your anxiety? Indeed, it is resentment that often makes you do so, is it not?

Does any good then—those of you, like me, who know how cowardly you are, how much resentment and envy and anxiety you bear—does any good then come from our cowardice?

Of course: in discovering cowardice in the presence of Christ, at the throne of the mercy seat, in the context of an accepting community, in the presence of another who acknowledges that she, that he, too, understands what cowardice is—in discovering our cowardice *in faith*, with the promises of Christ and the Spirit before us—and, yes, *in* us—we begin to come to self-knowledge and a *true* humility and to new life.[10]

Discovery of our cowardice can lead us to despair, self-deception, and self-rejection or to new trust in the mercy of God, a new recognition of why Christ died for us, a new reliance on God for what we need each hour and day of life.

It takes courage to admit that we are cowards.

It takes courage to begin to admit our fears and, really, to come in touch with them.

It takes courage to respond to our fears—neither by capitulating to them nor with a half-conscious fanatic aggressiveness. (Fanaticism, at

7. Pieper, *Four Cardinal Virtues*, 134.
8. Matthew 6:25 (RSV).
9. Zander, *Is This the Way?*, 2, quoting Macarius, *Starets of Optimo*.
10. Lewis, *Screwtape Letters*, 137–38.

bottom, is aggressive cowardice.) It takes courage to see the counselor or join the therapy group; to see the math instructor or the one in philosophy and religion; to quit that sport after all; to go out for that sport after all.

It takes courage to acknowledge our envy and resentment and anxiety—and even more courage to allow it to be removed from us, taken away.

It takes courage to admit we have done wrong—been in the wrong. Oh what courage it takes. Finally—only as I rely on forgiveness can I find the courage for that.

It takes courage to admit I don't have it together.

It takes courage to refuse to go along with the crowd when acceptability seems to depend on it.

It takes courage to *be happy, to be joyful*—yes, it takes courage, all the way, to be happy, to be joyful in a world in which pain, uncertainty and insecurity, failure, suffering and death are the lot of us all, present now, and along the way—until the kingdom comes. *It takes courage to be happy, to be joyful*: not that courage denies pain, uncertainty, insecurity, failure, suffering, death. On the contrary, courage takes them in, acknowledges them; the person with courage says, "Nevertheless. I shall receive the gifts."

Jesus does not tell us what we ought to do but cannot. He tells us what God has given us and promises still to give; and finally, as Dylan Thomas cries, "Death shall have no dominion."[11]

Our hearts are fixed on many things other than the gifts of God, other than God: we shall be pulled away—painfully—by the mercy of God, pulled away from the things on which we have fixed our hearts, in order that we may come to courage and happiness and joy in the presence of God.

Courage is to receive the gifts of this day and not to worry about tomorrow (not even when you are planning for it and doing what must be done in preparation for it).

You will be provided—you will be provided with courage.

Will you let go and give up to God your anxiety?

Will you let go and give up to God your resentment? And your envy?

If you are seeking a painless life—a life free of insecurity and uncertainty—it will be full of pain, fear, and, finally, terror.

But if you want real life, new life—well . . .

Christ is enough.

This Table is enough.

God's Word is enough.

Really? we say. Really?

---

11. Thomas, "And Death Shall Have No Dominion," 77.

Do not misunderstand me when I say Christ is enough, the Table is enough, God's Word is enough. Anyone who is honestly entering or seeking to continue the life of faith will find her intelligence, his intelligence sharpened. The life of faith is an education itself—in which the other pieces of education begin to fall into place (not to be left out).

But yes, Christ is enough, this Table is enough, God's Word is enough.

Someone who has followed Christ a long time will be asked, "Did you lack anything?" "Nothing, Lord. I lacked nothing," will be the response.[12]

May the God of hope fill you and me with all joy and peace in believing.

Let us take courage and come to this table to break bread and to drink wine together. For now it is enough. Be not anxious for tomorrow even as you think about tomorrow (for I know it is on your mind). But let courage follow courage: and let God be your God.

Amen.

---

12. Luke 22:35.

12

Who Then Is This?

January 9, 1983

WE ARE EACH LIVING a story. Of course each of us is part of many stories. We are in other people's stories—and they are in ours.

We hear from Mark's gospel part of the story of the Good News—a story which reaches out to include us in it, even as our story and the story of the Good News can become parts of one story.

I hope we may be able to connect—at least at some points—our story and this story of the boats and the storm on the sea.

> On that day, when evening had come, he said to them, "Let us go across to the other side." And leaving the crowd, they took him with them in the boat, just as he was. And other boats were with him. And a great storm of wind arose, and the waves beat into the boat, so that the boat was already filling. But he was in the stern, asleep on the cushion; and they woke him and said to him, "Teacher, do you not care if we perish?" And he awoke and rebuked the wind, and said to the sea, "Peace! Be still!" And the wind ceased, and there was a great calm. He said to them, "Why are you afraid? Have you no faith?" And they were filled with awe, and said to one another, "Who then is this, that even wind and sea obey him?" (Mark 4:35–41 RSV)

Evening has come to our civilization in important ways. The end of many of the ways of our civilization is a great blessing; the passing of its day, a relief.

But it is not all blessing and relief.

Someone has observed that children become more adult in these days (I did not say mature) and adults more childish (I did not say childlike). College students have anxieties about meaning and purpose and place—about whether life is worth living or not—more to be associated with a civilization at evening than at morning and its beckoning to a new day.

The shadows of nuclear anxiety . . .

The old has passed away, but the new has not yet come. Indeed, we understand the Advent hymns better than those of Christmas perhaps: "Watchman, tell us of the night, what its signs of promise are."

Notice—as we return to the story from Mark, which was our gospel lesson this morning—notice that for Jesus that evening has come does not seem to stymie him or stop him. (This does not mean, by the way, that Jesus does not know how to rest: he does know how—how to rest.) But when evening had come, he said, "Let us go across—to the other side."

"The sun shall not smite thee by day, nor the moon by night" (Psalm 121:6).

The disciples leave the crowd: they leave the crowd. We must, you know: we must leave the crowd. "Leaving the crowd, they took him with them, just as he was."

Will we have the wisdom to take him with us? To admit the Christ to our trip, our journey, our story?

They took him—just as he was. The statement is enigmatic. The one already identified in Mark's gospel as the one who says, "Listen!"; the one who speaks in parables; the one who many thought was "beside himself"; the one who has said, "Those who are well have no need of a physician, but those who are sick. I came not to call the righteous but sinners"; the one who says, "Follow me"; who says, "The time is fulfilled, the kingdom of God is at hand." Him they took—just as he was.

They get into a boat—and go into the sea.

What is the boat you are taking into the sea?

We all have our little boats, don't we? Some of us have made them as fit and sound as we can. Others of us have neglected our boats—they are leaky.

And it is good to have other boats out there on water, not too far away, as the dark of night comes up.

They push out into the sea—to get to the other side.

And a great storm of wind arises: the economy of our country—it is a storm of wind perhaps, the full velocity of which we have yet to feel?

Some of us began to feel a storm of wind at Christmas vacation time—in our family situation.

Some of us who are seniors begin to feel a storm of wind: this career business is beginning to blow.

Some of us begin to feel a storm of wind in this way: our childhood and high school faith—that little boat—we're beginning to wonder about it as we hear many views swirling and pressing around us.

Some of us have felt the wind of death blow into our lives—cold and terrible.

A storm of wind arises, and it affects us: the waves beat over and into the boat.

Our little boat is insufficient: the little boat so secure in quiet weather, at least adequate, even if we had not calked it. Now, even if we have, it makes no difference! It's beginning to fill. We have discovered what the *sea* really is.

Water is ultimately the image of new life. But first it is the image of chaos.

Chaos comes into our minds and hearts—we become confused, scared, even terrified; fuddled, even overwhelmed.

The boat is filling, heavy—even like our souls—heavy with water. It's not going to make it, our boat isn't. We've lost sight of the other boats. We're going to go under—overwhelmed by the storm, the storm of cultural forces, overwhelming ideas, friendships that have failed, our family's disintegration, personal suffering; overwhelmed by the heavy waters of lost motivation, we can't bail out our little boat fast enough. We're trying. But we're being overwhelmed.

And where is Jesus the Messiah in all of this? The one who, in some ultimate sense, has got us into this?

For that is what we feel, indeed we know, when the storm comes. We cry out, why? Where are you now, O God, the author of our lives, the director of our destiny?

It is you, O Christ, who in some overriding way made the proposal to go to the other side! It is you who got us out on this sea, defenseless in this poor boat of ours.

Where is the Savior so-called, our guide, our protector, in all of this? Where?

In the stern, asleep, asleep on the cushion. (That's where he is.)

"Do you not care if we perish?!" we cry.

There is no cultivated piety in these existential prayers. There is only need and anger and clear anxiety, even terror.

They wake him. They know who is to blame—and, strangely, who alone can help, though they cry out less from any trust or hope in help than from resentment. "Teacher, do you not care if we perish?"

Do you not care? we cry out—care that our civilization has gone into the darkness, into a storm we cannot handle or see the end of. Do you not care about the nuclear threat to human life? The ecological threat to the planet?

Do you not care that our family suffers and disintegrates, that, try as we may, we cannot put our family back together?

Do you not care that the friendships in which we placed so much hope have ended—in disappointment, betrayal even, shocking, depressing bereftness?

Do you not care that our faith has become dull and dead?

Do you not care that those who should not have died have died?

Do you not care that we suffer?

Do you not care that we are depressed?

Do you not care that we have lost our motivation and cannot find it again?

Do you not care that we are trying—and that it does no good?

Do you not care that we are overwhelmed? Aye, terrified, some of us?

They—and we—cry out to Jesus not so much to help but rather to express our question, our deepest of all questions to the stormy (or the empty) sky, to the darkness, to the void, to the apparently helpless or uncaring God who got us into the mess: Do you not care? Do you not care? Do you not care if we perish?

And here we must stop. For here the continuation of the story itself (the gospel account of the storm and of Jesus in the boat) becomes the problem. How can we go further? For here what follows (we cry out) is itself for us the "storm." Here what follows is itself, for us, the filling up of our boat. Here is where our resentment reaches its maximum intensity; the wind howls like a hurricane. How can we believe? How can we trust? Did what Mark reports really happen then? Can we follow the story any further? "Do you not care" if we cannot believe, if we cannot trust? That—the happy ending—is precisely what we doubt, yes, even despair of: "Teacher, do you not care if we perish?"

We've heard the rest of the story. And that has become for us a part, indeed, the very eye of the storm.

Do you know that in the eye of a hurricane there is peace, there is calm?

Will you acknowledge your resentment? Your helplessness? Your fear? Your suffering? Your dullness? Your insufficiency? Your inability to write the full story of your life? Your incapacity to bring about this happy ending?

Will you acknowledge your finitude (as the theologians say)? Your limits, *our* limits, the limits on you personally and on all of us together? Will you listen in the midst of the storm? Will you stop? Will you truly let your cry simply *be*? Will you simply let it be—your cry?

Will you accept the implications of your anger? Your fear? Your resentment? That your way and mine—our wisdom, our skill, our self-sufficiency—is not enough? Indeed, will you accept that glimpse of its finish?

Will you become open to a story that *includes* your story—includes your whole story—but that is more than your story, indeed, that takes up where your story comes to an end?

Will you accept the end of your story as you can write it and plan it and live it and be it?

We come to the end in our great cry (varied as may be our ways of crying it), we come to the end in our great cry: Do you not care? Do you not care if we perish?

Now it is—to remember another story like this one—now it is like walking on the water in the middle of the sea, in the middle of the night.

Now it is the beginning of what no eye has seen, nor ear heard, nor the heart of any of us conceived, what God has prepared for those who love God (1 Corinthians 2:9); let *us* simply say for those who will give up, who will open themselves to the story that includes our story—our whole story—but give ourselves up, open ourselves to the story beyond our power to write, beyond our power to make happen or to be.

Now we begin. Now we are, indeed, overwhelmed. Now we have only our doubt: bring it along; and our fear: bring it along; and our resentment: bring it along; and our total insufficiency—to believe or trust: bring it along.

Now we begin—with TV images filling our minds instead of peace and music intended to provide us oblivion shaping our souls instead of heavenly confidence. Bring it along. Now we begin—with our growing consciousness that for us it is impossible: bring it along. Now we begin—where our efforts are of no avail, no help: bring it along.

Now we begin the story—or, rather, continue it, but where we do not believe or trust.

He awoke, rebuked the wind, and said to the sea—to the chaos, the insurmountable and impenetrable chaos, even the chaos of our minds and perceptions, the chaos of our civilization and of our souls—"Peace! Be still!"

We are in the story. But our part is disbelief and distrust. (How humiliating.)

"Peace! Be still!" Beyond our powers to achieve or make happen—this peace, this stillness.

And the story goes on. The wind ceases. The boat does not go down. We are saved. And there is a great calm.

And then comes the question to our question. The question we are called to have courage simply to hear, simply to hear and to bear:

"Why are you afraid? Have you no faith?"

Why are you afraid? Have you no faith?

And we may remain silent and afraid and resentful. We may remain in our disbelief and our distrust.

Or it may come to pass that we, too, may be filled—notice filled, not create, not conjure up ourselves, but be filled with that which is a gift. We may be filled with awe, and say—even you and I, we may say to one another, "Who then is this?" Who then is this that even the storms and winds and sufferings and failures and rejections and disintegration and destruction of our life obey him—and fulfill his purposes?

It may come to pass that we are filled with awe and say to one another, "Who then is this that speaks and lives—to whom are obedient even the wind and the sea that destroy our faith and our hope and our love?"

Who indeed? That is the question from the story that lays claim to your story, and mine, this morning and in the evening.

Who indeed is this that all that would sink our little boats obeys him?

13

"I Am with You All the Days"

February 20, 1983

First—I'm going to use the word "elusive." The word means eluding clear perception or complete mental grasp.

Second—Lent began Wednesday. This is the first Sunday of Lent. Lent is the way the church calendar reminds us that we are on the way to the cross. Lent ends with Easter. And we enter into Lent because Christ has been raised from the dead, the victory won.

Third—two scriptural texts:

> For the love of Christ controls us, because we are convinced that one has died for all; therefore all have died. And he died for all, that those who live might live no longer for themselves but for him who for their sake died and was raised.
>
> From now on, therefore, we regard no one from a human point of view; even though we once regarded Christ from a human point of view, we regard him thus no longer. Therefore, if any one is in Christ, he is a new creation; the old has passed away, behold, the new has come.
>
> —2 Corinthians 5:14–17 (RSV)

> Now the eleven disciples went to Galilee, to the mountain to which Jesus had directed them. And when they saw him they worshipped him; but some doubted. And Jesus came and said to them, "All authority in heaven and on earth has been given to me. Go therefore and make disciples of all nations, baptizing

them in the name of the Father and of the Son and of the Holy Spirit, teaching them to observe all that I have commanded you; and lo, I am with you always, to the close of the age."
—Matthew 28:16-20 (RSV)

We wait for the Lord—until he comes: in glory, in power; until God dwells with us, and we are God's people—and God wipes away every tear from our eyes, and death shall be no more, neither shall there be mourning nor crying nor pain any more.[1]

When we eat bread together and drink the cup we proclaim the Lord's death until he comes: we wait for the Lord.[2]

We are acutely conscious, at times, of the absence of the Lord, of the absence of God. It is, *indeed*, as if God had gone into exile . . . or as if we had banished God—oh, not you perhaps, or her, or him, or me, or *them*, but all of us together, had banished God. In any event we are, at times—some of us, most of the time; some of us, all of the time—dimly aware or acutely conscious of the absence of the Lord, of the absence of God.

May we learn how to listen and to wait . . . indeed, to wait, as those coming awake . . . to wait for the Lord.

We are conscious of the absence of the Lord. May we wait—for the Lord—until he comes.

But we must respond to something no less momentous, no less decisive for us.

The risen Christ sends the Spirit; the risen Christ speaks to those who will hear—the marks of the nails in his hands, the open wound in his side, the one who has been spit upon, the one who has heard ring in his ears "crucify him," the one who has been betrayed, the one who has heard a close friend say of him, "I never knew the man"—the risen Christ speaks to those who will hear. Coming to a place to which we have been directed by him, there is in our midst both worship and doubt as we hear Jesus say, "All authority in heaven and on earth has been given to me."

What can that mean? In heaven perhaps. But what authority does he have on earth? At Colgate, for example?

Go therefore and make disciples of all peoples, of all types, baptizing them in the name of the Father, the Son, and the Holy Spirit, teaching them . . .

How shall we teach? And how shall we be taught?

. . . teaching them to observe all that I have commanded you.

---

1. See Revelation 21:1–4.
2. 1 Corinthians 11:26.

What is it to observe? That is, to practice what Jesus has commanded? And how—if we should hear ourselves addressed to do this—how do we teach another to observe, to practice what Jesus commands?

"And lo, I am with you always, to the close of the age"; literally, "lo, I am with you all the days."

Let this sermon be no comfort or encouragement to anti-intellectualization. But let it be said, nevertheless, Jesus the Christ is not an idea; not a philosophy; not even a philosophy of life; not even a theology; not even a religion.

There's an old gospel hymn that says something that's got to be said this morning: "What a friend we have in Jesus, all our sins and griefs to bear."

From the Gospel of John we have these words from the Christ about what we may expect: "If a person loves me, that person will keep my word, and my Father will love that person, and we will come to that person and make our home with that person. The person who does not love me does not keep my words."[3]

We know what it is to keep our word: it is to be true to what we have said. Christ says to keep his word: to be true to what he said.

"Brother, do you love my Jesus? Sister, do you love my Jesus?" That's the question we sang to each other.[4]

The words of Christ continue: "These things I have spoken to you, while I am still with you. But the Counselor, the Holy Spirit, whom God will send in my name, the Holy Spirit will teach you all things, and bring to your remembrance all that I have said to you. Peace, I leave with you; my peace I give to you; not as the world gives do I give to you. Let not your hearts be troubled, neither let them be afraid. You heard me say to you, 'I go away, and I will come to you.'"[5]

Jesus Christ is not an idea, not a philosophy of life, not a theology, not even a religion.

Paul Tillich has written that we are fragments and riddles to ourselves. Is it not so? "The more we experience and know that fact the more we are really human. St. Paul the Apostle experienced the breakdown of a system of life and thought which he believed to be a whole, a perfect truth without riddles or gaps. He then found himself buried under the pieces of his knowledge and his morals. But St. Paul never tried again to build up a new, comfortable house out of the pieces. He realized always that fragments remain

---

3. See John 14:23–24a.
4. "We Are Climbing Jacob's Ladder," v. 3.
5. John 14:25–28a.

fragments, even if one attempts to reorganize them. The unity to which they belong lies beyond them."[6]

St. Paul could live with a philosophy of life made up of fragments, a theology, and, yes, a religion of fragments because he had met Jesus the Christ; if it is not putting it in too homely a way, because he had a friend in Jesus; because the elusive presence of Jesus Christ he did not reject but allowed to become decisive for him.

What of us? What of me? What of you?

Jesus Christ is an *elusive* presence; an *elusive* friend; the friend who with God sends the Spirit into our midst; indeed, the friend, powerful, elusive, broken—and easily rejected—who promises to be born in us.

Jesus the Christ is better understood as a friend than as a philosophy. Can a philosophy eat and drink with you? (Can a religion, for that matter?) Can a philosophy or a religion bear your sins and your griefs? Can a philosophy or a religion die for you? Can a philosophy or religion accompany you and converse with you, and weep with you, and encourage, and beckon you on?

Jesus Christ may not answer every question that you ask or that I ask. Indeed, he will have his own questions for us. But what a friend we have in Jesus, all our sins and griefs to bear!

Being a Christian may not be to have the answer to the question: Why is there evil and suffering? Jesus Christ does *not* say, "I am the answer, the conclusion, and the end of questions." He says, "I am the way, and the truth, and the life."[7] Being a Christian is not necessarily to have answers as to why there is evil and suffering (though if we examine our hearts in the presence of Christ, we'll find some awful clues). Rather, being a Christian is having a friend, if an elusive friend; being a Christian is being part of a fragmented community of very ordinary folk—who have a friend, an elusive friend; who have heard (not just felt—perhaps not even primarily felt), who have heard the Spirit, the Healing Spirit, the Holy Spirit.

Is your strongest sense when with your friends your *feelings*? Sometimes yes; sometimes no. Often when we are most truly *with* our friends, we forget all about how we *feel*. For we are with them, and we are engaged in *doing* things with them—talking and acting: we are not preoccupied with ourselves, with our feelings. We are delivered from all of that, sometimes, when we are really with our friends.

Being a Christian is being part of a fragmented community of ordinary folk who have heard and even met the Spirit of Christ; who have a

---

6. See Tillich, "Knowledge through Love," 112–13.
7. John 14:6 (RSV).

friend, an elusive friend; and thus, although we do not bring questions to an end—including the question of suffering and evil—we can say, by the power of the Spirit, by the power of the presence of that friend: all things work together for good for those who love God.[8] For *all* things bring me closer to this elusive friend and to God.

A great German preacher whom the Nazis tried to silence has said something I must say this morning: A person who lets this friend, who lets Jesus only *halfway* into his heart is far poorer than a 100 percent worldling, far poorer than someone who has never met the Risen Christ, never known the Spirit. The person who lets Jesus Christ halfway but no further has no peace. That person does not receive the peace that passes all understanding; but what's more, that person loses the world's peace. (The world can provide a peace too.) That person loses the world's peace because his or her naiveté has been taken away. Therefore, a constant bickering goes on in that person's heart, and it is quite apparent that one day, in a fit of rage, the halfway person will slam the door on that quiet Figure, on that elusive Friend, who even then has continued to knock and seek entrance. The anti-Christian is always a half-Christian gone mad. This you can depend on. (And this drama illuminates, for those who have eyes to see, much of the intensity and anguish of our college and our culture: the anti-Christian is always a half-Christian gone mad.)[9]

I have referred to Jesus as an *elusive* friend. I do not think I mislead us in saying so. The Gospels are not treatises, elaborating a philosophy of life. They are accounts of Jesus, calling people into his friendship, and of Jesus being a friend. (Greater love has no one than this, that one lays down one's life for one's friends.)[10] But Jesus is elusive.

We read in Mark's Gospel that they were going up to Jerusalem, and Jesus was walking ahead of them; and they were amazed, and those who followed were afraid.[11]

Those who have ears to hear let them hear. To learn that Jesus walks ahead of us in our journey, leading us to death of the self, and new life—giving us his body, his blood along the way; to learn to observe what he has commanded—that this is that to which we have been called. ("What do you mean *we*?" someone says to himself, to herself.) It amazes us, and we are afraid.

---

8. See Romans 8:28.

9. This paragraph based upon Thielicke, "Parable of the Seed and the Soils," 57–58 (emphasis added).

10. John 15:13.

11. Mark 10:32.

Jesus the Christ is elusive. The wind—the Spirit blows where it wills, and you hear the sound of it, but you do not know whence it comes or whither it goes; so it is with everyone who is born of the Spirit.[12]

If you do not know that Jesus the Christ is elusive, I hope you will discover it as you become more acquainted with his words, and his questions to us. And we must take time for that. "'Who are my mother and my brothers?' And looking around on those who sat about him, he said, 'Here are my mother and my brothers! Whoever does the will of God is my brother, and sister, and mother.'"[13]

"What do you want me to do for you?" he asks on more than one occasion.[14] And what should we say?

We can do much thinking about these things, about Jesus the Christ, his claims, his gospel; about the Healing Spirit, the Holy Spirit. We can and we do, and often we should. But let us not be misled. Jesus Christ is not an idea, a concept—and not finally one who stands still while we think about it all. He is an elusive but actual friend. The Spirit does move: it does blow. And the Spirit moves us from philosophy and religion to a living relationship. Amidst the fragments of ideas, the Spirit moves us from detachment and half-heartedness to the beginnings of friendship and new life. We may then well be philosophers or theologians, but we would see Jesus: we will not be ashamed to say, in our own ways, what a friend we have in Jesus, all our sins and griefs to bear.

We wait for the Lord—until he comes. But the risen Christ speaks now from within our midst. For Christ comes into our midst and into our hearts, though we resist him, and fatefully.

He comes to us as he came in the flesh to those on a lakeside. As Albert Schweitzer testified,

> He speaks to us the same word: "Follow thou me!" and sets us to the tasks which He has to fulfill for our time. He commands. And to those who obey Him, whether they be wise or simple, He will reveal Himself in the toils, the conflicts, the sufferings which they shall pass through in His fellowship, and as an ineffable mystery, they shall learn in their own experience Who He is.[15]

---

12. See John 3:8.
13. See Mark 3:31–35.
14. See Mark 10:35–52.
15. Schweitzer, *Quest of the Historical Jesus*, 403.

We live in days and do not know what a day may bring. There are days of confident faith and days of sad blundering and terrible confusion and doubt. There are days when the birth of a child brings joy and days when illness and death bring anguish and sorrow. There are days of peace and days of war. There are days when life is music and days when despair wraps us in impenetrable mist. Says Jesus the Christ, "But, lo, I am with you always: I am with you all the days."

Amen.

14

Some Questions

An Epiphany Sermon

January 8, 1984

Now when Jesus was born in Bethlehem of Judea in the days of Herod the king, behold, wise men from the East came to Jerusalem, saying, "Where is he who has been born king of the Jews? For we have seen his star in the East, and have come to worship him." When Herod the king heard this, he was troubled, and all Jerusalem with him; and assembling all the chief priests and scribes of the people, he inquired of them where the Christ was to be born. They told him, "In Bethlehem of Judea; for so it is written by the prophet: 'And you, O Bethlehem, in the land of Judah, are by no means least among the rulers of Judah; for from you shall come a ruler who will govern my people Israel.'"

Then Herod summoned the wise men secretly and ascertained from them what time the star appeared; and he sent them to Bethlehem, saying, "Go and search diligently for the child, and when you have found him bring me word, that I too may come and worship him." When they had heard the king they went their way; and lo, the star which they had seen in the East went before them, till it came to rest over the place where the child was. When they saw the star, they rejoiced exceedingly with great joy; and going into the house they saw the child with Mary his mother, and they fell down and worshiped him. Then, opening their treasures, they offered him gifts, gold and frankincense and myrrh. And

> *being warned in a dream not to return to Herod, they departed to their own country by another way.*
> —Matthew 2:1–12 (RSV)

THE DANGERS IN HEARING the sermon this morning are two.

First—evasion. We'll be tempted to say, "It's for someone else, for the others." "It's for the students"—that's what those of us who are not students will be tempted to say. "It's for the believers," those of us full of doubt (and dismay) will be tempted to conclude. "It's for those who are 'real' religious," those of us who think ourselves not very religious can say: our evasion. "It's for those who *feel* this sort of thing," those of us who don't feel it much can counter. "It's for them, not for me," we can decide. Evasion—that's one of the dangers (for the preacher as well as anyone else).

The second danger is sentimentality: a little after-Christmas glow . . . perhaps like a TV Christmas special in January . . . a little nostalgia perhaps . . . perhaps even some good feelings. Good feelings are fine as long as they are not the cover for the sentimental illusion that if I *feel* something or *see* something or *understand* something then I won't have to let my life be changed; then I won't have to give up any of my ways . . . even my ways of feeling and seeing and understanding and doing . . . then I won't have to give up my priorities and reactions and routine . . . then I won't have to give up my detachment and my aloneness and my fear.

So—two dangers: evasion and sentimentality.

"What child is this who laid to rest, on Mary's lap is sleeping, whom angels greet with anthems sweet?" To whom do the wise bring their gifts? It is, of course, the babe who is born to die, the one who will cry out from a cross. The one who is born in us, meek and humble and full of light and beauty but whom we come to deny and crucify in us: for we know that the life of this one in us means death to a life lived unto and for ourselves.

May we overcome the dangers of evasion and sentimentality as we turn to the story of those wise men who came with their gifts.

There are a series of questions for you and me from the story.

First, where's your star? Or, perhaps better, what is the star which you follow?

The sermon is more about your gold and your frankincense and your myrrh than about the star you follow. But, believe me, you and I must ask ourselves, What star are we following?

There are baseball stars and movie stars and rock stars. There are the stars and stripes, of course. We are sometimes still told to follow *our* star.

And many of us want to *be* stars. Be careful. Remember the wise in our story, who did not seek to be stars; nor did they follow *their* star.

(And remember a star can only be seen when night falls, when darkness comes.)

So the first question from the story for you and me: What is the star which we follow?

The second question is this: Can we keep clear of Herod?

A true star guides us. We all have at least glimpsed it, I think—if only for a moment, between the clouds . . . or on one of those rare occasions when we looked unto the hills around and beyond our immediate and intense preoccupations.

We have at least glimpsed the true star—in the darkness. But then we come to Herod. Herod comes into our life. All Jerusalem is with him, all the world. Herod is the real world, the real world about which we talk. Herod is subtle: the real world, as we call it, is subtle. Herod knows the score. Knowing the score—the bottom line—isn't that what it is to come to terms with the real world? Herod does not reject us; nor does the real world. "You have seen a star?" we are asked. "Let me in on this." That is the craftiness of the so-called real world. The real world, as we call it, likes the language, even the feelings of idealism and morality, of reverence even . . . so long as Herod is fully included in whatever they are directed to. Herod's first instincts, if not his final ones, I think, are not to kill the Christ but to turn the business into that of "Christ and Herod," a partnership of sorts.

Can we keep clear of Herod? Of course we must meet with Herod, with what we call the real world. Notice that the wise men were neither naive nor reckless nor self-righteous rebels. In fact, they outfoxed Herod. Still, can we keep clear of Herod as the star leads on, focuses in over that barn, that manger—which the so-called real world holds of so little account.

The solitude of it all, the need the three had for each other, the *concentration* on the star and where the star was leading, and the capacity to *remember* what they had seen and known there in the presence of the babe and his mother, when they returned from their worship.

There is no avoiding Herod: "Go, pursue your quest," he says, "and when you have found what you are looking for, then bring me word—that I, too, may come and worship." "Christ and Herod," perhaps. But as the narrative goes on to make clear (though we seldom read that far): it is, finally, Christ *or* Herod.

Herod or the baby—to whom shall we be loyal? That is the real meaning of the question: Can we keep clear of Herod?

The wise go their way, and being warned—even in dreams—they do not return to Herod. They go another way: they go another way, even though all Jerusalem, all the world seems to be with Herod.

So—from the story—these questions to us: What is the star you follow? Can you keep clear of Herod's *will* even if you must, of course, meet and deal with Herod?

And this third question from the story: To what, to whom are you really bringing your gifts? The gifts of your life? Your gold and frankincense and myrrh?

We hardly know what joy and worship and the giving of our selves and the gifts of our life might be. Yet we seek to know. And thus this story in Matthew's Gospel. We enter it through imagination. May our imagination grasp us.

Here in this story, persons—indeed, we may see ourselves—come not, finally, to talk (though of course there were words) or even to see (though of course they saw) but to worship.

"Oh star of wonder, star of night," star coming to rest over the place of humility and quietness, where the baby is (even the child in us, the newborn, the newborn in us, the newborn Christ).

Worship is release to joy: "They rejoiced exceedingly with great joy."

And worship is *intimately* related to giving, to the giving of ourselves.

We—each of us—seek to give.

We must give or die!

But we are afraid that what we have to give will not be recognized, will not be appreciated, will not be accepted. So afraid.

And yet we continue to seek a way to give. We sense that if we cannot give, what we have and are will stagnate, rot, and die. We must give of what is in us.

We die if we cannot give . . . our gold, our frankincense, and our myrrh.

Gold is our excellence.

Gold does not rust, you know. Gold is the better for being refined—*by fire*. Our hearts quake, again and again, yours and mine, at being subjected to the furnace of life. But *if we have God to give it to*, our excellence is only made more plain and real in the furnace of life.

Gold is easily shaped. Excellence, too, is easily shaped. So beware. Herod wants excellent women and men. Excellence may serve Herod or the babe born to be the Suffering Servant. What *shapes* your excellence? what [sic] *shapes* your excellence?

Gold is our excellence. We each of us have gold ore in us. We each have excellence in us.

Oh, to find it, to let that ore be purified, to let it be refined—as by fire—and shaped according to the glory and will of God revealed in that baby's story; to fall on our knees in worshipful lives—and to give of our excellence to the One who, in quietness and love, triumphs over death and lives forever—and who is worthy—worthy of our gifts and gift: this One who comes into the stable of our hearts and the manger of our minds, yes, even to the places where we crucify Christ in us.

Gold is our excellence.

Frankincense is our *longing*, our terrific *longing*.

Frankincense is an aromatic gum resin, used for burning as an incense and as a fragrance. Our inmost and deepest longing is implied by it: our longing for a star, for mysterious night, for wonder, for joy—indeed the longing itself at times an aching joy; our longing for our true home, for that to which we can give open-hearted reverence: whether we *believe* in God or not, our longing for God.

Will we make our frankincense, our longing a gift? One of our *great* gifts? Will we bring our longing: will we bring our cry, "Guide us to perfect light"? Will we bring our unutterable longing to the newborn babe? To the One born to die that we might die to ourselves and begin to live at last, at last!

Gold is our excellence. Will we bring our excellence to that newborn baby?

Frankincense: our longing. Will we bring and give our great longing?

Gold, frankincense, and myrrh. Will we bring our myrrh, as well as our gold and frankincense?

Do you remember the carol? "Myrrh is mine; its bitter perfume / Breathes a life of gathering gloom: / Sorrowing, sighing, bleeding, dying, / Sealed in the stone-cold tomb."

Will we bring our bitterness, oh our bitterness at things and our resentment and our sorrow: our sorrow over what has been taken from us . . . our sorrow over the way we have lived?

Some of us have this gift to bring in greater measure than others. But the point is will we bring it as a *gift*? This too—perhaps, above all, this too.

For this is a gift fit for the babe, fit for the man born to die, fit for God: your bitterness, your resentment, your sorrow.

Will you hold on to it and let it harden you, poison you, and finally kill you? Or will you give it—your gift, perhaps your greatest gift—to the babe?

That which we think *keeps* us from worship, *keeps* us from joy, *keeps* us from love . . . will we bring it, bring it all?—resentment, bitterness, sorrow—and cry out, "Here, for you—my gift! Even when my excellence is destroyed and my longing is gone, I have a gift for you. And I give it to you. For it is mine; it is what I have and what I am. Receive it as my gift."

And it is received.

It is received.

Gold is our excellence.

Frankincense, our longing.

And myrrh, that strange perfume blended of our bitterness, our resentment, our sorrow.

We must give or die. We die if we hold on to our gifts.

Giving oneself and worship are intimately related; they are finally one.

And so our dangers: evasion—"it's for someone else, for the others." And sentimentality—that if I *feel* something or *see* something or *understand* something then I won't have to let my life be changed.

Then from the story come questions to us:

What *is* the star which, really, you follow?

And then: Herod or the child? To whom will you be loyal?

And then: To what, to whom are you bringing the gifts of your life?

And will you bring your gold, your frankincense, and your myrrh?

There is a wisdom that allows those held together by it to rejoice exceedingly with great joy. They have seen the star come to rest over where the child is.

They have come—to the beginning, the beginning of the new, the beginning of life.

With them we may enter in and see, and fall down and worship; free at last to bring our excellence, to bring our longing, to bring our bitterness, resentment and sorrow—to bring *ourselves*—to God, newborn in us; and thus to begin to love our neighbor as ourself . . . and to begin to love You, O God, and to enjoy You here and now and forever.

Amen.

15

Our Anger

March 11, 1984

Be angry, but sin not...

—Psalm 4:4a (RSV)

Therefore, putting away falsehood, let every one speak the truth with his neighbor, for we are members one of another. Be angry but do not sin; do not let the sun go down on your anger...
—Ephesians 4:25-26 (RSV)
See also Ephesians 3:14-21; 4:15 16

MANY OF US ARE feeling tired, very ragged. Why do we feel so tired, so ragged?

The short answer, for many of us: because we're so *angry*.

Underneath our fatigue, our disarray, our raggedness is *anger*.

What wears us out is not our work but our worry.

And worry is often shot through with anger (though we hardly acknowledge it). Or worry is something we find developing in us as we hide from our anger.

Anger is dangerous: we all know that—dangerous to others, dangerous to ourselves. We're not always eager to get in touch with our anger for fear it will tear us apart—or wreck our relations with others.

But my text this morning is: "Be angry, but sin not."

The confidence that makes possible such a strange proposal is this: God loves us, and God can use our anger to new and even glorious purposes. God can convert our anger from something destructive and self-destructive into something constructive and creative and life-giving.

Let's look more closely and name *some* of these angers.

We're angry because we have too much to do; angry because things seem coming in on us too fast: we can't find any real order or shape to it all.

We're angry because we feel betrayed by someone. Someone has—or people in general have—not lived up to our expectations.

We're angry because we confided something to another, but he or she did not understand—and now we feel foolish and alone.

We're angry because we've put ourselves on the line about something and did not prevail: we've been neglected or overruled.

We're angry because it's beginning to dawn on us—frighteningly—that we are not who we thought we were; others have not lived up to our expectations of them, *but also we have not lived up to our expectations of ourselves.* That scares us . . . and angers us.

We're angry—some of us—with the people, whoever they are, who are making the world so dangerous with nuclear weapons. We're angry that social ills do not get the attention we are convinced they deserve.

We're angry—some of us—because many Colgate students did not seem touched at all by the Charity Fund Drive appeal.

Some of us are angry at the idealists, "utopians" we may call them, because they won't see what appear to us to be facts about human nature—right before their eyes.

Some of us are angry—beneath our worry—about the employment prospects after May.

Some of us are angry—beneath our loneliness—about the way we're being treated on our floor or in our apartment.

Some of us are angry that the people at home keep fighting and tearing each other apart.

Some of us are angry for reasons that the preacher does not even seem to sense—and that makes us further angry.

"Be angry, but sin not." God can *convert* our anger from something destructive and self-destructive into something constructive, creative, and life-giving.

Let me hasten to make clear something I am *not* saying. I am *not* saying, "Go vent your anger on those who make you angry." I am *not* saying, "Let it all hang out." I am *not* saying, "Go give 'em a piece of your mind." I am interested that after several decades of that notion in popular psychology, the latest psychological research on anger suggests that counting to ten or one hundred . . . or a thousand—keeping control over anger at critical moments is usually much healthier than venting it, exploding with it.

So keep counting to ten or one hundred . . . or a thousand.

But it is vitally important to discover with *whom* we are angry; what, *really*, we are angry about; *why* we are angry.

Sometimes through reflection—courageous reflection—we can begin to get answers to these questions.

Sometimes we need to talk with others or another—friends, parents, a counselor.

For it is vitally important to get in touch with that anger beneath our fatigue and our worry.

We are simple—all of us—yet deep as well. Underneath our fatigue and worry is anger, and underneath the anger is fear: fear that we shall be excluded from life with others. And underneath our fear is our love!—our love of others, our longing to enter into solid, real human community.

As long as we are in the flesh, love must struggle to subdue and overcome fear. Love's great ally in that struggle is courage. Courage.

The *conversion* of anger is not its denial. We are not called to get rid of our anger. Our text is "Be angry . . . but sin not." God can convert our anger. *Sin* is to be separated from others, from our self, from God. The Bible is saying, be angry, but let not your anger separate you from anyone, or any group, by turning you to indifference or hate for that person or group. Let not your anger separate you from that deep love for all persons (indeed, all *things*) which dwells—however hidden—in your heart of hearts. Let not your anger separate you from God—from God to whom in moments of honesty we want to cry out in anger, "Why *me*, Lord?!" "Why is it *this* way?!" "Why don't you *do* something about it, Lord?!"

Bring your anger to God—as the psalmist does. Indeed, that is the beginning of the conversion of our anger: that we bring our anger to God. God can use our anger, use it wonderfully, use it mightily.

We have something of a suggestion of how that might be in Chesterton's hymn, which we sang together this morning:

> O God of earth and altar,
> Bow down and hear our cry;
> Our earthly rulers falter,
> Our people drift and die;

> The walls of gold entomb us,
> The swords of scorn divide;
> Take not thy thunder from us,
> But take away our pride.
>
> From all that terror teaches,
> From lies of tongue and pen,
> From all the easy speeches
> That comfort cruel men;
> From sale and profanation
> Of honor and the sword,
> From sleep and from damnation,
> Deliver us, good Lord![1]

When we're always losing our temper our anger gets spilled out to no good purpose usually, and often it makes for us and others some terrible messes. Probably there is a *deeper* anger *underneath* the immediate anger *felt*. And we do well to find that *deeper* anger out.

Fatigue and worry tell us often of anger that we have feared to acknowledge (but that we do well to discover).

But anger is life-giving as well as life-destroying. At least since Plato people have been aware that without "spirit," a disciplined use of anger, there can be no courage. *Courage is anger in the service of one's love.*

To resist injustice is not the same thing as rejecting or hating or becoming indifferent to those who oppose you. Indeed, you need anger, but anger with injustice itself, anger in the form of *courage* to resist injustice.

Anger removes inhibitions! Luther used to say he couldn't preach unless he were angry. Often we'll sit on our hands or chew on our lip until enough anger sets us free from our inhibitions to speak truth.

But a few verses before Paul said, "Be angry but do not sin," he said (significantly), "Speak the truth in love."

To speak the truth in hostility is no longer to speak the truth, really, according to the New Testament.

Speak the truth in love. *Be* angry but sin not. Your anger overcomes your inhibitions; your anger supplies you with courage—to be put in touch again with your neighbor, your enemy, yourself, your God.

---

1. Chesterton, "O God of Earth and Altar," vv. 1–2.

You see, the anger that we feel only as defense against hurt tosses us to and fro: it turns into what Nietzsche calls *resentment*. It leaves us bitter, manipulative, seething.

The anger that is "spirit," that gives form and motive to courage, is clean and liberating. It remembers the humanity of the other; it does not seek separation from the other.

"Oh, but preacher," we say, "that's so hard. I can't do that." Indeed. And here we come to the heart of the gospel this morning.

God *accepts* your angers and anger, yours and mine, accepts them now and in the days to come. To give ourselves to God, to give ourselves up to God is to bring our anger to God.

At the heart of the gospel is the news that God loves sinners, perhaps—scandalous as it strikes us when we really think about it—loves sinners *best* of all; loves the sinner that *I* am; loves the sinner that *you* are. The community into which we are called is not a community of the "righteous"—the "concerned" at Colgate, or whatever; no, the community into which we are called is a community of sinners. Of course we are all sinners in *different* ways. So *your* way of sinning may make me angry, and *mine* may make you angry. But we dwell together by forgiveness—the forgiveness of God and of each other—or we do not remain a community.

And God is a God of new life, a converting God, a transforming God.

Therefore, God would take your anger and take mine and convert our angers and our anger into courage!

God can re-form and redirect that anger of ours, overcome our fear of anger and our misuse of anger, indeed, overcome our becoming the victims of our own anger.

God does not want to tear us apart or to have us torn apart. But if you are being torn apart by your anger, know that *that*, too, that very anguish can bring you to God.

Let God take that anger and put it somewhere powerfully and positively: into humor, for some of us. God's still working on me in that regard—a tough shell to crack, but God will win the battle. Anger can become the motive to a creative humor if we let the anger out and let the anger be converted.

God can take our anger and begin to free us, by that same anger, from our inhibitions. Until we are in touch with some anger we often remain just "self-conscious," unable to serve the causes, to speak up in gentleness but firmness where we know ourselves called to speak—whether in personal life or on public issues.

God can take our anger and, converting it, use it to increase our self-esteem. If our anger never gets expressed our self-esteem drops. (If we never express our anger we become both more afraid of it and ashamed of ourselves as well.) But if our anger is given over to God's conversion of it, then our anger will become power in the service of a good cause.

Or our anger will help us to a new sense of self-esteem, help overcome our inhibitions, help give us humor.

Our anger in God's hands can give us back our power to make choices, to make decisions. For decisions always require something of the strength of anger: something must be *cut through* to make a decision.

Our anger, when transformed by the Spirit of God, turns compassion from sentimentality and mere feelings of sympathy into active work, into action.

God will, in short, take our anger and give it back to us as courage.

So *be* angry: *be* angry . . . but sin not.

That is, do not let your anger separate you from any other, or from yourself, or from God.

For God's Spirit can transform my anger and yours into courage: courage in the service of love . . . so that we can begin to live freely and decisively; the victory over fear beginning to be accomplished in us: the new life—God's life by the Spirit of Christ—beginning to be the life we actually *live*.

Even so, come Lord Jesus.

Amen.

16

You Can't Keep God Dead in Your Life

An Easter Sermon

APRIL 22, 1984

And when the Sabbath was past, Mary Magdalene, and Mary the mother of James, and Salome, bought spices, so that they might go and anoint him. And very early on the first day of the week they went to the tomb when the sun had risen. And they were saying to one another, "Who will roll away the stone for us from the door of the tomb?" And looking up, they saw that the stone was rolled back; for it was very large. And entering the tomb, they saw a young man sitting on the right side, dressed in a white robe; and they were amazed. And he said to them, "Do not be amazed; you seek Jesus of Nazareth, who was crucified. He has risen, he is not here; see the place where they laid him. But go, tell his disciples and Peter that he is going before you to Galilee; there you will see him, as he told you." And they went out and fled from the tomb; for trembling and astonishment had come upon them; and they said nothing to any one, for they were afraid.

—Mark 16:1–8 (RSV)

Let not your hearts be troubled; believe in God, believe also in me. In my Father's house are many rooms; if it were not so, would I have told you that I go to prepare a place for you? And when I go and prepare a place for you, I will come again and will take you to myself, that where I am you may be also. . . . Peace I leave with

> *you; my peace I give to you; not as the world gives do I give to you.
> Let not your hearts be troubled, neither let them be afraid.*
> —John 14:1–3, 27 (RSV)

From the Apostles' Creed: "He suffered under Pontius Pilate, was crucified, dead, and buried. He descended into hell . . ."

The very last words of the oldest text we have of the Gospel of Mark: "And they went out and fled from the tomb; for trembling and astonishment had come upon them; and they said nothing to any one, for they were afraid."

We here this morning can understand, I think, why the first response to the resurrection of Jesus Christ is fear.

For whatever else the resurrection of Jesus Christ means, it means—you can't keep God dead. You can't keep God dead in your life.

Deep down, *all* of us (*some* of the time) and *some* of us (*most* of the time) hope we *can* keep God dead, keep God dead in our life.

There is a question that comes to each of us: what are you doing with your life?

Our life itself is our answer.

On the last day, the question will be: what did you do with your life?

Our life itself will be our answer.

The question frightens us.

We try to hide our lives—certainly parts of our lives—from others and even to hide our lives from ourselves (sometimes *especially* from ourselves).

We try to avoid recognizing that we are called to give account for our lives.

We are tempted, in other words, to hope that the truth about our lives can be hidden—and that we can even hide from that truth ourselves.

What are you doing with your life?

Some of us spend a great deal of time drinking in order to avoid that question. Some of us spend a great deal of time in frantic sexual pursuit trying to avoid that question. Some of us spend a great deal of time keeping busy, even very busy, in order to avoid that question. Some of us spend a great deal of time working hard at religion in order to avoid that question. Some of us spend a great deal of time elaborating (even very elaborate) justifications for our life—and fantasies—in order to avoid that question.

At times we want so desperately to avoid having to give account for our lives that we imagine despair to be better than faith.

You know what despair is? "Nothing really makes any difference." That's despair.

We live in a culture riddled with it.

We fear being held accountable for the truth about our life—accountable for ourselves as really we are, our lives as really we are living them. And thus at times each of us hopes to keep God dead—whether we call ourselves believers or seekers or doubters.

Our will to keep God dead is often expressed in our greater counter-question. You know the question: "Who's to say?"

What ought you to do with your life?

"Who's to say?"

What are you *doing* with your life?

"Who's to say?"

And on the last day: what did you *do* with your life?

"Who's to say? It all depends on your point of view." That's despair.

We love to say there are no answers because we think we can thereby escape recognizing that *our life is our answer*. Our *life* is our *answer*.

We play with the fire of nihilism and despair when we play with the fire of an eternal "who's to say?"—when we play with the fire of an eternal "there are no answers." Our forbears referred to this as the fire of hell. Jesus calls it a place of torment. And so it is.

So we live days or weeks or years in a *kind* of despair, half-hidden—moving from one escape to another: hiding, running from the question: What are you doing with your life?

And we may come to feel more at home with what destroys us than with what restores us, more at home with our escapes than with the joy of trust and love, more at home with slow suicide, quiet self-destruction than with life.

We flee from accountability for our lives. We flee from recognizing that our lives are an answer to a question. We flee from remembering that everything matters: every sparrow that falls, every crushed woodchuck on the road; every lost toy, every lost dog or cat; every lonely, lost, or dying child; every lonely, lost, or dying one of us.

We flee because so much do we fear a judgment, *any* judgment on our lives. We flee from the question put to our life, we flee from accountability for our life because we fear we shall be condemned.

Whoever God is, whatever else we may say about God, God is the One from whom the truth of our life cannot be hid. Even when with great energy, subtlety, or both, we seek to hide from the truth of our lives, we know that the truth of it *remains* nevertheless.

Truth cannot be destroyed.

And so I repeat, we can understand, I think, why the first response to the resurrection of Jesus Christ is fear. For the resurrection of Jesus Christ means—you can't keep God dead. You can't keep God dead in your life.

But precisely thus the resurrection means more. It means you can kill God's love, but you cannot keep that love dead and buried.

I want to share with you something of a conversation some years ago between two persons—one a professional burglar and the other a psychoanalyst, a psychoanalyst for whom Jesus had the central place in his psychological orientation.

> The burglar, an illegitimate child, had undergone the miseries of a loveless childhood, cruel teenage years, and then a terrible struggle with unemployment. He had never known his father though he believed him to be a man of considerable wealth. Due to an accident—suffered in an attempted burglary—he had begun to talk to the analyst and to confess his feelings about his father. The burglar had acknowledged how much he hated his father for abandoning him. The analyst had told him in reply that he understood how much he hated his father. The analyst showed the burglar that he (the analyst) accepted him, with all his hatred and with his way of life expressing in many ways that hatred. The analyst told the burglar he could admit to him that if his father were here, he, the burglar, would destroy him inch by inch. And in that moment of honesty and anguish and acceptance, the burglar began to change: "Perhaps I wouldn't hate him," the burglar said. "He's an old man now, with trembling hands I suppose." The analyst replied: "If he could know your fate and what he did to your life, perhaps he would confess himself." "I hate him," answered the burglar, but then with another spirit, "yet I would ... perhaps I would like to know him."[1]

Let me summarize what this analyst then goes on to observe—by the light of Jesus Christ:

---

1. Adapted from Kunkel, *In Search of Maturity*, 3–9.

> Self-clarification, transformation of our lives begins with the decision not to fight against our failures, not to run away from them or conceal them, but to bring them into the light; and this decision enables us to confess. None of us can truly and thoroughly confess as long as we judge, condemn, excuse or praise ourselves. In doing that we shall repress or forget the most important part of our life and therefore never discover the truth. But if our desire to be honest can become greater than our desire to be good or bad, then the terrific power of our failures will become clear, and behind the repeated failure—and the hostility that surrounds it—the old forgotten fear will turn up: the fear of being excluded from life; and behind the fear, the pain—the pain of not being loved; and behind this pain of loneliness, the deepest and most powerful and hidden of all human desires: the desire to love, to give oneself, and to be part of the living stream that we call human unity. And when that love is discovered behind hostility, hostility disappears. The transmutation of power is brought about by the discovery of truth. But truth cannot be taught in words. It must actually be experienced within our hearts. Furthermore, it cannot be experienced without confession, and confession needs a confessor who becomes a friend through suffering, fear, anxiety, anguish and pain.[2]

We flee, in various ways and in our many relationships, from the One who calls us to account. We flee from the One who poses to us the question, What are you doing with your life? And, on the last day: What did you do with it? We flee but then begin to recognize such flight to be flight into emptiness and despair. And so we hesitate, and begin to lurk around, afraid to leave, but afraid to confess—I suppose rather like Jesus' friends did when he was finally on the cross. We don't want to run completely away, but we don't want to get too near.

The tomb—ah, there's a fitting place to go. We'll linger there awhile, sing some sad old songs, perhaps, and then return to our busyness, our cogitations, our fabrications, our binges and affairs, to our compulsive quest for security and power and prestige (even in good causes). We'll return to our never-finished efforts to justify our lives.

But we do begin to *wonder* about our escape to the trivial. And we begin to recognize the lies we try to believe about ourselves and the deceptions by which we seek to deceive others and, even more, ourselves.

---

2. Adapted from Kunkel, *In Search of Maturity*, 3–9.

It's healthy—this self-recognition. It's healthy, it's the beginning of freedom to feel guilt about our failures as friends and acquaintances, as parents and children, as people of Colgate (for Colgate is us)—to feel guilt about our failures as citizens of our nation, as citizens of the world, as men and women.

The only thing that is unhealthy is our failure to believe that there is more mercy in God than sin in us!

I don't know, finally, why sin is such a bad word. Obviously, we're all sinners—the more so we try to deny it. But that's not the issue. At issue is whether there is more mercy in God than sin in us.

As love is stronger than death, so forgiveness is stronger than sin.

The tomb is empty. You can't keep God dead. You can't keep God dead in your life. The first preaching of the resurrection announced the heart of its meaning—the forgiveness of sins.

All of us are forgiven. We are not relieved of the consequences of our *sin*, but of the consequences of being sinners. It is not that we are no longer sinners but that we are sinners *forgiven*.

Instead of any longer trying to prove or, worse, to justify ourselves, we can begin to confess, to express, and, yes, even to *be* ourselves—courageous, vulnerable, confused, dedicated, joyous, stumbling followers of our crucified and risen Lord.

Sometimes we imagine that if we had no accountability to give, we would be free. Such freedom is like the freedom to fall through space forever: a modern image of hell.

No, we are accountable for our lives. Everything does matter. But when we fall, it is not forever but into the everlasting arms of God.

The word of Easter: God is alive, not in the tomb, and going to meet us in familiar territory, where we are doing our things and living our lives—going to meet us, with judgment . . . and mercy.

The judgment of God brings to an end all our self-deceptions, the "games," the rationalizations, the self-justifications, the *self*-righteousness; it brings to an end our attempt to hide from our lives by asking "who's to say?" and brings to an end the devil's comfort that nothing matters. The judgment of God is the end of all that. With power it falls upon us suddenly or gradually, as the case may be; but the resurrection of Christ means we have confidence *today*—for *this* day of judgment—and for the *last* day, the last day of judgment.

You and I are beckoned to come out of the darkness in which we hide, into the light. You and I are called to let our hearts become warm and melt again and to cry human tears again—men and women—and with joy. For courage and forgiveness and love are not dead in us after all.

I meet you, says the risen Christ, in the familiar places of your life, where you are under threat, under duress, under pressure, grieved, angry, afraid. I will meet you in those places and guide you and be with you. Look for your brothers and sisters. I will be there. And with me there is mercy and forgiveness.

Hear these words written very near the end of a life of remarkable accomplishment by a genial and courageous person, a person of towering intellect and marvelous skepticism:

> Looking back, I have no serious complaints about anyone or anything: except my own failures today, yesterday, the day before yesterday and the day before that—I mean my failures in real gratitude. Perhaps I still have bitter days ahead, and certainly my death is coming. One thing remains, for me to remember and impress upon myself, in respect of yesterday and all the days which have now gone before, and again in respect of all those which may follow, and of that last day which is certainly coming: "Do not forget the good that he [God] has done!" . . . How do I know whether I shall die easily or with difficulty? I only know that my dying, too, is part of my life. . . . And then—this is the destination, the limit and the goal for all of us—I shall no longer "be," but I shall be made manifest before the judgment seat of Christ, in and with my whole "being," with all the real good and the real evil that I have thought, said and done, with all the bitterness that I have suffered and all the beauty that I have enjoyed. There I shall only be able to stand as the failure that I doubtless was in all things, but by virtue of his promise, as a sinner justified, as a sinner forgiven. And as that I shall be able to stand. Then . . . in the light of grace, all that is now dark will become very clear.[3]

My brothers and sisters, we cannot keep God dead. We cannot keep God dead in our lives: no matter how hard we work at it, even if we die trying.

The word of Christ to us this Easter morning is this: Even when you crucify me and I die and you put me in a tomb, yet I will come again and take you to myself—if you will have me—that where I am you may be also. Receive my love. Receive my peace. Peace I leave with you; my peace I

---

3. Busch, *Karl Barth*, 499.

give to you. Not as the world gives do I give to you. Let not your hearts be troubled. Neither let them any longer be afraid.

With that word of Christ addressed to us, let us reach out now one to another as a sign of his presence—and exchange the peace of God.

17

Homecoming and Our True Home

A Sermon for Homecoming Sunday

OCTOBER 21, 1984

> *But, as it is written,*
> *"What no eye has seen, nor ear heard,*
> *nor the heart of man conceived,*
> *what God has prepared for those who love him,"*
> *God has revealed to us through the Spirit. For the Spirit searches everything, even the depths of God.*
> —1 Corinthians 2:9–10 (RSV)

THIS IS HOMECOMING WEEKEND. It's wonderful to see so many alums back with the University Church today.

But let's admit that homecoming doesn't mean much to lots of undergraduates—and that *most* of those alums who have returned to Colgate for homecoming are either asleep, beginning slowly to get into brunch somewhere, or have already left.

Then let's admit another sort of thing: that most of us, so far as we are conscious, are more concerned about whether there's life-after-Colgate, or life after retirement, or life after this term's over, than we are about whether there's life after death. (Although that's not true of all of us.)

But then let's admit further that there is in the idea of homecoming—and in that word, "home"—deep power.

Country music expresses, exploits even, the depth and power of home. One of the most plaintive of the country music classics is put on the lips of a man in prison, a murderer apparently, condemned to execution, who dreams:

> The old hometown looks the same
> as I step down from the train . . .
> Yes, they'll all come to meet me . . .
> It's so good to touch the green, green grass of home . . .
>
> Then I awake and look around me
> At four gray walls that surround me.
> And I realize that I was only dreaming . . .
> They'll all come to see me in the shade of that old oak tree,
> As they lay me 'neath the green, green grass of home.[1]

Some of us may remember from the musical *West Side Story* a more hopeful song—one that I have recalled from this pulpit before. The word "home" is not used, and yet the song cries out in longing for home, for a new home, like none that those who sing have ever known before, yet for which they hope:

> There's a place for us,
>   somewhere a place for us. . . .
> Hold my hand and we're halfway there:
>   hold my hand and I'll take you there,
> somehow, someday, somewhere.[2]

One of my earliest recollections of my father is his singing that old drinking song—singing it, though, with a kind of tenderness which I cannot forget:

> Show me the way to go home,
> I'm tired and I want to go to bed.
> I had a little drink about an hour ago,
> and it went right to my head.
> Wherever I may roam,
> on land, or sea, or foam,

1. Putman, *Green, Green Grass of Home*, vv. 1, 3.
2. Bernstein and Sondheim, "Somewhere."

you can always hear me singing this song:
Show me the way to go,
show me the way to go,
Show me the way to go home.

What is home? What is it to come home?

Few words are more powerful than "home." But like all powerful words, like all powerful symbols, it may cut more than one way.

Any pastor knows that Christmas (how many weeks now till Christmas?) is one of the *hardest* times for many folks: for most alcoholics, for example, for many of the elderly, and for many others, perhaps for you. Christmas in America has been made into a powerful material drama of the home, of a certain kind of ideal home, and usually of home in the past. Christmas becomes a time, for many, of intense nostalgia, of loneliness intensified, of regret and resentment—often justifiable resentment, I say. For if anything, home at its best means that no longer is one an outsider. And yet Christmas often becomes a time when many feel with especial poignancy that they are outside, that they are, in deep meanings of the term, homeless.

The word "home" can cut more than one way. The very *word*—"home"—can leave us with the sense that we are traveling *away* from life, that home is only in a receding past, that home has gone, and that we are now only outsiders.

Let me be very clear then: home is dangerous.

After all, according to both Genesis and Jesus, we are all called in some sense to leave parents, to leave home.[3] Maturity is recognition at the right time in the right way that, in certain profound respects, we cannot go home again. Or better, the day comes when we must leave home in order, truly, to go home.

Moreover, home can be the source of ethical failure; home can collapse our courage. "Why was there not more resistance from within Germany to the Nazis?" people ask naively. To resist injustice and evil is *usually* to risk the security of home. Why has there not been more resistance to racism in America by men and women—White and Black—who have wanted racial justice? Because it might cost them their homes.

How many wars have been fought basically by appeal to the feeling for home? And there has been incalculable injustice tolerated because of love for home. Is it so today?

---

3. See Genesis 2:24; Mark 10:6-8 (or Matthew 19:4-5).

Jesus' followers left him when his showdown came. Where did his disciples go? They went home. Even as he foresaw: "You will be scattered, every one to his home, and will leave me alone."[4]

Deep feeling for home may lead us away from our self as well as bring us to ourself.

And what is our true home?

There has been, probably, too much preaching about the furniture of heaven and the temperature of hell.

To talk *too easily* about heaven as our true home can betray faith and love . . . rather than witness to it. A friend of mine, who became one of the most effective ministers I ever knew, lost his father when he was about nine years old. Such a loss cannot be calculated. Various persons in the church took this boy aside to tell him about heaven—or their idea of it. Someone told him that his dad had died because God wanted him so much; but all the boy could think of was that he wanted his dad too—as much as God, he reckoned. His feelings toward God only became charged with resentment after that conversation. Heaven was no consolation for him. He remembers that what helped sustain him was a man, an elder in the church, who put his arm around his shoulder and said simply, in effect, "I don't know why your Dad died, but I miss him terribly, and I know you do," and became the boy's friend.

As those of you who have passed through or now live with grief discover, if healing is to begin, what must be acknowledged someday, in its mysterious depth, is this: he-she-the one I love is dead.

It is instructive, I think, that the writers of the great Christian creeds experienced this, knew this. In the Apostles' Creed they confess *thus* their faith in Jesus Christ: "Conceived by the Holy Ghost, born of the Virgin Mary, suffered under Pontius Pilate," he was "crucified, *dead*, and buried."

Only when we begin to face the mystery and reality of death can we begin to enter into resurrection faith.

There is a deep word from Kierkegaard that I am constrained to share at this moment: "Whether a person has been helped . . . depends essentially upon the degree of intellectual passion he has employed to understand that help was impossible, and next upon how *honest* he is toward the Power which helped him nevertheless."[5]

---

4. John 16:32 (RSV).

5. Kierkegaard, *Sickness Unto Death*, 172.

The word "home" may well arouse in us only nostalgia and loneliness; I understand that very well. Or "home" may lead us to cowardice, to betrayal of our responsibility to do justice, to resist injustice: I understand that, too.

But the symbol, the word "home" may also help *open* us to the rule of God, to the kingdom of heaven, to what Martin Luther King Jr. dreamed and called Beloved Community.

The New Testament writers beheld in the *death* of Jesus God's purpose to bring us home to ourselves, to one another, and, yes, to God. Christ, approaching his death, says this: "Let not your hearts be troubled; believe in God, believe also in me. In my Father's house are many rooms; if it were not so, would I have told you that I go to prepare a place for you? And when I go and prepare a place for you, I will come again and take you to myself, that where I am you may be also."[6]

Home, our *true* home; yet how can we speak it?

Robert Frost helps me in the impossible task with his poem "The Death of the Hired Man." Silas, a single man, an ordinary and not particularly outstanding man, has come back ill and ready to die to a farm home where he has worked as hired help before. Warren, the decent owner of the farm, is not happy that Silas has come back; Silas has let him down in the past. He relents only so far as to admit that "home is the place where, when you have to go there, they have to take you in." But Mary, his wife, goes further, and she says of home, "I should have called it something you somehow haven't to deserve."[7]

Mary is right. If we have to *earn* our home, our true home, what chance have we?

What can we say of our true home? *You* must speak for yourself. There will be clues in the home you've had but also in the home you've *never* had. Let *me* say this: There will be privacy there as well as togetherness; there will be work—satisfying tasks for which we have had some chance to become competent; and there will be leisure, and we shall learn to play again. And, yes, there will be the special others—whose very names become more hallowed with the years; I cannot conceive it otherwise. But not only they are there.

For there will be *other* homes in our true home—homes *linked* to homes, and many *kinds* of homes, not just those created by a man and a woman and their children. And there will be gatherings and celebrations. And we shall learn to worship.

---

6. John 14:1–3 (RSV).
7. Frost, "Death of the Hired Man," 38.

It will be familiar, and renewing, and ever new. It is not just "*gemütlichkeit*," not just friendliness and warmth and welcome—because love without justice is not fully love; but justice without love is not even justice.

So there will be a welcome there without having to earn it: *and forgiveness.*

And so I dream of our true home, even as I remember, remember death, and what Matthew Arnold calls "the eternal note of sadness."[8]

Some of you have worried about becoming sad during this sermon, and some of you have fought it. Indeed, there are at least two dangers in matters like these: *sentimentality* is one . . . a little religious emotion, a little nostalgia, a little pie in the sky by and by, and then back to business as usual. But the second danger in the face of sadness is *refusal* of it with a quiet *coldness*—in fact, a certain kind of nihilism, if a very conventional nihilism. We will not allow the sadness to enter because dreams of home and justice and love threaten our "management" of our lives, and so we turn cold; we stare intently as into a black hole, and seek to steel ourselves, and feel nothing except the cold, indeed to feel nothing . . . except nothing.

To those of us in this second danger—and it can be any and all of us—to you I say, *for God's sake* allow the sadness, even the eternal note of sadness in! It is a way back, perhaps the only way back.

So you find the notion of our true home an impossible dream, and talk of heaven impossible to follow or to feel, *all right*! But let the sadness that is linked in this world to our dreams and hopes for home, let that sadness *be*.

Homecoming is a *symbol*. Home is a *symbol*. Heaven is a *symbol*.

"*Just* symbols?" someone asks.

Of course not *just* symbols!

Like all true symbols, homecoming and home participate in that which is too deep for words, in that "which no eye has seen, nor ear heard, nor the heart of man conceived," in that which has been "revealed to us through the Spirit. For the Spirit searches everything, even the depths of God."

Will you hope with me that prayers, like my father's very secular but very tender prayer—"show me the way to go home"—that my Dad, who at eight years old watched his mother die, and lost his childhood home there at the foot of her bed, that he and *all like him* will, verily, be shown the way to go home—to a true and real home?

Will you hope with me—and translate hope into *action*, those of you who think the sermon has been escapist—will you hope and work for prisoners, *some* kind of prisoners, and perhaps even real criminals and

---

8. Arnold, "Dover Beach," 112.

would-be criminals, that they may find—and not merely six feet under—the green, green grass of home?

Will you hope, will you work and hope, pray and work and hope that there may be a place for us, for *all* of us, somewhere a place for us, for (dare I say it, in the face of their awful suffering?) for the starving of Africa and the countless homeless of our great cities, and the burnt out, including the burnt out right here at Colgate? Will you take on *commitment* to the hope that peace and quiet and open air wait for us, somewhere? Can you let your life *turn around* so that your *life* shows your dream of that home where there begins to be time together with time to spare, time to learn, time to care? Will you dare hope together that we will find a new way of living, that we will find a way of forgiving?

There may be no way without tears; increasingly I think so, but I don't know. Save us from sentimentality, O God! But save us no less from a shallow positive thinking! And save us from the coldness that denies the symbols, the words, the dreams in which sadness and *joy*, sadness and *hope*, sadness and *courage*, sadness and *love* are inseparable! Save us from that coldness which we *prefer* in order that all our problems can remain "manageable"! How can we "manage" heartache and death and joy and our human longing for a real homecoming, a real home?

Well, listen to something a guy I know has written:

> The gospel shouts the good news that God is making his home with us, that we are homeless wanderers no more. We are not yet home, but we are going home. Going home to that homecoming banquet where elder brother and prodigal son, father and son, mother and daughter, exile and stranger, man and woman, white and Black, East and West, Arab and Jew, poor and rich, lion and lamb will sit down together in peace. The biblical word of new creation, of resurrection, suggests that all our history—personal and communal, over all the aeons, over all the earth and throughout the entire cosmos—is not lost or forgotten. Rather, all is gathered up, restored, offered, celebrated, shared, brought into communion. As in the . . . Creed, "I look for the resurrection of the dead and the life of the world to come." Yes, I look and keep on looking, and sometimes I think I glimpse it from afar. And if someone tells me that "eternity is in an hour" and that homeland heaven is available right now on homeland earth, I will nod and celebrate and enjoy. But I will still wonder about the mystery which is to come—the mystery in which we shall all be changed, the mystery of that communion of the

saints streaming in the gates of home when no one will be on the outside, ever again.[9]

So let's turn to our neighbors and offer them "the peace of God."

And may we hear our neighbor's greeting to us as a *call* to live as those who know life to be on the way home; to live in anticipation of our great homecoming; to live *revealing* the hope that one day no one will be on the outside ever again.

"The peace of God be with you."

---

9. Raines, *Going Home*, 145.

18

Zaccheaus

NOVEMBER 24, 1985

He entered Jericho and was passing through. And there was a man named Zacchaeus; he was a chief tax collector, and rich. And he sought to see who Jesus was, but could not, on account of the crowd, because he was small of stature. So he ran on ahead and climbed up into a sycamore tree to see him, for he was to pass that way. And when Jesus came to the place, he looked up and said to him, "Zacchaeus, make haste and come down; for I must stay at your house today." So he made haste and came down, and received him joyfully. And when they saw it they all murmured, "He has gone in to be the guest of a man who is a sinner." And Zacchaeus stood and said to the Lord, "Behold, Lord, the half of my goods I give to the poor; and if I have defrauded any one of anything, I restore it fourfold." And Jesus said to him, "Today salvation has come to this house, since he also is a son of Abraham. For the Son of man came to seek and to save the lost."

—Luke 19:1-10 (RSV)

THE TEXT THIS MORNING: "For the Son of man"—Jesus the Christ—"came to seek and to save the lost."

Let us pray.

O God, that you come to seek and to save those who, like me, are lost without You, gives us confidence to pray that You will accept the words of my mouth and the meditations of our hearts, O Lord, our Strength and our Redeemer. Amen.

When our children were young we used to sing about Zacchaeus, the fellow we heard about in our New Testament lesson this morning. Jesus looks up and sees Zacchaeus there in his tree and tells him to hurry and come down. Then the refrain of the song has Jesus' word: "For I'm coming to your house today."

"For I'm coming to your house today." We don't have to be psychoanalysts to get something of what that's about, do we? Your house, your house—where you're at, where you set your priorities, where your *real* desires and your *real* wishes and your *real* fears are to be found.

Jesus is coming into Zacchaeus's house to have dinner with him: Christ is coming into Zacchaeus's life. Perhaps Zacchaeus will even say with Paul the Apostle, "It is no longer I who live, but Christ who lives in me."

Perhaps. But let's get back to this story of Zacchaeus. I want us to get inside this story a little and maybe, by the grace of God, this story will get into us. But I want to warn you, it's one of those stories that may tempt us to say the preacher went from the sublime to the ridiculous. (Or maybe he went from the ridiculous to the sublime and then to the even more ridiculous.) Both you and the preacher—well, we each have to take our chances, don't we?

And that's, of course, the very opening atmosphere of the story. Jesus has entered Jericho and he's passing through. He's not staying long. He's passing through. One does not have forever to see him, let alone show him hospitality. He is passing through! In life our chances come—and our chances go. We all know that. Let us not assume it to be different here in these matters we take up together this morning. I'm not embarrassed to say with the old evangelical preachers, Jesus is passing through these parts, these environs, this morning. And most are asleep or at brunch—and even those of us who aren't may not see our chance because we don't get it that the environment is the environment of our own soul . . . and that where we are this morning is fateful.

Which brings us to Zacchaeus.

The song we used to sing at home said Zacchaeus was a "little" man. Well, that may or may not be true: that Zacchaeus was small. There may be textual problems with that. But there's one thing about Zacchaeus that there are no textual problems about: he was rich. He knew how to make money, and he was rich.

Zacchaeus

He was the chief tax collector of Jericho. We're not quite sure what that meant. We have no other references from that time to the office of "chief tax collector." But the business went something like this. You got a contract with the Roman government. You gave an agreed amount to Rome. Anything more you collected you kept.

Tax collectors were collaborators, then, with the Roman occupation of Palestine. A lot of commentators point out how tax collectors thus were outcasts. Now I don't want to deny that. For strong Jewish nationalists, for the very pious and the very poor—and if there weren't too many of the very pious, there were a good many of the very poor—Zacchaeus was certainly an outcast. And there were probably other people, too, who didn't like Zacchaeus for the way he'd cut into *their* profits.

But when we're rich, "successful," as we say, when we've "done well"—as we say—people have a wonderful way of overlooking *what* we've done well, in *what* it is that we are successful or *how* we got our money. Now this isn't said very often in church. But it needs to be said.

This is a money-culture. Men and women in your home city or town and in this town and at this college often appraise each other by how much they make, how much they have, or what they can afford to do. Not always, to be sure—and less, maybe, when we're twenty than when we're forty (which helps explain some of the pressures college students may feel from parents). And not always because we really *want* to appraise people and life that way . . . but . . . because we lose and forget the other ways to measure and appraise. And let's face it: we *do* often appraise each other, deep down, by the standard of money—and for powerful reasons. Do you know Robert Frost's poem "Provide, Provide"?

> The witch that came (the withered hag)
> To wash the steps with pail and rag
> Was once the beauty Abishag,
>
> The picture pride of Hollywood.
> Too many fall from great and good
> For you to doubt the likelihood.
>
> Die early and avoid the fate.
> Or if predestined to die late,
> Make up your mind to die in state.
>
> Make the whole stock exchange your own!
> If need be occupy a throne,
> Where nobody can call you crone.

> Some have relied on what they knew,
> Others on being simply true.
> What worked for them *might* work for you.
>
> No memory of having starred
> Atones for later disregard,
> Or keeps the end from being hard.
>
> Better to go down dignified
> With *boughten* friendship at your side
> Than none at all. Provide, provide![1]

Frost's poem penetrates deeply the fright hid secret in our psyches—yours and mine. Do we not sense *how—in our own ways—*we *aspire* to be, indeed, are beginning to become, the chief tax collector of Jericho?

Zacchaeus was often treated with respect. And he had some friends, I reckon: enough anyway for some dignity.

But remember the atmosphere of this story. Jesus is passing through.

And for some reason Zacchaeus sought to see who Jesus was.

But he could not—he could not see on account of the crowd. We understand that, don't we? Even if we want, even *when* we want—want to see Jesus, whatever that means; want to find something more to life than what life, the way we're living it, seems to be adding up to; want to see something good that lasts—something that promises courage and joy and freedom; even when we want—we may admit in our most private heart—want to see the face of God . . . even when we want thus to see—we cannot . . . we cannot, on account of the crowd.

Need I really say more about that? We cannot see Jesus because of the crowd—because of our crowd.

We don't know why Zacchaeus wanted to see Jesus. Maybe he'd met him once or heard him somewhere or heard *about* him. Maybe he was just curious. Maybe he didn't even know why he wanted to see him. Maybe he wanted to see him because he was beginning to recognize that there were a lot of other things he couldn't see very well and that he was, somehow, impoverished.

Whatever the reason, Zacchaeus did want to see Jesus—though he couldn't because of the crowd.

He is fully aware of *one* thing: Jesus is passing by. Jesus is not lingering. He is passing by.

---

1. Frost, "Provide, Provide," 307 (emphasis added).

Jesus is passing by us . . . this morning. Passing by where I am and passing by where you are. I believe that.

Zacchaeus wanted to see him. And here we come to ridiculousness number one. Zacchaeus did something ridiculous for a successful business person to do—ridiculous, I suppose, for anybody but a child to do. It was definitely not cool for the chief tax collector of Jericho to be up in a tree—"out of his tree," I imagine not a few who saw him thought.

About sycamore trees you should know this: the figs they produce aren't much to write home about. But the wood—the wood is the most durable.

Zacchaeus needed help from something durable that could hold him, hold him up so that he could catch a glimpse of Jesus passing by.

The Christian church in all of its pathos: its figs sometimes aren't much to write home about either. It is often wooden, isn't it? (We prefer plastic today.) It may not turn us on like rock or alcohol or poetry or money or success. But by the grace of God the church endures. It is *durable* wood. And it will endure. And the church gives us access to see. So, yes, the church is a sycamore tree: nothing more, nothing less. (Like St. Paul calling the church a clay pot. But in that pot, the treasure.) And from up in a sycamore tree, Zacchaeus suddenly can see—over the crowd, suddenly can see Jesus the hidden messiah passing by.

And yet our text does not dwell on Zacchaeus seeing Jesus. Rather, we learn that when Jesus came to the place, to that sycamore tree, he looked up and said, "Zacchaeus, hurry up and come down. For I'm coming to your house today."

To come truly to oneself is to find Christ at home in oneself.

Zacchaeus *had had* the savvy, the smarts, the guts to fulfill whatever first-century version there was of Robert Frost's advice: "Better to go down dignified with boughten friendship at your side than none at all. Provide, provide!"

But Zacchaeus had the gift to go *beyond* his savvy, his smarts, his guts and hard ambition. Zacchaeus when he went up that sycamore tree had a gift beyond hardness. He had the gift to be simple—even the child's gift. Perhaps he was no longer ridiculous because he no longer cared whether or not he was ridiculous. He wanted to see—to see the face of God. And when Jesus told Zacchaeus to hurry up and come down from there, "For I'm coming to your house today," Zacchaeus scrambled and came down. And our text tells us that he received Jesus with joy. With joy.

Of course, the crowd comes back into the picture now. It always does, you know. "The crowd murmured," it says. They all murmured. What are they murmuring about around *you* these days? They murmured against Zacchaeus as a man unworthy. And they murmured against Jesus because he chose to go to the home of Zacchaeus, of all people.

Which brings us to the dinner scene. Jesus has come home; Jesus has come home to Zacchaeus, the one who received him with joy. And Zacchaeus stands up, and he says to the one the text for the first time refers to as "Lord"—the one to whom he has, in his joy, become accountable, accountable for himself and his life—he says, "Look, look, Lord. Half of my goods I give to the poor... and, well, if I have... have defrauded anyone of anything ... I restore it... fourfold."

And so the sermon comes down—to the "even more ridiculous"—and the sermon comes *back* to us ... as all real sermons must.

One need not be a Marxist or a socialist to see that the poor of this land and the world are hurting, hurting so badly they are often desperate and despairing. Those who are called down out of their trees by Jesus are called to set what they can right.

Those called by Jesus may have more respect for one kind of economic system than another. But more than defenders of any economic system, they will be defenders of the defrauded, of the poor and the hurting. And partly because they know themselves to be poor also—no matter how rich. Whether socialists or capitalists, they will be *critics* of mumbo jumbo, rationalizations, evasions, cruelties, and lies in their own system.

In a system like ours, this means for those of us in business or going into business: profits, OK; *maximization* of profits, no ... no way.

Oh, I know that's not "realistic," as we say. Love in this world never is. Or is it? What is *real*, anyway?

"Maximization of profits" means by definition that when profit clashes with any other claim, profit must have—within the law—the final word. This is to deny the very meaning of persons. Only the "maximization" of personality, of persons, can be justified before the face of Christ. There can be no justification in the presence of Christ for the maximization of profits as either corporate policy or personal ambition.

Maximization of profits is *rationalized* by the system. You know, "the system, working as it does, is really best for everybody even when some people have to be hurt" (the same thing the Marxists say about theirs). Such rationalization is, before the face of the poor even in and around Hamilton, New York, let alone in the Bronx or Brazil, as preposterous as Marxist double-talk about getting rid of bourgeois consciousness—often really, that is, getting rid of middle-class people—in order to benefit "everybody." Both Marxist elimination of the middle class and capitalist maximization of profits are transparent willingness to trash whoever may be hurt or destroyed by *that* system's demands.

God is not mocked. Christ is not fooled.

Fraud can be perfectly legal, as we all know in our heart of hearts. Fraud is to take advantage—not *of* our opportunities, but *with* them, and thereby take advantage of others who are confused, unlucky, powerless, or helpless.

When we defraud we are called to restore fourfold.

And in the selection and conduct of our *vocations*—something we are all thinking about in some way—we are called, in the presence of Christ, to begin to *break* with the measure of money (or "what money can buy") as the measure of success and meaning. We have *some* freedom while we make our friends in childhood, in high school, and in college to know that money is not really the measure. Yet often as we move toward our careers or get settled in them, we find ourselves—like cattle—entering the narrow chute of a corral where that measure of money becomes, if not the only measure, then the most important one of all.

My point is not to do something we aren't fit for or couldn't be happy doing. (Though in this matter of what *really* makes for happiness we are all in need of more thinking, I reckon.) My point is that in order to enter or sustain a vocation we can really believe in or practice a profession or conduct our career the way we think it ought to be practiced, we may be called to cut our income expectations even in half; or, out of a large income, even to give half to help others; or to make our investments where they will help most, with even the possibility of half as much financial return. We are called to conduct our business, our professional practice, to live our lives revealing that we understand that the bottom line is people, not profits—as we, again in our heart of hearts, all well know.

"Well, Coleman Brown," some of us are saying now, "the sermon was going all right until this last stuff about money and profits, maybe even cutting my *income* expectations in half. You can't really expect to be taken seriously with *that*, can you? Anyway, then it really *did* become, like you said, 'ridiculous.'"

Only after that part of the story does Jesus Christ say of Zacchaeus, "Today salvation has come to this house." Only after Zacchaeus, somehow aware of his *own* poverty, begins to discover, in his joy, the *freedom* to respond and care. And in a way that is *explicit, empirical*, and has to do with *money*. Money (or as we prefer, "the things money can buy") has, you see, the *power* to *occupy*—to *take over*—our house, to take over our self, our dreams, our hopes; to shape our highs and lows. (We know that with grades sometimes: our anxiety about grades is often the shadow that money as the standard of meaning casts into our lives.) The power of money can so take over our house that even should it be that we are able to get to church and leave the crowd and climb a sycamore tree and see Jesus, *yet* when he says to us, "Friend, hurry up and come down, for I'm coming to your house today," we shall simply sit there in our tree. And Jesus shall pass on, shall pass by. And it shall be so inscribed in the book of life.

There is a last word: the last word in our text, from Jesus: "For the Son of man"—and Jesus refers here to himself—"the Son of man came to seek and to save the lost."

What does it take to get us down out of our trees? To help us let go of money as the measure of life and let go of being "the chief" as our only aspiration, the only thing worth living for? What does it take to bring us to life? Must we all die in our fright, clutching?

The road goes on, you see, from Jericho to Jerusalem, to another tree—as sometimes it's been called: to the cross. To get us out of our trees, Jesus goes up that tree, goes up upon a cross.

Zacchaeus was far-seeing. Somehow, from that sycamore tree in Jericho, I think he could see Jerusalem and the cross and the love there. Yes, I think he began somehow to understand: "It is no longer I who live, but Christ who lives in me."

Zacchaeus had seen (in the face of Christ) that he was confused, hurting, helpless, and poor and yet that he was acceptable. So he came down to begin to be with Christ in a life shared with the confused, the hurting, the helpless, and the poor.

Come down out of your tree. Christ is passing by. Christ would come into *our* house and eat and drink with us. Christ invites us to take up again the new way—in which we discover that to become poorer is to become richer . . . to become vulnerable is to become free . . . and to take the terrible risk of love—love of God and of one another—is to begin to find security . . . the *only* security finally there is.

Amen.

19

A Spirit Which Affects Us for Ill— and Our Empty House

A Parents' Weekend Sermon

NOVEMBER 2, 1986

When the unclean spirit has gone out of a person, it passes through waterless places seeking rest, but it finds none. Then it says, "I will return to my house from which I came." And when it comes it finds the house empty, swept, and put in order. Then it goes and brings with it seven other spirits more evil than itself, and they enter and dwell there; and the last state of that person becomes worse than the first. So shall it be also with this evil generation.
—Matthew 12:43–45 (RSV)

Behold, I stand at the door and knock; if any one hears my voice and opens the door, I will come in to him and eat with him, and he with me.
—Revelation 3:20 (RSV)

THIS PARABLE SEEMS VERY foreign and long ago to us—as perhaps, this morning, Christ and God do, too: foreign and long ago.

But we have some sense of a spirit which affects us for ill, a spirit which gets hold of us and messes things up. It may be a spirit of quarrelsomeness;

a compulsive need for revenge—to get back. It may be a spirit of self-pity: we are in the grip of such a spirit this morning, perhaps. Some of us are alcoholics—I hope we are alcoholics who have found Alcoholics Anonymous and have recognized that we are not going to be rid of that unclean spirit but have to live with it—but with our feet on its neck rather than its feet on our neck.

That is part of what I want to preach on this morning—living with our unclean spirit.

What is yours?

Perhaps you are a *work*aholic. And there is no Workaholics Anonymous yet, is there?

Has the unclean spirit affected this Parents' Weekend for some of you—the same old family tension? The same old topics making for discomfort and grief?

For some of us the unclean spirit is desires we regret but cannot subdue.

For some of us the unclean spirit is that we seem in the grip of a range of things that it seems we must do; yet those things seem to have no point, no meaning.

Jesus' parable may seem strange, foreign, and far away. Yet you and I—we know what an unclean spirit is. We know what it is to have an unclean spirit in the house—even in the house of our souls, in the house of who we are.

Sometimes the unclean spirit will leave for a while, be gone. But the unclean spirit in each of us is restless—if you will, it is not satisfied to be gone. The unclean spirit says, in its own way, "I will return to my house from which I came." The spirit which gets hold of us and affects us for ill and messes things up returns. Most of us know that experience, I believe.

And here we begin to approach the center of Jesus' parable. Jesus is not simplistic. Jesus is not a perfectionist. Jesus is under no illusions about your life—or mine. The spirit which gets hold of us and affects us for ill returns to us. "So what else is new?" Jesus is not surprised. Nor does Jesus condemn.

Rather, the question the Christ is putting to us is: *What happens then, when that spirit returns?*

One commentator has admitted that Jesus' story is a story to chill the blood.

We come to the moment when, for a while, that spirit which affects us for ill is gone. Our soul, our self is portrayed by Jesus as a house: the house is cleaned up now, vacuumed, restored, the windows gleam again; there is fine linen, and tapestries, and works of our favorite art; the stereo has all new components, good tapes are neatly stacked; the desk is in order again, the computer is working perfectly, the house smells fresh; a fine car—more than one, perhaps—stands outside; there is a good school to attend (or arrangements for the children to attend good schools have been made); church now and then (after all, you never know—tradition is nice). Everything is clean, swept, put in order . . . and empty.

Here is the crisis of Jesus' story.

And what makes more than one hearer of it recognize that it is a story to chill the blood is recognition that *if your house is empty, you're a setup for possession!*

The warning in Jesus' story goes like this, remember: when that unclean spirit returns (as it will) and finds your house put in order, swept and empty—it goes back out and then brings home with it seven other spirits worse than itself; they all enter, and the last condition of that person "becomes worse than the first." Jesus adds then these words to his story: "So shall it be also with this generation."

I repeat what I guess is my first point: *if your house is empty, you're a setup for possession*—by a whole range of destructive spirits even worse than the one you're already well acquainted with.

It is awesome, overwhelming in many ways, to preach the gospel of Jesus Christ in a time of widespread and massive distrust—distrust of the gospel and distrust of God. None of us is spared that distrust, none of us, including the preacher.

Is it not true that we are more worried about getting a good grade in that midterm or seeing that stock recover; that we are more worried about that sorority or fraternity bid or whether our contract will be renewed; that we are more worried about interviewing well, about getting a good job; is it not true that we who are parents (and I am the father of four, two still in college) worried more about whether our children got into Middlebury or Colgate than whether they are entering the kingdom of God? Is it not true that we, too, contemplate more about whether they know what career they want, interview well, and get a good job than that—whether they live or whether they die—they are the Lord's?

What do we think is happening and going to happen to us—this "generation" (to use Jesus' word), this generation which includes us *all*? What is going to happen to a people, to a civilization that treats spiritual depth as something about as important as occasionally roasting marshmallows or checking out a local church when there's time?

We live in a culture that will not let Jesus Christ simply speak to us of his hopes and fears for us. Either we wrap Jesus in the American flag, assuring ourselves of how he blesses (or at least doesn't really mind) our indifference to the poor, our trust in military power, our consumer itch, or we try to enlist Jesus for our new spirituality, which boils down to: whatever feels good, whatever you *like* thinking, *whatever* is optimistic, *whatever* gives you some much-needed self-esteem—let that be your gospel.

The gospel of Jesus Christ has not been refuted. It has not grown stale. It has not worn out. But we are tired of hearing it and of *not* being transformed by it: we are tired of our own resistance to it, tired of our own beginning to open the door of our house to Christ but then hesitating yet once more: of that we *are* tired; that *is* wearing us out!

We are tired of our own double-mindedness.

We are tired of our own emptiness!

With all the things we have and all the things we have to do! And, God, we have so much to do, don't we? Even now, many of us are half occupied about how we'll get to brunch on time and back on the road or back to our work (neglected this weekend because of so many *other* things to do). We have so much—and so much to do! And yet: both as individuals and as a culture (look at so much of what occupies us on television, look even into the house of your own soul, your own self)—we are often so empty, so appallingly empty.

Now, the question must come: To whom does your soul, your self belong?

And if you answer, "It belongs to me, my soul is mine," then, this morning, hear only this—there is not time to say more—you are naive, though not wonderfully, joyfully naive—not naive like the child—but naive in a chilling and terrible way. (Naive, I was going to say, as sophomores are sometimes naive—except I feared I would offend the sophomores. But "sophomore," remember, means wise fool.) We are too much—each of us—too much, too rich, too complex to be mastered by ourselves.

To whom does the house of your self belong?

Notice in Jesus' parable, when the unclean spirit returns, what it says; the unclean spirit refers to that house as "my house."

How shall I say it this morning? The spirits which affect us for ill are persistent and productive: they do not give up in the face of your claims or mine.

Nature—and human nature—abhors a vacuum!

Empty houses never remain empty! Empty houses never remain empty.

There is going to be one kind of party—or another; one kind of celebration—or another—in the house of our culture and (finally, perhaps even more importantly) in the house of yourself: one kind of party, one kind of dance or another. The celebration by the seven unclean spirits worse than the one that already troubles you—or the celebration of the kingdom of God, the Lord's Supper, the celebration of the arrival of Christ.

Now that *one* unclean spirit, with which we began, may still be around, probably will be, I venture—trying to make a place for itself even at the Lord's Supper, trying to look casual, peering out from under the table even. Perhaps not, but I reckon so.

The alcoholics among us understand what I mean. When you join Alcoholics Anonymous, you acknowledge that "once an alcoholic, always an alcoholic." You need the continual help of the AA community and the healing spirit there to keep that one unclean spirit from bringing all its friends and taking over the house, and you say, "once an alcoholic, always an alcoholic"—even when you haven't had a drink for fifteen years.

Perhaps it's also "once a workaholic, always a workaholic," even if you take an hour for yourself every day and make time for your family and friends every week.

That's my second point: *the dangers of perfectionism.*

If your house is empty, you're a setup for possession: that was the first point.

And the second is: the point of life is *not* to have a clean, well-swept, empty house. That's perfectionism. And it betrays us every time. The unclean spirit comes back—every time. The question is, What will it find when it returns? What will that spirit which gets hold of us and messes things up find when it returns to you? That spirit of quarrelsomeness, that revengeful spirit you know so well, that spirit of self-pity (so powerful), the unclean spirit *you* know most intimately—what will it find? A clean, beautifully arranged, empty self?

In that case you will find the end of your story a tragedy.

Or—or . . .

We are empty houses of various kinds, you and I. And we try not to hear—we distance ourselves from—we *deny* that we hear (indeed, we deny in order *somehow* to fill the emptiness)—we turn up the volume against the one who speaks both to our empty culture and to each of us personally in the emptiness of our house.

In spite of the preacher, in spite of all the busyness we attend to, in spite of all we do to tune out the one who stands at the door of our emptiness, we understand: "Behold, I stand at the door. If anyone hears my voice and opens the door, I will come in to you and eat with you—and you with me."

As one person has put it, Jesus Christ suffered unto the death, not that we might not suffer but that our sufferings might become like his.

No longer empty, our sufferings, but full of meaning and compassion and understanding and hope—even in the midst of failure; full of love in the midst of conflict and, yes, affliction—even affliction by that spirit which affects us for ill, gets hold of us and messes things up.

We hear Christ in our very emptiness. We hear Christ in the very wonder we have at our own loneliness.

The empty house *will* be filled.

The unclean spirit will return. Either we are a house—torn up, perhaps, afflicted by our unclean spirit, sure—but a house in which the spirit of the Suffering Servant of God can come home, or we shall be in bondage to a whole array of unclean spirits ever more powerful than ourselves.

If your house is empty, you're a setup for possession by the powerful and, yes, finally empty spirits of the day.

But don't be a perfectionist, as if having a clean, well-swept, *empty* house were life's point.

When shall we learn that our personality, yes, our very selves are made for the indwelling of Christ? Yes, I mean exactly that—our souls, our selves are made for the Spirit of God to be received, to enter, and to become at home. Our souls, our world are made for that—and, finally, for nothing else.

We feel Christ's presence even when we turn up the volume of our interior music, even as we turn back into our empty house—and busy ourselves—hoping that no unclean spirit or anything else will knock.

We hear the voice of one whom we often treat as dead but who is alive—even at the door of our souls—one who lives and will not depart. And that one says—and we know it is that one who says it—that one says something like: "Behold, I stand at the door and knock; if you hear my voice and open the door, I will come in and eat with you and you with me."

You shall not be empty anymore. And even in your troubles you shall no longer despair.

20

God Believes in You

A Communion Sermon

December 7, 1986

And Mary said, "My soul magnifies the Lord, and my spirit rejoices in God my Savior, for he has regarded the low estate of his handmaiden. For behold henceforth all generations will call me blessed; for he who is mighty has done great things for me, and holy is his name. And his mercy is on those who fear him from generation to generation. He has shown strength with his arm, he has scattered the proud in the imagination of their hearts, he has put down the mighty from their thrones, and exalted those of low degree; he has filled the hungry with good things, and the rich he has sent empty away. He has helped his servant Israel, in remembrance of his mercy, as he spoke to our fathers, to Abraham and to his posterity for ever."
—Luke 1:46–55 (RSV)
See also Luke 1:26–35; 2 Corinthians 5:14–16

LET ME TELL YOU what I'm going to preach today: You may not think much of yourself, but God believes in you. God believes in you.

You may be discouraged—even deeply discouraged—about your life, but in God's eyes you are favored.

Abraham Heschel, a great Jewish wiseman and saint of our times, observed this as he studied the Bible: "The great problem" in our life "is whether to trust, to have faith in God. The great problem in the life of God is whether to trust, to have faith" in us.

"The central issue," Heschel went on to say, is not our "decision to extend formal recognition to God, to furnish God with a certificate that [God] exists, but the realization of our importance to God's design; *not to prove that God is alive, but to prove that . . . [we are] not dead!*"[1]

The birth of Christ in our lives—the *real* Christmas—is the great chance God gives you and me to prove that we are not dead.

You and I are (let's get it plain)—you and I are part of God's design: you and I are part of God's hope and, yes, God's faith.

Entering into Advent is a way of recognizing that whatever your discouragements, however dead you may have become to anything but your own plans and personal worries, God trusts that you and I may prove not to be dead but willing to give birth to life and love in this hurting, unjust world—this hurting, unjust world that God enters in order to save. And mark it plain—*how* God enters this world of ours: by calling us to give birth to the Christ with gentle care and terrific courage.

The Scriptures are not only a record but revelation. When we open ourselves both with simplicity and with imagination that is undefensive, the Advent and Christmas stories become revelation of what is to come in our story. The Scriptures can reveal to you who you are and what you are called to do and how much God believes in you and trusts you.

Do you know the story of the man who was going down from Jerusalem to Jericho? He fell among robbers who stripped and beat him and then ran, leaving him half-dead. Then various people came down the road but passed by on the other side, until a Samaritan (despised by most Jews at that time) came by and saved the man, was neighbor to the man (Luke 10:29–37). Well now, women as well as men can identify with that man who fell among robbers and found a neighbor even there.

And I say to you this morning that men as well as women can identify with Mary the mother of Jesus. For we are all—women and men—called, *chosen* to give birth, to bear the Christ: the Christ so vulnerable yet so desperately needed—to bear the Christ in this often terrifying, lonely world of ours.

Let me put it very straight: whatever our motives for being here today, I believe God has brought us to this service to hear this: you shall conceive

---

1. Heschel, "Idols in the Temples," 67 (emphasis added).

and bear in yourself the Messiah, bear in you the Christ whom God sends into these tumultuous *times* of ours and into the very *places* in which you are daily living out your life. That is why you have been brought—"by will and by grace," as Jewelnel Davis[2] used to say—to this service, to receive, if you will, the body and blood of Christ, to receive the "peace of God" from someone you may not even know, to receive friends and strangers here and receive God's word *to you*.

Why? Simply so that you can have a little religious lift before tumbling back to papers and exams or whatever?

No—for more than that: in order that you and I become strong enough and courageous enough *to give birth* . . . to give birth to what is conceived *in you* by the Holy Spirit, to what even now you bear in yourself: the Christ who has come into the world that first Christmas and yet for whom we wait in such deep need this morning—and for whom all the world longs in the secret of our aching hearts. That one for whom all of us wait is conceived in you, that one you are called to bear into life and time.

Do I speak in symbols? Of course. How else can we speak of God and the transformation of life which God seeks through entering, truly and literally, into human life; which God seeks, believing in you and me?

The story of Mary *reveals* to us the central activity to which you and I are called as *our* stories unfold. Whoever has ears to hear, let that person hear.

Christ is conceived and to be born in our lives.

A good parent does not confuse herself, himself with the child. (Of course it takes most parents a long time to become good parents.) A good parent nurtures and disciplines and lets be: as the child grows, increasingly lets the child be who the child is.

So with us as we conceive and bear Christ in our lives.

Luther said we are to be Christ to our neighbors. And Thomas à Kempis said we are to imitate Christ. All right, but be careful. I reckon we may do better to imitate Mary—men and women—and be Mary to our neighbors; that is, recognize that I am not Christ. No, I am the handmaiden, I am the hod carrier of the Lord.

I am not Christ—you are not Christ—yet in and through our lives we can give birth to the Christ who precisely thus enters into life among us. We can give birth to Christ and, in our actual lives, let Christ grow and develop, become fully who Christ really is: our guide and our savior. In our own lives we can let God be God.

---

2. Assistant Chaplain from 1983 to 1985.

You and I can begin to live in *honest* relationship to God and in faithful recognition that *everyone* is a child of God—no matter what they presently believe (or think they believe), no matter how they live! You and I are called to conceive and to bear for the world the Christ of God, the One who saves people—in countless different ways—from hating themselves and others, who saves people from despair and unending distrust and the death of love and death. So much confidence does God have in you and me!

"Hail, O favored one, the Lord is with you!"

But to hear addressed to us what was first addressed to Mary fills us with fear as it filled her first with fear.

Why? Because it begins to take away from us all our self-set purposes. Because we must go through travail and being misunderstood. Because we must learn patience. Because we must learn yet much better how to care for another and for others than ourselves. Moreover, as an old man said to Mary when Jesus was still a very tiny baby, this child will be spoken against—"and a sword will pierce through your own soul also"—for by this Jesus, "thoughts out of many hearts will be revealed."[3]

The messenger of God says, Do not be afraid. You have found favor! You have a vocation, a calling—a calling to life whose benefits will go out beyond your own place and time.

But Mary protests. Look, she cries, I don't even have a husband. This is frightening business. And we understand. We, too, protest. We, too, are frightened. Essentially we say what Mary says: What will happen to me if the Christ is conceived in my life and I am to bear Christ into the world?

"I feel totally inadequate," we cry. "I'm too young"—or "too old." (In our own eyes, we spend half our life, I think, feeling too young for what we are called to do . . . and half our life feeling too old for what we are called to do.) "I'm too inexperienced," we cry. Or, "I've *already* messed up my life too much."

Some of us cry out, "I'm not even sure I believe in God, let alone that I can bear the justice and joy of God to others and the world."

One way or another—like Mary—we all protest. "I'm only a first-year student." Or, "I haven't even figured out what I'm going to do next summer." Or, "I don't even know my major yet." "*I* haven't even figured out how to have a relationship yet." "My parents are getting a divorce." "I'm flunking out of school." "I've just joined a sorority." "I've still go to do graduate school."

But this God we may not even know whether we believe in or not—this God is a God who believes in us—who believes in us whether *we* believe

---

3. See Luke 2:25–35.

or not; however inadequate we may feel; whatever our age; whatever our experience; however much we have messed up our lives! Whatever we may do next summer... or major in; however it is with us in relationships; whatever the struggles at or with home; regardless of our failures and flunking! Whoever our associates—whatever our plans.

God believes in us. All our feelings and evidences and arguments to the contrary are beside the point. God believes in us, has confidence in us, chooses and calls us, and in us conceives the Christ.

Our responsibility is greater than we can understand. It is—I use the overused word—it is awesome, our responsibility is.

Yet surrounding our awesome responsibility, with Christ conceived in us, the implication of God's message to us is this: Take comfort. Be confident. Be confident in God's confidence in you, even though you do not share that confidence yourself yet—that confidence in yourself.

You are to bear Christ into the world. This that you bear is greater than you. (Mary grasped that.) This that you bear is bigger than your identity. (Mary grasped that.)

This is not, finally, so much a matter of effort as it is, over and over again, a matter of consent. You and I are to let the power of the Most High God—the One who believes in you and in me—overshadow us. For thus says the Lord God, the Holy One: "In returning and rest you shall be saved; in quietness and in trust shall be your strength."[4]

And we are called to say with Mary, let it be. *Not* que será, será—not *whatever* will be, will be. But, *let* it be. Let it be—your mysterious will, O God, that we, that I should bear Christ into the world.

And we are brought near to God to say with Mary:

> My soul magnifies the Lord,
>
> and my spirit rejoices in God my Savior,
>
> for God has regarded me in my low estate.
>
> For, henceforth, all generations will call me blessed;
>
> for the One who is mighty has done mighty things for me—and in me.
>
> And hallowed be God's name.
>
> God's mercy is on those who reverence God from generation to generation.
>
> God shows strength (through our weakness)
>
> and scatters the proud in the
>
> imagination of their hearts.

---

4. Isaiah 30:15.

There is, you see, the imagination of our lonely arrogance and there is the imagination of God's presence in us.

> God puts down the mighty.
> God exalts those who are called low or of no account,
> God fills the hungry with good things;
> the rich he sends empty away.

The song of Mary is a song that shakes the status quo, a song of social justice. It is harder, the *Christ* will say, for the rich to enter God's realm than for a camel to go through the eye of a needle.[5]

God remembers mercy: never forgets it, not forever.

Consent to bear and give birth to what is conceived in you by the Holy Spirit—the Christ of God—helpless, weak, unformed as that in you is.

Of course it is completely human—bone of your bone, flesh of your flesh. Have you not heard?! God has become completely human! That is the Christmas coming! That is the miracle.

And we wait in anticipation for the birth in you and me, from the womb of our contemporary life together, for the birth of Christ.

The annunciation to Mary—and a Mary you are, every one of you, I am and you are—the annunciation is the good news that there is more mercy and faith in God than sin and despair in us.

Advent and Christmas are actual expressions of God's hope and faith and love. God believes in us. God loves us. Let us begin to believe as God believes and then—may it be—love even as God loves.

---

5. See Mark 10:24.

21

"Weeping May Tarry for the Night, but Joy Comes with the Morning"

FEBRUARY 15, 1987

I will extol thee, O LORD, for thou hast drawn me up, and hast not let my foes rejoice over me. O LORD my God, I cried to thee for help, and thou hast healed me. O LORD, thou hast brought up my soul from Sheol, restored me to life from among those gone down to the Pit. Sing praises to the LORD, O you his saints, and give thanks to his holy name. For his anger is but for a moment, and his favor is for a lifetime. Weeping may tarry for the night, but joy comes with the morning.

—Psalm 30:1–5 (RSV)

Who shall separate us from the love of Christ? Shall tribulation, or distress, or persecution, or famine, or nakedness, or peril, or sword? As it is written,

> *"For thy sake we are being killed all the day long;*
> *we are regarded as sheep to be slaughtered."*

No, in all these things we are more than conquerors through him who loved us. For I am sure that neither death, nor life, nor angels, nor principalities, nor things present, nor things to come, nor powers, nor height, nor depth, nor anything else in all creation, will be able to separate us from the love of God in Christ Jesus our Lord.

—Romans 8:35–39 (RSV)

"Nothing can separate us from the love of God." That is the *first* text this morning. And I want you to know what that means: God can reach you. God can reach you. And so *joy* is possible, whatever we feel or think this morning. Joy is possible because joy, finally, is this God who loves you—reaching you. The reality of everyday life, what seems "*really* real" to you, is not so far from God that God cannot reach you. That's the bottom line of what I want to say this morning.

This is Black History month, I remind you. And some know, but some may not, that the experience of Black people in America has been profoundly shaped by Jesus—and by the church. And the Black churches have been, so often, strangely, churches of gladness, churches of joy.

In Black churches people usually know that whatever else you may think about life, we're in it together. Life is finally not a private matter—important as solitude is and important as the right to privacy is: life is finally not a private matter; we're in it together.

And in the Black churches people usually know something else that all of us who want to be happy, who want to be glad, who seek joy must come to know: joy cannot be segregated from sorrow. Joy cannot be segregated from sorrow. If you want to be happy, if you want to be glad, if you want to enter joy, you're going to have to start being kinder to sorrow: kinder to your own sorrow, kinder to the sorrows of others, kinder to the sorrows of the world. Joy cannot be segregated from sorrow.

Some of us heard together Martin Luther King's powerful preaching, from a recording, in January at a service in the Judd Chapel downstairs. And I want us this morning to remember some of the things he said one Sunday (in the late Sixties) to a congregation of Black people struggling with life.

> Death is not a period which ends this great sentence of life but a comma that punctuates it to more lofty significance. Death is not a blind alley that leads the human race into a state of nothingness but an open door that leads us into life eternal.
>
> "I am persuaded that neither death nor life . . . nor anything else in all creation can separate us from the love of God in Christ Jesus our Lord."
>
> However dark it is now, morning will come.
>
> Our slave foreparents taught us so much in their beautiful sorrow songs . . . They looked at the midnight surrounding their days, and they knew that there was sorrow and agony and hurt all around. And when they thought about midnight, they would sing, "Nobody knows the trouble I've seen, nobody knows but Jesus." And pretty soon something reminded them that morning

would come and they started singing, "I'm so glad [that] trouble don't last always."

Centuries ago Jeremiah, the great prophet, raised a very profound question: he looked at the inequities around and he noticed a lot of things; he noticed the good people so often suffering and the evil people so often prospering. Jeremiah raised the question: "Is there no balm [no healing medicine] in Gilead [the place where the healing medicine was made]? Is there no physician there?"

Centuries later our slave foreparents came along and they too confronted the problems of life. They had nothing to look forward to morning after morning but the sizzling heat, the rawhide whip of the overseer, long rows of cotton. But they did an *amazing* thing: they looked back across the centuries and they took Jeremiah's question mark and straightened it into an exclamation point! And they could sing, "There *is* a balm in Gilead to make the wounded whole. There *is* a balm in Gilead to heal the sin-sick soul." Then they came with another verse: "Sometimes I feel discouraged . . .

(Dr. King got discouraged.)

. . . and feel my work's in vain. But then the Holy Spirit *revives* my soul again. There *is* a balm in Gilead." And so I can sing that, and another song comes to me—"I've seen the lightning flash. I've heard the thunder roll. I've felt sin breakers dashing, trying to conquer my soul. But I heard the voice of Jesus say still to fight on. He promised never to leave me, never to leave me alone![1]

We live in a culture hypnotized by death, not a culture awed and mystified by life: we live in a culture that holds death, not to be a comma, but a period; not to be a boundary but the end—THE END—the everlasting, eternal end. H. Richard Niebuhr is right when he says this is "the great overarching myth . . . the almost unconquerable picture in the mind"—the mind that reaches into us all, that we all share with our culture to some degree: in the "past forgotten, dead generations." And there is an "image of myself" and all society "coming to that future when there is no more future." Niebuhr calls this, in all its forms, our "mythology of death."[2]

Because we have been overwhelmed by the myth of death; because our culture holds death to be THE END, the everlasting, eternal end, we cannot,

---

1. King, *Knock at Midnight*.
2. Niebuhr, *Responsible Self*, 106–7.

many of us, sing tenderly and vulnerably, with tears streaming down our faces, about the everlasting arms; we cannot sing "leaning, leaning on the everlasting arms"; we cannot sing, with Martin Luther King Jr., "Precious Lord, take my hand"; we cannot sing with the Black churches—as Jewelnel Davis taught us to sing—"This is my story, this is my song . . ."

And so the church must become the *skeptic*—we must become *the skeptics*—skeptical of the powerful myths of our day, which often are at the bottom of both our beer commercials and our methods of literary criticism, our politics and our very views of human well-being.

Segregating life and death—and living in a culture that holds to the myth of death as the last word—we segregate joy and sorrow. And we segregate them desperately; we segregate them, desperately trying to keep the vision of nothingness out of our days and ways, trying to keep sorrow out of our joy.

But something strange happens as we try to keep sorrow out of joy: we lose the joy.

To segregate joy from sorrow is a desperate thing to do: joy and sorrow seek each other; they are friends; they are bound by love; they are, if you will, kind to each other.

But so often we desperately try to segregate them. We become desperate for happiness, for pleasure, for contentment—so desperate that we make ourselves unhappy in our *insistence* on happiness; so desperate that we often end up vomiting after a night of so-called pleasure; so desperate to be undisturbed in our pursuit of contentment that we become jittery, irritable, even enraged. It *is* possible to find contentment (at times), pleasure (at times), happiness (at times) if we can give up our desperation—*and give up our insistent segregation of joy and sorrow*: if we will let them be—and let them find each other in our lives, and treat them kindly, both joy and sorrow—then happiness and pleasure and contentment will make their place with us at times and we shall welcome them like good friends who, like all good friends, come and go.

We shall only be happy with happiness, *enjoy* our pleasures, and find contentment with being content when we have allowed joy into our lives: and joy will not come without sorrow. If we try to overcome sorrow by a stiff upper lip or by turning ourselves cold to life; or refusing to feel anymore; or by denying that we even know sorrow—or by frantic, desperate attempts to run from sorrow—we shall never know joy and we shall turn happiness, pleasure, and contentment into *shallow* things, things we cannot even trust.

The second text today is "weeping may tarry for the night, but joy comes with the morning."

Sometimes the night is short and the dawn comes soon. Sometimes the night is long and we wait for the dawn more than military sentries on a night like last night, out of doors, frozen, watch for the morning light and relief from their posts.

Indeed, keeping in mind the Black experience in America and the Black church, life itself can at times seem a long night: that's why from the Black church could come the song, "There's going to be a great day!"

The night of nuclear fear is upon us and we can only remember and trust that finally the light that overcomes the night is not—is not, I say—the light of that disaster which, if it comes, will only be deeper night, but the light of the true day, of the new day that God will bring according to God's own promise, beyond every disaster, personal or worldwide.

Now here, I know, I touch our sensitive nerves. For here we discover again how powerful over us and in us is the myth of death; here we discover (yes, again) how weak, how little is our faith. And those who tell us glibly that *they* have *much* faith—and that they have come to it easily—we *suspect*; fanaticism is not faith, we know. And glib assurance we envy, perhaps, but still its very glibness takes away its power to assure.

Here is where we recognize that only grace under pressure can testify with power. We are made to pause when Martin Luther King Jr., on the night before his death—when the threats were out, FBI protection reduced—tells us, "I'm happy tonight. I'm not worried about anything. I'm not fearing any man. 'Mine eyes have seen the glory of the coming of the Lord.'"[3]

The joy of believing must let the sorrow in in order to become belief, and believable. The joy of faith, of trust in God has an open heart to sorrow and treats sorrow so kindly that sorrow is finally not chilled out or denied or rejected, but *transformed*—as the night sky begins to be transformed by the first hues of morning light.

Joy is an awesome mystery. "Now we see in a mirror dimly"—in the darkness—but then face to face. "Now I know in part"—as my participation in life begins to disclose to me those first signs of light that lead me to trust that a morning does come, someday, not just for me, but for us all.[4]

Joy is a mystery. We have taste of, a sense of, have intimations of joy at various times, in various ways. We have known it in the grandeur of nature; at Christmastime; in haunting memories of childhood; when we learned that she survived the operation and that she's going to get well.

3. King, *Knock at Midnight*.
4. 1 Corinthians 13:12.

What I want to say now about joy, and thus about happiness and pleasure and contentment, which, while they are not joy, are its weaker friends—yes, joy is strong . . . *too* strong for us at times: as I've tried to say, always strong enough to be kind to sorrow, indeed, to allow sorrow to be—but what I want now to say about joy as I'm beginning to come down to the end of this sermon requires something dangerous and difficult to say; or better, I have to say something dangerous and difficult to make the way for joy.

What's difficult and dangerous to say—dangerous because so easy to misunderstand and misappropriate—is something about, not the relation between reason and faith but about the relation between reason and God. Let me go slowly.

There's no place for anti-intellectualism in Christian faith: it's as wrong to be against our minds as it is to be against our emotions or our bodies. Our minds should be treated no less than our bodies as temples of the Holy Spirit. And we should all—much more than we do—seek *excellence* of mind, especially about the things we believe most deeply, hope most dearly, love most truly. Faith should be able to reason well—at least as well as one can possibly reason.

But finally a deep difference must be made clear: the difference between trusting in reason—which is to trust only in that which you can explain and illuminate—and trusting in God, which is to trust in the source and end of all things, the One who brought *you* into being. (Who knows why *you* and not someone else? "God only knows.")

To meet God is to experience not an explanation but love.

Finally a deep difference must be made clear: the difference between trusting in our powers of reason and trusting in God, who is the source of reason and all things.

I have not forgotten about joy. For that is what the energy of joy is. Joy is found where we begin to trust that sorrow and joy cannot be segregated—*reasonable* as it seems to do that; joy is found where we begin to trust that weeping may tarry for the night but joy comes with the morning; joy is found where we begin to trust that the name of the Mystery is not death and emptiness, but . . . but everlasting arms and love . . . joy is where we begin to trust that *true* humanity is not in slavedrivers and cruelty and indifference . . . but in Jesus, crucified and, yes, alive.

It is one of the greatest Black preachers of our day, Gardner C. Taylor, who has said as well, perhaps, as it can be said what must be said:

> The great and rich promises of God stagger us. What is more, the Gospel story of God's love for us seems too good to be true. This is why many people cannot accept it. If God's grace was

not so freely given, if His love for us was not so unconditional, if we could see more of our human trait of driving a bargain, we would feel more understanding. Jesus says that God "maketh his sun to rise on the evil and on the good." We look at the passage which says, "Fear thou not; for I am with thee; be not dismayed; for I am thy God: I will strengthen thee; yea, I will help thee; yea, I will uphold thee with the right hand of my righteousness," and we wonder why God would say such a thing. Is it true? Does this represent the mind of the Eternal? If so, why would He make such a promise as this? It is almost too good to be true.

We grope toward some understanding as to why this almost unbelievable promise is reasonable. It is habitual for our minds to cry out for some logical explanation why this is so or that is true. It is one of the strengths and it is one of the weaknesses of the European mentality, and of those of us who have been influenced by it, to believe that everything can be grasped by the mind and if something is real, it must make sense by our standards . . .

Now, let me try to weaken my case before I advance it. The greatest things in life are not reasonable. The mind may make sensible comments about these greatest things in life, but they are not reasonable. The love of a mother for her child has reasons, but it is not reasonable. The love of a man for a woman, and the other way around, is surely not reasonable. Beauty, a sunset, the great plunging torrents of Niagara, the final tremendous thunders of the "Hallelujahs" in Handel's *Messiah*, the catch in the throat when the sun sets over the sea striking a line of gold on the calm waters touch us at a different level from logic and reason.

And the love of God for us is not reasonable. Heaven knows it must be accepted on faith. If we merited God's love, we could readily understand it. If we were sufficiently attractive, that would make sense. As it is, it is a mystery.[5]

Finally, let me say this, for it became clearer to me than ever it has been as I struggled with this sermon: The issue is not for you this morning to try to believe what you don't believe. The issue is, Will you receive it when it comes? Will you receive it when it comes?

God is better than we think. God can reach us. God can reach us. Reach us right here in this life and in this *everyday* life of ours. And that is joy—joy that you can experience.

---

5. Taylor, "Making a Great Promise Reasonable," 50–51.

The Black church is a testimony—may Black people (both here and not here) not forsake it, and white people (both here and not here) not overlook or, God forbid, despise it—a testimony to God's power to give joy.

It may be night for you this morning—morning literally, but *really* night: a night of self-preoccupation, worry, uncertainty, confusion, defeat ... And the night may be short or long.

Weeping may *tarry* for the night—but joy comes with the morning! That is God's promise. And God can reach you. God can reach you. That's also God's promise.

22

"I Desire Mercy..."

A Communion Sermon

SEPTEMBER 11, 1988

> *And as he sat at table in the house, behold, many tax collectors and sinners came and sat down with Jesus and his disciples. And when the Pharisees saw this, they said to his disciples, "Why does your teacher eat with tax collectors and sinners?" But when he heard it, he said, "Those who are well have no need of a physician, but those who are sick. Go and learn what this means, 'I desire mercy, and not sacrifice.' For I came not to call the righteous, but sinners."*
>
> —Matthew 9:10–13 (RSV)

I WANT TO TELL you a story, a simple story, a true story of a woman and her minister. The woman's husband had lost his job and her baby had been hospitalized. She came to see the minister; this is what she told him: "After last week"—when her husband lost his job and the baby had become so ill—

> I came into church Sunday and looked at you up there in that robe and thought, "God is in a black robe like a judge, ready to judge me." And I got angry at God. I could see God standing in heaven saying, "Give her husband a pink slip and make her baby sick." Then you came down out of the pulpit and sat next to me and put your arm behind me in the pew while we listened to the solo. And the reason I cried was not because of anything in

particular in the sermon or the prayers, but because when you put your arm around me at the back of the pew, I thought, *God loves me. God's not angry with me*, and I was so glad, I couldn't help crying.[1]

We do not live in a religious world. We live in a world one person has described this way: a "world of broken human relationships, of unfair parents who demand what children cannot give, and of tragic deaths."[2]

Someone *here* has seen a parent or close relation lose a job. Someone here has known the anguish of the child gone in the night to the hospital. Someone here has known directly the tragic death. Some of you are children of unfair parents who—much as you love them and they love you—demand what you cannot give. And all of us know something of the brokenness of human relationships.

Jesus never forgets what kind of world it is. He cuts through the stuff, the little ways we divide up people—in part divide them up in order to protect ourselves from the uncertainty of the world and to hide from death.

But Jesus in this text we've heard comes and sits down—and he eats and drinks with people . . . as they are, whoever they are.

"Tax collectors and sinners"? How can we understand who they are? Think of the people, or the kind of people, you honestly think just unacceptable, the kind of people the world can really do without, in your opinion. It's disturbing for us to think that they're there too, at the table with Jesus.

When we put on our moral but merciless glasses we can't see how Jesus could be with such people, those "tax collectors and sinners."

And somebody—and often some part of ourself—will inevitably ask, How could that be? Why *is* that?

Jesus' answer discloses something, something powerful and frightening and wondrous: Jesus is a healer, a healer of human souls.

You and I? We are human souls.

With great irony—greater irony than we can at first understand—Jesus says, "I came not to call the righteous." If you've got it all together, then I didn't come to call you. I came to call the unacceptable, the separated, the sick, the sinners. Jesus wants us to think about that—and about who, if anyone, has it together.

---

1. Troeger, *Creating Fresh Images*, 42–43.
2. Troeger, *Creating Fresh Images*, 57.

And in the midst of his reply, he quotes one of the prophets who heard God say, "I desire mercy and not sacrifice." "I desire mercy and not sacrifice."[3]

Here in the midst of the world as it *is*—not as we should like it to be—with people acting like they do act, not as we should like them to act, the word of God is this: "I desire mercy." Mercy.

Mercy and not sacrifice.

Now Jesus isn't saying we won't have to make or don't have to make sacrifices. And he is not saying, nor was the prophet Hosea whom he quoted, that rituals and worship are not pleasing to God.

What Jesus is saying is this: I desire mercy and not whatever thing you do—no matter how good that thing is, no matter how good it is—that thing by which you get out of doing mercy.

When we hear "I desire mercy and not sacrifice," we hear God say to us, I desire mercy and not something second best, not whatever you have devised, no matter how good in itself, to *escape* from being merciful.

Now notice carefully exactly what Jesus says; he says, "*Go and learn what this means.*"

We here this morning all are set these days to go about learning things, all sorts of things. I'm trying to learn for new responsibilities I have this year. First-year students have heard a lot about how to learn ever since they arrived on campus. We've heard in introductions to courses about what we're going to learn this semester. Many of us, young and old, are trying to learn how to deal with new stages in our life, with new people—and all sorts of things.

And Jesus Christ—this Teacher-Savior, this Savior-Teacher, this One whom we know only as we allow the Spirit of God to get into us, inside of us—this Jesus says to us, amidst all we are trying to learn, "Go and learn what *this* means, 'I desire mercy and not'" whatever you are doing—no matter how good it is!—by which you get yourself out of doing mercy.

We have to go and *learn* mercy. As we go, let us realize immediately that mercy is not the same as niceness, though sometimes being nice may express mercy. But sometimes being nice can be a way of evading mercy; mercy is at times very matter-of-fact, unsentimental, rough, even *unnice*—but mercy is hanging in there.

Mercy *often* is hanging in there with others.

Mercy is not possessive: mercy is not a way in which we bind people to us—even as it is not a rejection, a pushing people away.

---

3. See Hosea 6:6.

With mercy we assume the other hurts too—that the other is vulnerable too (even when we can't see it or the other is obnoxious).

With mercy we are alert for opportunities not to *appear* good but to *be* kind, supportive, forgiving.

It is vital to recognize that mercy is a threefold way of life; it is not a one-dimensional way we are to go and learn but a three-dimensional way:

One. Go and learn mercy toward yourself. Hear that? Go and learn mercy toward yourself.

Two. Go and learn mercy toward others in your close personal relationships. In your close personal relationships.

Three. Go and learn mercy toward others in the social, political, economic order: mercy in the way you analyze and in what you are for (and against) in public life and policy.

Let's go back over the three dimensions.

Go and learn mercy toward yourself.

Some of us know we're very hard on ourselves. (Secretly we're sometimes kind of proud of it.)

We're hard on ourselves because we won't forgive ourselves for not being who we sometimes wish we were—but aren't.

We're hard on ourselves because we won't forgive ourselves for not being who we sometimes wish we were—but aren't.

We often say, "I should *have* . . . I should have succeeded . . . I should have done better . . . I should have . . ."

Many of us are really angry and harsh and merciless with ourselves.

Often when this is so it is because our parents (again, with the best intentions in the world) haven't accepted us for being who we are but, instead, keep on dreaming of us becoming who they wish we were. This is hard.

Or some crowd of peers rejects us for being who we are. As if that weren't hard enough. But then we "blame" ourselves! We get down on ourselves. Psychologically and socially we must go and learn what it is to show mercy toward ourselves. (*Some* of us will only be able to learn mercy toward others after we have begun to learn mercy toward ourselves.)

Being hard on yourself is no virtue. Being self-disciplined or hardworking may be a virtue. Being able to repent, to say "I'm sorry," may well be a virtue. But being merciless on yourself is finally conceit. It is refusal to forgive ourselves for being who we *really* are rather than being the fantasy we sometimes wish we were.

The second dimension: go and learn mercy toward others in your close personal relationships.

Mercy here is not going to bed with someone because we feel sorry for them or because they want us to so badly. Or giving someone who's drunk another drink because they're groaning for it. Or helping someone cheat on an exam or a paper because they're so scared of what will happen if they fail. Nor is mercy being given a B+ when the work is C- work.

Mercy in close personal relationships requires us to *learn* how to *listen* to others. Mercy requires attention to the other, rather than calculation. Attention rather than calculation. Mercy requires us to be more imaginative: how would I feel in that situation? How would I feel if that were happening to me? How would I feel if I were making such an ass of myself? And then the *courage* to respond with mercy's imagination.

The third dimension: go and learn mercy toward others in the social, political, economic order.

Here mercy requires that we go and learn where others are coming from.

Here mercy is steady insistence on justice.

Justice without mercy only breeds new animosity, new defensiveness, new conflicts. The New Testament knows something we forget at peril to our social causes and hopes for the world: justice without mercy only breeds new animosity. But mercy without justice is not mercy!

The assumption of the Bible is that—with exceptions that prove the rule—when a person or a people stand in need of mercy from others it is not because they have failed but because they have been wronged.

We *all* stand in need of the mercy of God.

But there is a deeply unbiblical, un-Christian notion at work in American culture that when people are down and out, homeless, poor, unemployed, illiterate, living in slums, there's something wrong with them. The assumption of the Scriptures is that something wrong has been *done* to them.

A lot of us—whatever our racial and ethnic background—have been taught to say, "I don't want mercy, just a chance." It *sounds* pretty good. And it has some truth in it. But the problem is that such an approach often leads parents, albeit unintentionally, to become merciless with their children and to teach their children to be merciless. Many of us have been raised for success, not mercy—even in Christian homes. We know that inside of ourselves.

Now success is not evil in itself, even as sacrifice—ritual and worship—are not.

But Jesus challenges us—in order to save us from despair: "I desire mercy and not sacrifice!" I desire mercy and not success. I desire mercy and not whatever it is—no matter how respectable and well argued and socially acceptable—whatever it is you practice in order to evade mercy.

We can hear the living Christ against the background of all the computers and against all the noise that we seem to need to escape his quiet voice and against all the propaganda that "if you get yours you'll be secure," we can hear Christ say, "I desire mercy in your nation." In the spirit of Martin Luther King Jr. we can say, there will be neither domestic peace nor tranquility until you do justice and *love* mercy and walk *humbly* with your God.[4]

Go and learn what this means: I desire mercy toward others in the social, political, economic order.

Go and learn what this means: I desire mercy toward others in your close, personal relationships. Listen your way in, learn your way in, imagine your way in to your neighbor's shoes and head and heart, especially that neighbor most unacceptable to you.

And go and learn what this means: I desire mercy in your relationship to yourself. Come off it. You're not so perfect or so good that you have always to be coming down so cruelly on yourself whenever you discover who you really are. We're more at home with the tax collectors and sinners—and, yes, with the sick—than yet we've accepted. We, too, stand in need of healing. But notice: that is where the true conviviality is; that is where Jesus has sat down and makes himself at home, to eat and drink. And listen to him: I came not to call the righteous but to call those who don't have it together. I desire mercy in your relationship to yourself.

You are to go and learn mercy toward yourself, to recognize that with all your defects, you are still acceptable; that you have been hurt and have hurt others in return—and still you are loved.

Mercy is an attitude, an orientation, toward those in Bangladesh and South Africa, those in the city, and in the hills surrounding Hamilton, those in your sorority or dorm—including those of whom you thought, "asshole." And mercy is an attitude toward yourself.

To go and learn mercy is to begin a new life. The community Jesus is working this morning to fashion, and will till the end of the age, is a community of mercy.

"Oh yeah," we say, and yawn, tempted to wander off in mind and heart. But go and learn that God, the Mystery itself, our Father, the One who loves us with a mother's love, desires mercy so that we may know from inside of us God's mercy toward us and the peace and power of mercy.

---

4. King, *Knock at Midnight*. See Micah 6:8 (often quoted by King).

You and I have much to learn this term, this year, this life. Go, says Jesus, and *learn* what *this* means, I desire mercy and not whatever it is that you have devised, no matter how good, to escape from being merciful . . . and to escape the mercy of God, its peace and its power.

The meaning of this poor service of worship is that God is merciful—even when we, especially when we cry out in anger and hurt and fear, cry out, "O God, where is your mercy? I don't feel it. I don't see it. I don't understand it."

God is not angry with you, even if you are angry with God.

The heart of God breaks, and in a voice human and broken we hear, Take, eat, this is my body broken for you. This cup—drink of it, any who will—for this is my blood which is poured out for the forgiveness of sins.

23

Strong at the Broken Places

NOVEMBER 6, 1988

Jacob left Beer-sheba, and went toward Haran. And he came to a certain place, and stayed there that night, because the sun had set. Taking one of the stones of the place, he put it under his head and lay down in that place to sleep. And he dreamed that there was a ladder set up on the earth, and the top of it reached to heaven; and behold, the angels of God were ascending and descending on it! And behold, the Lord stood above it and said, "I am the Lord, the God of Abraham your father and the God of Isaac . . . Behold, I am with you and will keep you wherever you go, and will bring you back to this land; for I will not leave you until I have done that of which I have spoken to you." Then Jacob awoke from his sleep and said, "Surely the Lord is in this place; and I did not know it." And he was afraid, and said, "How awesome is this place! This is none other than the house of God, and this is the gate of heaven."
—Genesis 28:10–13a; 15–17 (RSV)

Now when [Jesus] heard that John had been arrested, he withdrew into Galilee; and leaving Nazareth he went and dwelt in Capernaum by the sea, in the territory of Zebulun and Naphtali, that what was spoken by the prophet Isaiah might be fulfilled:

"The land of Zebulun and the land of Naphtali,
toward the sea, across the Jordan,
Galilee of the Gentiles—

> *the people who sat in darkness*
> *have seen a great light,*
> *and for those who sat in the region and shadow of death*
> *light has dawned."*
>
> *From that time Jesus began to preach, saying, "Repent, for the kingdom of heaven is at hand."*
>
> —Matthew 4:12-17 (RSV)

THERE'S A PASSAGE FROM Hemingway I'd like to read: "If people bring so much courage to the world the world has to kill them to break them, so of course it kills them. The world breaks every one and afterward many are strong at the broken places."[1]

The world breaks all of us.

What I'm *looking for* is *the strength* that comes—at our broken places.

I realize it's hard sometimes to listen to someone while he looks for something. We wonder, underneath, to ourselves sometimes, Who really is this guy, preaching? What does he know? The questions are reasonable.

Last week Irene and I were at Middlebury College. I preached there. Our son, Brad, was graduated from Middlebury last May; and he's a freshman football coach there this fall. And I was moved almost to tears, in thankfulness, as I looked out on the little congregation there to see Irene and our son Bradford Coleman Brown. And this morning we are thinking of Brad and of Brad's younger brother, Joshua (whom a few of you know), a sophomore at Brown. Josh this week is over at Middlebury visiting Brad; we are thinking of those two, our youngest—"the little boys," as Susan used to call them—and of Susan, our daughter out in Santa Cruz, and of Justin, our oldest, at Harvard: Susan and Justin have worked very hard this decade—taking care of little children and retarded people and the homeless. But have we, have I always understood what they were up to?

Who is this guy preaching today? What does he know?

He knows, as he said on Parents' Weekend but as once he did not know, that all parents curse as well as bless their children. And *each* of us (for *all* of us are children of parents) must work that out by the grace of God. The preacher knows not only what it is to laugh and to preach and to teach and to counsel but what it is to cry and to pout and to screw up and to have to keep learning how to grow up and to have to keep learning how to receive heaven as a little child in order to enter into it.

---

1. Hemingway, *Farewell to Arms*, 249.

And the preacher knows—*I* know—that what I've been saying about family and myself and all may arouse in us (whatever our interest) a little embarrassment; and we wonder, indeed, we hope the preacher may be a bit embarrassed now and get on with it.

Friends, we have to be able to risk embarrassment—yes, I'll say, *suffer* embarrassment—if we're going to do anything worth doing.

We put so much energy into keeping ourselves from being embarrassed that we are out of touch with most of life—with the deep wells of our own creativity and power and love.

To be cool—or something like it—is too often all we think we want said about our lives: that we're poised, we're not embarrassed about anything we do or are. Right?

Wrong.

To care, really and deeply to care, about *any*thing or *any*one is to risk embarrassment, often to *suffer* embarrassment over whom and what we care about. To do anything worth doing—whether it's shooting baskets, or learning how to care for another in a relationship, or making your life count in the few, short years given you—anything worth doing involves passing through an embarrassment barrier, as high-speed planes must pass through a sound barrier. An embarrassment barrier.

I think Abraham Heschel, the great Jewish theologian, is right when he says, "Faith begins in embarrassment." And, I confess, Heschel speaks for me when he cries out, "I shudder to think of a generation devoid of a sense of wonder and mystery, devoid of a sense of inadequacy and embarrassment."[2]

We're dying inside partly because we'd rather die than be embarrassed.

We shall become strong at a broken place when embarrassment breaks over us and we discover that there is something we care for far more than whether we are embarrassed or not.

It's time, by the way, relative to the election Tuesday, to stop blaming it on George Bush or Michael Dukakis or the media or the pollsters ... and to begin to be embarrassed: embarrassed for ourselves and how little care *we* have taken for the life of our nation. We get what we deserve, candidates, media, pollsters and all.

It's not really a political sermon today. But I wonder how many going into business here this morning understand that if they are going to keep their souls they must be part of a business reformation in America: those who really believe the bottom line is the bottom line destroy their children and their country.

2. Heschel, "Idols in the Temples," 67; "Children and Youth," 47.

And I wonder how many future high school and college teachers there are here this morning, how many people who will train well for prison work or work with low-income people or the homeless or in local government, in diplomacy or environmental reformation.

I wonder who here is beginning to resist a new wave of racism in America that *can* be met and turned back, but only by people willing to sit in the sackcloth and ashes of education about the terrible history of slavery and exclusion that really happened in the American past whose consequences continue to detonate today. (The past is always with us, perhaps most of all when we forget it.) It is an education about what really happened and continues to happen in our psyches and institutions but which—that racism—if it isn't met by women and men here this morning with a new willingness to learn, with new courage and sacrifice, today and in the years to come, has the clear possibility of destroying everything about Colgate and America that we're proud of! And I'm talking about us here this morning, not somebody else.

So I began by telling you just a little something about myself and about a few of the people I care about; and that I am willing to embarrass myself, and Irene perhaps, to try to indicate to you that I, like you, am dependent on the presence and the memories and the love and the forgiveness and the friendship and the dedication of others in order to live my life. I've gone on to say that I believe we can't do anything in this world without risking and suffering embarrassment. And then I guess by a few remarks I've said we've got hard and concrete things to do, though you, as I, must listen in quietness and storm for your own call. The world breaks everyone . . . but many are strong at the broken places. Christian faith is finally heroic faith—though there are no heroes, only men and women who begin to recognize themselves and what life is really about and to laugh and cry at what they see, who begin to enter into the darkness with fear and trembling and yet with strangely cheerful hearts to do what they don't know how to do and yet know they, with Jesus beside them, are called to do.

Which brings me to our Old and New Testament lessons. Jacob was in the dark when he dreamed and saw that ladder leading up to the light of heaven. Angels of God were climbing up it—toward the light. And angels were climbing down, sent by God, into the night. Good news and the presence of God comes to people who are in darkness. If we attend carefully to the unfolding of our gospel lesson, we see they are the ones who are given the amazing grace for repentance; they are the ones to whom Jesus brings the amazing possibility: "I can change, in the depths of my life, I can change."

Jesus comes to those in darkness and brings them to see light shining in, and over, things they would rather forget or deny—or, otherwise, fail to perceive.

We sit in the darkness of our anger, for example. But can we catch sight of the light shining in our anger? Anger in the *service* of what we love, in the *service* of love itself, is necessary for creativity and healing: *channeled* anger, *rightly used* anger is what we often call "spirit"; it's *courage*.

I'm not talking about cheap self-indulgence, the adopting of anger as a way of manipulating people. I'm talking about disciplined anger.

There can be no courage—courage to change yourself (which often begins with a kind of disgust with what one is doing to one's life), or courage to change anything else—without entering into the darkness of your anger. For the light of courage only comes to us in that darkness.

Some of us this morning sit in the darkness of resentment. We seem unable to get up. There is some suffering in our life—vague or clear—that, at deep places in us, leads us to resentment; to ask bitterly in what we suffer, "Why me? Why me?"

It is finally only God of whom, really, we ask that question, "Why me?" when we suffer. Who else could answer it? The *terror* of our question, when we get to the bottom of our resentment, is that only in reconciliation to God is there any answer to it. You and I? We can't overturn our own deep resentments on our own. But the gospel is light beaming with hope for all of us who know we have questions we cannot answer, and resentments we cannot overturn on our own—and yet who long for acceptance just as we are and for reconciliation in the midst of our resentment and pain.

You see the problem, friends, the problem I am trying to address is a terrifying one—though usually we *feel* it as something *boring*. Yes, boring.

But the terrifying fact of our lives today at Colgate and across vast sectors of our culture is that we have become bored, bored with God, bored with the very question of the meaning of our lives and our destiny. I quote Heschel again: "The central issue is not to prove that God is alive but to prove that we are not dead."[3]

We are bored with God, believers sometimes as much or more as nonbelievers. Why? Because God is not real for us.

Deep down, we know, if God is not real for us, nothing else in heaven or earth will save us.

And sometimes we know how much we long for God.

Yet God is not real for us.

---

3. Heschel, "Idols in the Temples," 67.

If God is not real for us, we will die in our sins, an earlier generation would have said. How would we say it today?

If God is not real for us, we will die of boredom, of indifference; we will die of trivia. Some of us are trivializing ourselves to death. Some of us *may* die having lived lives that amounted to little more than working hard for the money to keep ourselves entertained . . . until we die. *We* are becoming unreal.

We run the risk of dying no longer capable of being ashamed—ashamed that we don't seem, much of the time, to feel anything except our worries about our work and our compulsive need to be entertained. We run the risk of no longer even being ashamed that we don't seem to care enough to *change* anything, to *resist* anything, to *do* anything—but go with the flow, laughingly or silently as circumstances require.

The mercy of God is *finally* deliverance from shame. But be thankful for stabs of shame along the way. They are not enough—but they are glimmers of light and life.

We long for God, every one of us. But God is not real for us.

God is not real for us because we will not go to that "certain place" in the night where the ladder is raised and a way to light is opened—and a way *from* the light to *us* is opened. We do not accept that we are people who lie or sit in darkness.

God is not real for us because we turn away from the darkness of our time in which men and women like ourselves have need for us—and need for what we can do to help. God is not real for us because we deny that darkness in our own souls. We flee from it at first glimpse.

God won't have anything to do with anything—except what is real. God won't have anything to do with anything—except what is real.

God will not deal with you in the unreal places of your life or deal with me in the unreal places of mine. Neither will God be with us when we flee from the reality of the challenges of our personal lives and flee from the challenges of our times. God simply *remains* with those realities—and waits for us.

There's a line in an Arthur Miller play: "Good God, why are the grievances the only truths that stick?"[4] Our grievances at least are real. And God will be there—with whatever truths in your life really "stick." God will transform those truths, perhaps take those truths away from you in a sense and make different meaning for them than you are trying so hard to mean.

---

4. Miller, *After the Fall*.

But if you will begin to listen and trust only just a little, God will begin to transform the matters that are real for you.

Your shame about yourself—don't keep running from it. Our shame may bring us back from trivializing our lives and back to *feeling* and to taking risks on behalf of what we believe, deep down, and hope—and love.

Your sadness: your sadness will lead you to discover that in sorrow we can *share*, that others have been there before you and are waiting for you with their friendship. At the depths of our sadness we may learn, at last, compassion, and be grasped by the power to forgive. I don't know. But I know we try and try to forgive—and can't. Sadness and sorrow may sweep away our grievances against one another and bring us freedom to love again.

God is there—in the darkness of the matters that are *real* for you.

Where your confidence in yourself has broken down: it may be like Anton Boisen, subject to psychotic episodes. These episodes—which he experienced all his life—led him to be a parent of modern pastoral counseling with its compassion and gospel recognition of human darkness.[5]

In weaknesses or addictions or patterns of self-destroying behavior too strong for you: as it is for those in Alcoholics Anonymous, those weaknesses so real and powerful in your life can lead you to a real human community of persons who know what you know and to a role and a mission to others for which you are especially qualified.

Yes, God is there in the darkness of a sense of hopelessness someone may be feeling this morning: shining in that far light of what you know you really *want*—what you honestly, really know you *really* want.[6]

God is there in some awful hardship, shining how? Shining in the loyalty and love you feel called to express despite your bewilderment and fear: a loyalty and love that is not just "using" another for your own satisfaction—no more of that—or just feeling good about yourself, but that's real loyalty and love. It's in you, that light.

In the darkness of injustice and unmet needs, a light shines: the light of *activity* for the common good that you can take up—not primarily for the resumé or out of some sentimental idealism but because—what else can you do when there's injustice like *that* to fight, or need in others like *that* to meet?!

God comes to us where it's real—and that certainly means to the night within us. Jesus is a person of sorrows and acquainted with grief.[7] God is acquainted with the darkness, intimately acquainted. God comes down to

---

5. See Boisen, *Out of the Depths*.
6. See, for example, Lynch, *Images of Hope*.
7. See Isaiah 53:3.

us in the dark. God takes in our darkest moments—into God's own Spirit and communion.

What is it to repent? It is to act on new possibility. It is to act on new responsibility.

A sterner preacher than I has said what I must increasingly believe: "Everything comes home. It comes home in calamity if you do not take it home in repentance," that is, if you do not honestly acknowledge who you are and do not accept the power to act on new possibility in your life. But "everything comes home."[8]

"Everything that does not go through us like a transforming storm remains dead," unreal.[9]

My friends, God will be a bore for you and me until we turn to the real matters in our life we have fled. In *those* matters we shall meet God. There God gets "interesting" again.

The world breaks everyone. That's the fact.

But afterward many are strong at the broken places.

We find the strength at our broken places as, in the dark, we start to climb a ladder toward light; or, if we are not strong enough yet for that, as we begin to accept the light of God come down to us in our night.

Heaven is at hand for those who know their darkness—*our* darkness—and know God comes to us in what is real—yes, in the dark.

---

8. Forsyth, "Preacher and the Age," 153.
9. Thielicke, "Parable of the Seed and the Soils," 57.

24

He Looks Around on All That Can Be Seen

A Palm Sunday Sermon

MARCH 19, 1989

> And when they drew near to Jerusalem, to Bethphage and Bethany, at the Mount of Olives, he sent two of his disciples, and said to them, "Go into the village opposite you, and immediately as you enter it you will find a colt tied, on which no one has ever sat; untie it and bring it. If any one says to you, 'Why are you doing this?' say, 'The Lord has need of it and will send it back here immediately.'" And they went away, and found a colt tied at the door out in the open street; and they untied it. And those who stood there said to them, "What are you doing, untying the colt?" And they told them what Jesus had said; and they let them go. And they brought the colt to Jesus, and threw their garments on it; and he sat upon it. And many spread their garments on the road, and others spread leafy branches which they had cut from the fields. And those who went before and those who followed cried out, "Hosanna! Blessed be he who comes in the name of the Lord! Blessed be the kingdom of our father David that is coming! Hosanna in the highest!"
>
> And he entered Jerusalem, and went into the temple; and when he had looked round at everything, as it was already late, he went out to Bethany with the twelve.
>
> —Mark 11:1-11 (RSV)

Let us pray.

> O Love that will not let us go,
> We rest our weary souls in Thee.
> We lay in dust life's glory dead,
> And from the ground there blossoms red
> Life that shall endless be.[1]
>
> O Holy Spirit, come into this gathering
> and into our hearts
> that we may hear Your word for us today
> and be made new.
> Help us to see ourselves as You see us,
> confident that Your love for us does truly
> bear all things, believe all things,
> hope all things, endure all things,
> that Your love never ends.[2]
> Thanks be to You, O God,
> our Creator, Redeemer and Friend.
> Amen.

Of course God is not a cheap friend but a dear friend. God means to take death out of us—take out of us both our fear of death and our sick love of what finally chokes our spirit and messes up our freedom to be a friend to others. And because we resist what God means to do with us, God will, usually, at some important time seem our enemy. But God is our friend, our dear friend, though never a cheap friend.

If that seems somewhat confusing, then at least we've got the right day. For Palm Sunday is a somewhat confusing day.

Palm Sunday is festive, full of happy shouts. It is, in some ways, a day of triumph. And we do well to sing "All Glory, Laud and Honor to Thee, Redeemer, King." And to remember, perhaps, with the palms in our hands, the delight of children at a celebration they don't quite understand but are glad to be part of. In many ways we are still—all of us—those children. Thank God! For that is good. That is wonderful.

But Palm Sunday is a celebration with awful things only days away.

---

1. Adapted from the Matheson and Peace hymn, "O Love That Wilt Not Let Me Go."
2. See 1 Corinthians 13:7.

Don't be afraid of the happy shouts. But remember with one of the great Black preachers of our day—remember "with what a shudder... these happy shouts end, making many to understand the lament of some simple people whose words haunt the world. 'Sometimes it causes me to tremble, tremble, tremble.'"[3]

The tumult and the shouting dies. The palms are left in the dust. The crowd disperses. The colt, we may assume, is returned to its owner.

Jesus has entered the great city, the city of Jerusalem, city of the world, Jerusalem—the city where he will die.

And he goes to the temple, the great temple of the city.

There is, as we know, a literal meaning to things. And then there is a deeper, hidden meaning to things—a second message beneath the surface.

Usually we must pause, and let go, and begin to enter other regions of our mind if we are going to hear the second message—the deeper, hidden meaning of something.

Jerusalem? The temple? What is the deeper, hidden meaning there? The second message?

Jerusalem was, that first Palm Sunday, and is today one of the great cities of the world: a place of culture, of conflict, of religious diversity, a place of tradition and innovation, of trade, business and economic vitality, political intensity, military presence, a place of study, work, "interaction" on a large scale; a great pluralistic center, it reminds us of all the cities of modern civilization—full of good and evil.

And what does Jesus cry out as he approaches Jerusalem? "Jerusalem, Jerusalem... how often would I have gathered your children together as a hen gathers her brood under her wings—but you would not!"[4]

Even though we're out in the country here at Colgate, we are a part of Jerusalem: of our great modern urban culture, with its complex infrastructures and economy, its swollen rich, its multitudes of poor, its diversity, its sophistication, its injustice, its terrific interaction—full of good and evil. We all are a part of it.

Of course some of us may remember the vision of John in the book of Revelation: Then "I saw the holy city, *new* Jerusalem, coming down out of heaven from God... and I heard a great voice... saying, 'Behold, the dwelling of God is with people.'" God will be there. And in the new Jerusalem "God will wipe away every tear from their eyes, and death shall be no more,

---

3. Taylor, "Judgment and Mercy at Palm Sunday," 85.
4. See Luke 13:34 (Matthew 23:37).

neither shall there be mourning nor crying nor pain any more, for the old things have passed away."[5]

We heard that at Karen Ehlers's funeral Wednesday.[6]

The deeper, hidden meaning of our civilization—as of every civilization—is that it is doomed until . . . until the great day we find a center—not in ourselves, or in anything we devise, but in the mysterious source of our wonder and reverence and awe and joy and trust and love.

Jesus enters the temple.

What is the deeper, hidden meaning of the temple? What is the second message here? Listen to The First Letter of Peter: "Come to him, to that living stone"—rejected by the wise and powerful of the world—"but in God's sight chosen and precious; and like living stones be yourselves built into a spiritual house," into a real community; become yourselves a real temple.[7]

Like images in a dream or in a modern work of art, you and I are each a temple and at the same time part of a larger temple. For are we not part of each other, even as we are individuals? Each of us, an individual—and yet none of us able to maintain our hope or our sanity or able long to live at all without one another.[8]

Jesus Christ enters Jerusalem and goes into the temple.

You are the temple, by yourself *and* together with others.

And what happens? Before Jesus leaves the temple what did we hear he does? It was in our Scripture lesson. Before he goes out to Bethany, *he looks around on everything*. Before he leaves, *he looks around on everything*.

The shouting is over. It is very quiet now. Jesus says nothing. He says nothing at all. But he looks around on everything. One scholar translates it this way: *he looks around on all that can be seen*.[9]

Jesus Christ has made it to where we are. He has come into Jerusalem, into our civilization. Some have welcomed him. Many more, of course, have not. But he has come into the great, complex, pluralistic world in which we live—into the place where the economic and political and information power is, where slums and great institutions are alike to be found, rich and

---

5. Revelation 21:2–4 (emphasis added).

6. Karen Ehlers, eighteen, died in her dorm room of apparently natural causes and was found at 1 o'clock in the afternoon. She was the fourth Colgate student to die that academic year; she was predeceased by two who perished in the terrorist bombing of Pan Am flight 103 over Scotland, and another in a car accident traveling back from winter break. See Killian, "Colgate Students Mourn Yet Another Death."

7. 1 Peter 2:4–5 (RSV).

8. See 1 Corinthians 3:16–17; Ephesians 2:19–21.

9. Taylor, *Gospel according to St. Mark*, 457–58.

poor, the comfortable and the exploited and those who are not sure which they are.

And now he has come into the temple.

Some other time—not now—he may come into this temple that we are and drive out the buying and selling there and overturn the money changers and say, "'My house shall be called a house of prayer' . . . But you have made it" into a place of corruption—"a den of robbers."[10] But not now. Now in silence he looks around at everything.

Some other time the blind and the lame will come because they have heard that he is here and therefore they enter the temple with hope; and we shall be witnesses to healing—perhaps our own, if we are still stones here, still helping uphold a community where Jesus Christ can do his thing, can heal.[11]

But not now.

Now it is very quiet. Jesus Christ has come but he says no word. He simply looks around on all that can be seen.

There's an old poem by Burns: "A child's among you taking notes." "A child's among you taking notes."[12]

Jesus Christ who says, "Unless you become as little children you shall not enter"[13] the new Jerusalem, you shall not see the power and rule and glory of God—Jesus Christ, like that child who can enter, is here in the temple of your life and mine, a child among us taking notes. He is looking around on all that can be seen in us and going on between us.

It is a fragile yet awesome moment.

It is not just a moment in an ancient story—between the triumphal entry into Jerusalem and the cross there at Golgotha, the garbage dump of Jerusalem.

It is a moment in *our* story. We are seen. It is a moment in our story—when there is a wondrous hush that some of us can sense.

Jesus has come into our very temple, into our very lives, into our very hearts, not to condemn or to instruct or to plead, not to tell us anything but simply with the eyes of God and the eyes of a child to look around on all that can be seen in your heart and life, and mine.

---

10. See Mark 11:17 (Matthew 21:13; Luke 19:45–46).
11. See Matthew 21:14.
12. See Luccock, "St. Mark," 827.
13. See Matthew 19:13–15 (Mark 10:13–16; Luke 18:15–17).

Do we believe that our human affairs, international, national, local, individual, any of them, go on with no eyes to gaze upon them?[14]

Some of us have turned away from wonder and faith and now, as Gardner Taylor reminds us, we have only "a nameless sadness" as we try to push out of our minds "the loneliness, the uncertainty, the pathos of life with no sense of God to steady" us and keep us.[15] But having done so we become so defensive we can hardly bear a word. Jesus comes into our temple and simply looks around at everything before he leaves.

Others have another kind of situation: we feel very much alone, abandoned as we bear grief or homesickness, loneliness; as we keep trying to do our best but with little success; as we seek a way but find none. Jesus looks around on all that can be seen—our hearts are known; our relationships; how it is with us. He will do what he can. We are seen. We are heard but by one so quiet now before he goes to the cross that *we* shall miss the moment of that presence if we do not stop to see all that can be seen.

The Spirit of God, the Holy Spirit, the healing Spirit of God, comes into the temple that you are and that *we* are—whether we have desecrated it or cry out in it our lonely prayers; whatever our condition—strong or weak. We are seen and heard by one who takes it all in, by one who looks around on everything in our lives and sees and hears it all.

Sees and hears it all: the games we play with ourselves and one another; subtle games—games whereby we deceive ourselves into thinking we are wholly innocent, the fault all with the others.

The cowardice we practice by persuading ourselves that the power to change things belongs to someone else when *we* have been called to begin to bring about the changes.

The way we drift with the crowd.

All is seen and heard.

But that means also seen and heard is the great love still in us, the hope that returns unbidden, a trust sometimes also so subtle that we hardly recognize it: our commitments to others, our devotion to right.

In any event what *really* we value, believe in, love, is seen for what it is, for what it really is!

What really do you value?

What really do you believe in?

What, whom do you really love?

---

14. Taylor, "Judgment and Mercy," 88.
15. Taylor, "Judgment and Mercy," 89.

Can you, in the silence—with Christ watching and listening to you—begin to *unfold* the answers to those questions? And *remember* what you begin to unfold? And *carry it* with you, what you find, more in touch with the secret wells of your heart and life?

What really do you value?

What really do you believe in?

What, whom do you really love?

And look around on the community, on the larger temple of which, as a stone, you are a *part*. Do we seek our security only in separating ourselves from those who cause us pain and stress? "Of course people disappoint and disgust us." But "we disappoint and disgust" others too.[16]

Jesus Christ sees and hears how we disappoint others and how we have been disappointed by them.

Christ has come on Palm Sunday in acclamation, but it is short-lived. And it is not his final acclamation. This week he will teach some more, hold a last supper with his friends; then, betrayed and denied by his friends, he will go forth to be broken . . . "broken for you," as we remember at communion.[17]

But he will not forget what he has seen and heard in the temple of our hearts. He will carry it all with him to the cross. And when he cries out, "O Lord, forgive them, for they know not what they do," he is remembering us and what he has seen in the temple of our lives when he looked around on everything. And when he cries out, "Unto Thee I commit my spirit," his spirit remembers *us*. And when he cries out, "My God, my God, why hast Thou forsaken me?" he is remembering us and crying out our cry, remembering what he has seen and heard in your soul and mine.[18] And when he comes in before God, he is bringing with him what he has seen and heard in that very human temple of which we are stones and, yes, the temple that each of us in some deep sense is ourself.

What memories is Jesus the Suffering Servant storing up as he sees in my life and yours all that can be seen, all that is there?

And will we watch him more closely in our lives—through study and new discipline and worship and prayer—watch him carrying in his heart all that he has seen and heard? More closely watch him suffer and die with all that he has come to know of us engraved now on his life?

---

16. Taylor, "Judgment and Mercy," 87.
17. 1 Corinthians 11:23–26.
18. Luke 23:34, 46; Mark 15:34 (see also Matthew 27:46).

And will we more fully—even as for the first time?!—receive him from the dead, back into the temple, our community and ourselves?

Receive him back where he shall begin to teach us how to understand ourselves and one another—and how to love one another? How to give up what is destroying us and how to hold firm to what gives life? And how to tell the difference?

For when we receive Christ into our lives, he comes as one who already knows us, knows us better than we know ourselves. He comes as one who has, in silence, already looked around in the temple of our lives on all that we are and feel and think and then in mercy taken it all with him to the cross, that we too might pass from death to life—and begin today to live as those no longer afraid of death, as those no longer afraid of sin—our own or others'!—but, rather, confident in the power of God in Christ to see us through and through; to bear us all in all; and to take us, as we are, and turn us at last into the persons we were always meant to be, persons beginning at last a life worth living and a life that lasts forever.

Amen.

25

None of Us Have It Together and We Are the Salt of the Earth

Last sermon as University Chaplain

MAY 7, 1989

And as he sat at table in his house, many tax collectors and sinners were sitting with Jesus and his disciples; for there were many who followed him. And the scribes of the Pharisees, when they saw that he was eating with sinners and tax collectors, said to his disciples, "Why does he eat with tax collectors and sinners?" And when Jesus heard it, he said to them, "Those who are well have no need of a physician, but those who are sick; I came not to call the righteous, but sinners."

—Mark 2:15–17 (RSV)

"You are the salt of the earth; but if salt has lost its taste, how shall its saltness be restored? It is no longer good for anything except to be thrown out and trodden under foot by men."

—Matthew 5:13 (RSV)

None of Us Have It Together and We Are the Salt of the Earth 171

THE OPENING HYMN WAS Steve Hartshorne's favorite hymn.¹ Those who know me and the University Church and Colgate know what a presence Steve is this morning. God be with us, Ruth.

We just sang, "'Tis grace hath brought us safe thus far, and grace will lead us home"²—and from the opening hymn, "God of the coming years, through paths unknown we follow thee; / When we are strong, Lord, leave us not alone; our refuge be. / Be thou for us in life our daily bread, / Our heart's true home"—our heart's true home—"when all our years have sped."³

Last sermons are dangerous. If I swing from my heels for the home run, we'll all regret seeing the preacher strike out.

What I hope to do is lay a good bunt down the third base line and beat it out to first and trust that you will bring me home.

We're here in all kinds of conditions this morning. I know that very well. Such a sense of community as we find in our time, certainly in a modern university, is fleeting. It is full of conflicts. It is a community of fragments. And I preach out of the fragments of my own life to you who know the conflicts where you are or here at Colgate; the fragments of your own life; and who know that you are part of a fragment, not part of a whole. I preach comforted and encouraged by this description of St. Paul the Apostle:

> Paul found himself buried under the fragments of his knowledge and his morals. But Paul never tried to build up a new, comfortable house out of the pieces. He lived with the pieces. He realized always that fragments remain fragments, even if one attempts to reorganize them. The unity to which they belong lies beyond them. It is grasped, but not face to face.
>
> How could Paul endure life which lay in fragments? He endured it because the fragments bore a new meaning. The power

---

1. Professor Marion Holmes "Steve" Hartshorne, Harry Emerson Fosdick professor emeritus of philosophy and religion, died May 10, 1988. One of the very greatest teachers in Colgate's history (from his arrival in 1946), Professor Hartshorne retired in 1975 but continued to teach there, from time to time, after retirement. He and his beloved wife, Ruth, who survived him, were among the most loyal and active members of the University Church from its inception. Moreover, Professor Hartshorne, an ordained Presbyterian minister, preached regularly (and unforgettably) to the University Church over the years—his last sermon, November 15, 1987. His favorite hymn was "God of Our Life, Through All the Circling Years."
2. From Newton, "Amazing Grace," v. 3.
3. Kerr and Purday, "God of Our Life, Through All the Circling Years," v. 3.

of love transformed the tragic fragments of life into symbols of the whole.⁴

May it be so among us this morning—by the power of love.

We're here in all kinds of conditions this morning, I say again. And even if we're tired of the Prayer of Confession or have never said it before today, we may recognize something of our condition in it. I ask you to turn to it again with me (to hear part of it):

> We are before You this morning as broken men and women in need of forgiveness—having come from anguished moments in the night, and betrayals in the day; having said cutting words—or no words.
>
> Often bewildered by the obvious or subtle suffering that we see—or that is our own—we have been uncertain. We have concentrated on defense of ourselves, and have found the condemnation of others easy. We have not received others simply as they are, nor met them as ourselves.
>
> Hear our various inward cries. Forgive us and heal us. Alone we cannot be healed.⁵

And, of course, we who are gathered here this morning include seekers and doubters and believers. We may remember having heard that description before . . . and recognize it—and our selves. And perhaps even recognize that in each of us is a seeker and a doubter and a believer.

No preaching—no word, I should better say—ever reaches us (neither a word of condemnation . . . nor a word of joy, a word from "our true home"), no word ever reaches us unless it reaches our inner person: unless it reaches inside you . . . unless it reaches inside me.

And you know, there are no techniques for that. There really aren't.

Whether you or I are reached in our inner person, in our secret heart, is something mysterious, not under anyone's ultimate control. I would say it depends on the Spirit of God.

The words whereby we are reached are like windows through which light comes. We can clean them . . . throw open the drapes over them—or keep the drapes drawn. And it makes a difference whether in that house we call our self we turn *toward* that window through which light may come—or not. But *whether* or not light comes through—whether light comes through into our souls—depends on whether there *is any* light out there in the night,

---

4. Quotation and adaptation of Tillich, "Knowledge through Love," 112–13.

5. From the "Prayer of Confession for the Colgate University Church," included in this book.

whether the streaks of real dawn will ever start to come or not. Therefore, I ask you to pray with me:

> *You without whose love for us we cannot trust you, we cannot believe; You whose name is Truth which in our true and deepest doubting is what we seek; You whose name is too holy for us to know yet whom to know is to know a true mother's and a true father's presence, we have heard that You are Spirit and that those who worship You must worship You in spirit and in truth. Make that possible for us. Clean the windows of our heart. Turn us around. And reach us in our inner person, in our secret heart, that we may not live toward despair, but toward You to whom now we pray. Amen.*

One of the most haunting texts—aside from Scripture—that I have heard in my fifteen years as University Chaplain may be these words of Wittgenstein: "Tell me *how* you seek and I will tell you *what* you are seeking."[6] I'm not sure I understand those words; and be assured I'm not going to try to explain them. But this morning I've been attending and want to keep attending more to *how* we seek and doubt and believe than to *what* we seek and doubt and believe.

And that is often to what Jesus turns—*how*, how we seek and doubt and believe.

Which brings us back to the texts that we have heard this morning. And let me summarize them and, in doing so, summarize the heart of this sermon: *none of us have it together . . . and you are the salt of the earth.*

None of us have it together and we are the salt of the earth.

The other night at the Service Awards Dinner it occurred to me to observe how much drama—poignant, mysterious, sad, wonderful—there is in the lives . . . in the lives of any who gather at any time . . . in the lives, I now say, of us who gather here this morning. You know, if a great writer knew your story—the story of *each* of us here this morning—there is not one story that would not be a great novel—or a great TV series. We laugh. But it's true. The very quiet heroism, the sufferings, the fears, the failures, the obstacles, the obstacles overcome, the betrayals borne, the sense of humor recovered and shared again, the devotion, the friendship, yes, the love present here among us: this gathering is charged, it's full—as *every* gathering of human beings is—to those who have eyes to see . . . or better, to those

---

6. Wittgenstein, *Philosophical Grammar*, 370, quoted in Holmer, *Grammar of Faith*, 185.

who have hearts willing to be broken and yet strangely filled—those broken hearts—by love for those with whom we share this short life.

There is, my friends, enough hurt here in this Chapel—and, yes, sin in each of us, beginning with the preacher—to break the heart of God. And enough potential and poignancy and power and love in each of us, right here, to move God to keep the world going another day if ever God decided to give up on the world.

Which brings me back to our texts: None of us have it together . . . and you are the salt of the earth.

Now those of us who consider ourselves religious or moral (or, God forbid, both), those of us *in* religious communities often, and those *outside* such communities (often with the same sense of moral superiority so familiar in the religious), those outside who've found a moral cause—those of us in religious communities and those outside—often *presume*, deep down, and make it clear to others, whether subtly or directly, that we *do* know how to live . . . that we . . . *do* have it together . . . and that if a "sinner" is someone separated from her self, him self; if a sinner is someone separated from others by his own life, by her own life; if a sinner is someone separated from whatever ultimately counts . . . those of us *in* religious communities and those of us *outside* often make it clear that we . . . are . . . not *sinners* (at least not very often). We could do better, yes—we'll entertain that abstract proposition. But we, comparatively speaking, are doing pretty well. We know how to live—and, if not yet quite successfully, we just about have it together.

What can we say when we hear Jesus tell us, "I came not to call the righteous," and say in effect, "If you have it together, if you know how to live, you have no need of me"? Those whose religion (*or* those whose *repudiation* of religious life because of all the corruption inherent in religion) has made them better than other people; those who have worked out all their inner conflicts or conflicts with others; those who know what their priorities are and always live by them; those who know how to raise children; those who manage always to love their neighbor just like they've been taught; those who believe they treat everybody just about as they should; those whose lives almost always honor their God or whatever high value they treat as God: I did not come to call such people, Jesus says. You don't need me. You've already made it. You don't need me or the kind of community I'm hoping to create. I would be a waste of your time. I came not to call those who know how to live, those who have it together, but those who don't; those who are still trying to figure out how to live. They are welcome in my home and maybe I am welcome in theirs.

Those who are suffering uncertainty about their calling, their vocation, whether nineteen or twenty-nine or forty-nine or sixty-nine.

Those who still wonder who they are.

Those who feel condemned unjustly—or for good reasons.

I came, says Jesus, not to call the righteous, but those who don't have it together. Those who have it together have no need of a physician, no need for me. But those of you who don't have it together, let's go find the others who also don't—and let us be at home with one another. And judge not the "righteous," for aren't you always trying to establish that you're one of them too when the heat's on and you're afraid—and love's gone out of you?

But then just as we start to feel at home—if indeed we do at all—Jesus gets up from where he has been sitting with us and turns to those who are still with him in whatever way, and he speaks to us with hope and confidence and affection, yet speaks to us knowing how much he must challenge us for the sake of the world and for our sakes. You are the salt of the earth, my friends; but if salt loses its taste, how shall its saltness come back? It is no longer good for anything except to be thrown away.

Salt. "You are the salt of the earth." Again, as with most of Jesus' words, we'll have to dig for it—and mostly *after the sermon*—if you or I are ever going to begin to know. But we are those being addressed, I believe. You are the salt of the earth, I believe—and you and I must dig for what that means after the sermon, I believe, if our lives are not to be found worthless.

Notice, for starters, that Jesus did not say you are the honey or the sugar or the saccharine of the earth.[7]

In first-century Palestine (and much of the world still) salt is indispensable for the preservation of food. In the words of William Sloane Coffin to the graduates of Colgate a decade ago: Remember, "You are precious, you are unprecedented, you are irrepeatable, and in the divine dispensation, you are indispensable."[8]

And just a little salt, remember, changes the taste of the whole loaf—changes the whole quality of the dough or other food. The salt of the earth will be reckoned not by their numbers—but by their saltness. They change the taste of the whole.

And where are we reminded of the salt that is in us?

Some of us will be turned off or cynical at the familiarity of the answer. In our sweat. In our tears. In our blood.

---

7. See Thielicke, "Salt, Not the Honey," 24–34; Buttrick, "St. Matthew," 288–89.
8. See Coffin, "Baccalaureate Sermon."

I guess sweat speaks for itself. There will be no preservation of community or life without work—and I mean work for something besides ourselves.

Let me read something from Robert Bellah:

> Some of us often feel, and most of us sometimes feel, that we are only someone if we have "made it" and can look down on those who have not. The American dream is often a very private dream of being the star, the uniquely successful and admirable one, the one who stands out from the crowd of ordinary folk who don't know how. And since we have believed in that dream for a long time and worked very hard to make it come true, it is hard for us to give it up, even though it contradicts another dream that we have—that of living in a society that would really be worth living in.[9]

Our sweat for something besides our own advancement and security.

Our tears—the tears we shed out of regret and compassion. And I am not sure we shall ever learn compassion until we have learned regret. I am bold to say, God help us if we have never regretted anything.

But I know we can only bear regret when we are assured of acceptance and forgiveness. May we assure one another and be assured and learn compassion.

May we taste the salt in the tears we shed for those near and far from whom we have insulated our lives. And may those tears free us to tear down that insulation, break down that isolation—in our families and in our world.

And though we must each find our own way in that and be careful of too easily telling others what their call and mission and responsibility is, yet I urge us to know much better than we do the story—a story that makes us weep for various reasons, depending who we are—but the story of the suffering, the story (past and present) of African-Americans on this continent. May I say the same for the Latino/Latina communities at Colgate and in all the Americas. We must enter into the tears and frustration of one another. "You are the salt of the earth." The injustice being suffered by many women in regard to pay and place in our society; the injustice being suffered by single women parents. The violence being suffered by gay men and lesbians as well; the simply unjustifiable ostracization suffered by some people simply because of how they express the eros that all of us know.

But I'm not going to make myself a list of causes here and have you wait till I name yours or be offended because I don't.

---

9. Bellah et al., *Habits of the Heart*, 285.

To be salt requires specificity and sacrifice in your life and mine. It means the salt that comes from tears of mutual forbearance, deeper and more honest and more caring dialog. To be salt means to begin to preserve life better where you are—and to consider being at a better place than now you are, in order to preserve life.

Sweat—tears—blood: that's where the salt is. I have not shed my blood for the faith that is in me. Here all of us who have not must recognize that the blood of the martyrs is the seed of what Martin Luther King Jr. called "Beloved Community." And also remember that all birth involves blood.

We all have our wounds: self-inflicted and inflicted by others. There will be no healing of our wounds until they are brought into the fresh air for healing (Will we find the courage to do that?) *and* until we reach the forgiveness hidden deep beneath our fear of being excluded; and beneath that fear, the pain of not being loved, and beneath that pain and fear, the deepest and most hidden of all human desires: our desire for a rebirth of love; our desire to forgive, to give of ourselves and to be part of this diverse, fragmented living stream whose goal is that Beloved Community we dimly sense from time to time, that home where no one is outside ever again.[10]

How shall we seek and doubt and believe?

Let me only say this:

When you recognize you don't have it together but have forgotten *you are the salt of the earth, then you have forgotten the deep hopes your friends have for you, the deep need the world has for you—and why you were born.*

When you know you are the salt of the earth and have forgotten *you don't have it together, then you have lost your saltness and are henceforth good for nothing but to be thrown out.*

Well, I hope I finally got to first on that bunt and that with God's help *you* will bring my poor words home.

And, more, that we'll all with God's help work to help each other home.

And that when all our years have sped we shall all—with everyone—come at last to "our heart's true home."

Acknowledgments Made by Coleman B. Brown before the Sermon

I cannot, I find, acknowledge all the people that I ought to this morning. It is too much. It really is. I must trust that they know it, that you know it. That my ministry at Colgate without certain persons would simply have been

10. See Kunkel, *In Search of Maturity*, 8–9.

impossible I think *everybody* knows. The primary blessing I have been to many is that I have introduced them to Irene Brown, or Justin or Susan or Brad or Josh.

We do not forget yesterday's University Chaplains who served so many here so well and whose service endures: Ken Morgan, Bob Smith, and their colleagues in ministry.

I must acknowledge my dear friend Donna Mapes, secretary to the chaplains, my sidekick, even while she also has served General Education courses and helped keep a department running—friend and help to so many of you, Donna Mapes, without whom I know I could hardly complete anything around here—adequate or inadequate.

And if anyone thinks I can do justice—or will even try—to these great friends of mine: Chris Thomforde, with whom I began the chaplaincy, and Chellie Hammer and Charles Rice, with whom I finish—well, I must simply disappoint you . . . except to say I love them.

And what if I were to go back and rehearse the contributions not only of Chris Thomforde and Chellie Hammer and Charles Rice but also of Pat Dutcher and Marie Lindhorst and Jewelnel Davis and Kristine Anderson? All I can say is, Grace upon grace.[11]

And to thank all of you who have made possible this day, this service of worship, I shall only mention a few of those whom I've begun to "catch on" to. Beyond those I've already mentioned—Vicki Sheridan and Paul Barbins[12] and the Outreach Committee, not to speak of deans and a president and their colleagues.

And how could I not thank Colgate's wonderful Sojourners Gospel Choir?!

So *finally*, you know, when we applaud, we applaud each other. And *finally* when we are set free to give thanks—thanks to God—we thank God for all those, known and unknown, who have, yes, graced our lives and made it possible for us to live in some trust, and to hope and to love.

---

11. Those named in this paragraph served as Assistant Chaplain at various points in Brown's chaplaincy.

12. Cochairs of the student-led University Church Outreach Committee, advised by Brown et al.

26

An Ordination Sermon[1]

Preached at the Ordination of Michael Granzen, '80
The Fourth Presbyterian Church,
South Boston, Massachusetts

JUNE 1, 1986

MICHAEL, IT'S A GOOD sign: see how many people for whom *you* are more important than the Boston Celtics.

But it's not, perhaps, a good sign that the preacher from Colgate is not known for short sermons.

I want immediately to say how thankful I am to be here this afternoon—with this congregation with whom I had the privilege to worship this morning and who have been so cordial; with others from the community who visit today; in the company of this presbytery, and clergy and lay people from other churches; with family and friends of the one to be ordained (some of them very special friends of mine); to be here with an old and unbeatable friend from an inner-city church I served in Chicago—and now a new friend of yours, Michael; to be here with my beloved wife and son; and to be here with you, Michael, my dear friend . . . This is a goodly company, and I am filled with thankfulness.

1. Author's note: "This ordination sermon is included here, not because I esteem Michael Granzen more than the other ministers whose ordination sermons I have preached, but because I believe that this sermon may have somewhat more interest to a greater variety of persons than those other ordination sermons" (Brown, *Our Hearts Are Restless*, 151).

We are, in fact, surrounded by a great cloud of witnesses.

There will be those of us who may find what I preach this afternoon platitudinous. I preach this afternoon with a real and justified sense of inadequacy. I have been gone from the urban ministry for eighteen years. Moreover, I confess before you all and the one to be ordained I have been reading a book called *Ministry Burnout*.

I asked myself, "How shall I preach at the ordination of Michael Granzen to the Ministry of the Word?"

With St. Paul I say, "I am not ashamed of the gospel."[2] And an answer came to my question: "How are you to preach? You are to preach with compassion. With compassion."

We're all sinners, and we're all gonna die. To face *one* of those realities—and for some of us this afternoon one or both of those realities is very present—to face *one* of those realities is enough to drive us out of our right mind; and *both* seem unbearable.

So how to preach? With compassion—because we're all sinners (and we all know, deep down, that we are, even after we've discovered neurotic or patriarchal or other *socially* induced inner sources of self-condemnation). We're all sinners. And we're all folk on our way toward death, the death of this body and of this achingly familiar identity which—with all its fuzziness and its defects and tribulations—can mean so much to us. We're going to lose ourselves, and what's worse, we're going to lose each other.

A kind of common sense of compassion sometimes wells up in us for one another when we lose (even if just for a while) our dryness and our defensiveness and our judgmental spirit and our self-preoccupation, and we recognize our common condition and the humanity of our neighbor.

How much more grasp on us does that compassion have when the gospel sinks home to us.

Oh, we should recognize the ways we corrupt the compassion of the gospel into "cheap grace" and moral cowardice and sentimentality. And those of us who have learned to recognize how widespread is the taint of ideology, and how subtle "bad faith" can be, have special sentry duties to stand, I know: but let even those occupying those stern posts remember that the gospel is compassion, upsetting and transforming the very judgment of the world, including that judgment which earnest Christians and *post*-Christians might pronounce (whatever our various labels—liberal or conservative, liberationist, feminist or evangelical, neo-orthodox or radical).

We can only preach with compassion if we remember who *we* are and how it is with *all* who hear the gospel. With compassion . . . and with

---

2. Romans 1:16.

humility. For what one of us is in any way equal to, commensurate with (as some might say), let alone remotely worthy of the scandal of the gospel—the word from God and by God to us—that "*your* sins are forgiven," yours and mine? Lay that burden down. Lay that burden down.

As for death—"the *last* enemy to be destroyed is death," but destroyed. "Death is swallowed up in victory."[3]

Thanks be to God who gives us—gives *us*, you know, the special sentries among us and just ordinary burnt-out, vulnerable, wounded, defensive, doubtful, often bitter and self-serving people—people like me and, perhaps, like you (*whatever* post we occupy)—thanks be to God who *gives* to us the victory over sin and death, *gives* to us the victory through our crucified sovereign Jesus Christ, whose very power to change us is compassion.

Some of us preach, literally, from pulpits—as, Michael, you do and will. But all of us—whether from pulpits or picket lines, in parlors or bedrooms or supermarkets, from our places of work and leisure (seekers, believers and doubters; ordained or not)—all of us are always preaching with our lives.

I learned that from my children, I think. For the momentous preaching that our lives convey—unavoidably convey; for the necessary preaching to which God calls some of us in the ministry of the Word: preach—with compassion.

Now I've come a ways with what I want to say this afternoon, but I confess—I've still got a ways to go.

There are rules about preaching, honed by experience, tested by trial. I try to honor those rules; and I hope, Michael, that you will too. Yet today—as you, my sisters and brothers of the clergy, already sense—I violate some of the rules. I wanted to start by giving *thanks* for all of us (and to bring some greetings as well). And then I wanted to say what I believe God has tried to tell me all my adult life and may have begun at last to get through to me about *how, how* we are to preach our sermons . . . and our lives. "I desire mercy, and not sacrifice,"[4] says the Lord. Go, *learn how* to be compassionate, Jesus Christ says. Learn how to be compassionate.

But the sermon critic—and I'm one too—can say the sermon was more like a catalog—and that will have to do: First "this," and then "that." And then "another thing."

But even through a catalog gifts may be found; at least they may be pointed out.

---

3. 1 Corinthians 15:26, 54.
4. Matthew 9:13.

So keeping always in mind that we are all to be thankful for each other, and that we are all sinners and going to die, and that we all are called to learn how to be compassionate by the common sense of our humanity and by Jesus Christ our Lord, I want to say something about our use of words.

I want, for a moment, especially to address the members of the Fourth Presbyterian Church.

I don't want you worrying each other or Michael Granzen too much about swelling the membership rolls of the church. If that happens, praise God. But in small churches, growth can be one of those "fixations" that Michael mentioned in his sermon this morning. The issue is not growth but faithfulness. You already know that.

And the next thing I'm going to say you already know, too—but it's well to be reminded of it at an ordination. Don't make too much of it if you and the minister differ on, say, whether to put in new toilets or not; or because he went off to a retreat or a consultation or something when a bazaar was being held. (*I know* bazaars help raise money for pastors' salaries.)

And I know it's human to have a strong opinion about—what was it?—toilets. And those who worked the bazaar wore themselves out, and next year the minister—we'll hope—can drop in on that.

But let us all keep in mind what drives the Holy Spirit out of the community of faith: it is scandal—but not the glorious scandal of the gospel about which St. Paul writes (that your sins, and mine, are forgiven! that death is not going to have the last word over you or over me!), not the glorious scandal of the gospel; not the scandal of *notorious* sinners coming into the congregation (after all, the rest of us are just not so notorious), but the scandal of pettiness . . . and indulging our oversensitive feelings . . . and mountains made out of molehills: that is what drives out the Spirit.

And so I come back to the words we heard from the letter of James—and I speak not only to the members here but to the visitors and, yes, very much to my fellow clergy: "The tongue is fire . . . every kind of beast can be tamed, and has been tamed . . . but no human being can tame the tongue—a restless evil, full of deadly poison. With it we bless God, and with it we curse each other, who are made in the likeness of God."[5]

How do we curse with our tongues? I'm not talking of oaths we may mutter watching the Celtics lose (a rare occasion, I realize). The frequency of four-letter vulgarities is not even what I have in mind. Rather, what I have in mind is *gossip*, both personal gossip and gossip by groups about other groups. We *curse* each other . . . with gossip.

---

5. James 3:6–9.

Now those who are gossips have the same promise of forgiveness—of generous acceptance by Christ—as those who have become thieves, or adulterers, or liars. And the word holds, "Whoever is without sin among you, cast the first stone"[6]—at the one who gossips.

We *all* have delighted in passing on malicious information or fantasy (if only we knew) about someone or another group. After all, gossip is exciting. It quickens our blood. We feel lost passions. It gives release to resentment and irritation, to frustration and boredom. Women gossip. Men gossip. Conservatives gossip; radicals gossip. The old gossip; but so do the young.

And sometimes when we gossip we destroy children's parents, and children, yes, and families, and ministers (and fellow clergy) and others in the church of God; yes, we destroy the churches, and, all unknowingly, we destroy ourselves.

Gossip can become as addictive as heroin or alcohol. We have Alcoholics Anonymous and Gamblers Anonymous. (I hope there may be chapters meeting in this church.) I'm serious when I suggest that some of us need "Gossips Anonymous" so that our *tongues* may be tamed.

All of us do well to pray for the conversion of our tongues.

Most gossip is neither innocent nor trivial. A good test, of course, is simply this: Would I speak thus about that person (or those persons) in the presence of someone who loves them? Would I speak that way about them in the presence of God?

Let us instead learn how to pray. Prayer—that's the next thing.

A person whose dear friend had died—*albeit a troublesome friend*—wrote, "I need another afternoon with her, to sit among spring flowers and listen to her fears"[7]—and listen to her fears.

How shall we find the freedom to spend an afternoon in the presence of others or another and, with love, listen to their fears?

We are entered into an age, I believe, where we must learn to pray or die.

Those who would live the good life must learn to pray. Those who would make peace must learn to pray. Those who would make it a world fit for children must learn to pray; those who claim they love children must learn to pray.

---

6. John 8:7.

7. Author's note: I regret that I have not retained the article from which these poignant lines are taken.

Those who would *become* themselves must learn to pray. Those who would *forget* themselves must learn to pray. Those who would resist injustice—racism and sexism and national priorities that sacrifice the lives of the poor for extra vacations for the rich—those who would resist must learn to pray. Those who would hope must learn to pray. And those who would be happy—they must learn to pray.

We must learn to pray, not as a way to become pious or to indicate our piety. (The nub of Jesus' teaching about piety seems to be: *hide it*.[8]) Not learn to pray as a way to piety—but as a way to life, a way to life instead of death.

But someone says quietly to herself, to himself (someone ordained as likely as anyone else), "I can't pray . . . I can't pray anymore. The words go up to the ceiling and drop aimless, harmless, dead."

"I need another afternoon with her, to sit among spring flowers and listen to her fears."

Will you let such words, but words of *your own*—*such* as those—pierce your heart?

Then you shall have begun to pray. For *never* are your *real* words aimless, harmless, or dead. Your question is whether or not you can dare *approach* your *real* words, the words in your heart.

Prayer begins in receiving your own real words.

But prayer is more. "The Spirit—the Spirit intercedes for us with sighs too deep for words."[9] *The Spirit takes up our praying.* "O God," cries the Spirit deeper than our own spirit, "this poor failure at prayer has nothing left—no hope or faith or joy. Raise from the dead the words and the life of this one." *God's own cry* on our behalf.

Therefore, we can be directed to pray. Pray for other people. Try that again. Hold others in prayer. Those of you who keep lists or have special directories—pray for those on your lists, and in your directories—even name by name by name.

Pray for those you love. Pray for those you feel uncomfortable with.

Pray for the one who has let you down so terribly.

Pray for the SOBs in your life. We all know what SOBs are. Admit in anguish and anger, and with any humor you can find, that they are, for you, indeed SOBs, but pray for them—not necessarily that you will feel differently about them, not necessarily that they'll change—but that God will be their good God, their good God and yours. Pray for the SOBs in your life . . . and maybe somewhere, someone will be praying for you in the same way.

8. Matthew 6:5–6.
9. Romans 8:26.

Admit your hatreds, but pray. Cry out that you have been let down, but pray. Admit you are uncomfortable—but pray. Don't take those you love for granted anymore—pray for them.

And I said that those who would make peace, who would make it a world fit for children, who would resist injustice must learn to pray.

But—someone wants to cry out: prayer is no substitute for work!

No, indeed it is not.

But work is no substitute for prayer!

Prayer is the transformation of our work. Prayer brings our work from death to life.

I believe God can accomplish great, *if hidden*, things through us all. We do not—any of us—know how to pray as we ought. But the Spirit helps us in our weakness—takes up our prayers, makes a home in us, sticks with us, and intercedes for us—yes, with sighs too deep for words.

It's been my assumption throughout that we are *all* sinners and sufferers. Whether we're pastors or church agency people, homemakers or homeless, steamfitters or unemployed, lawyers or computer programmers, students or teachers makes no difference; no difference whether we're women or men; lesbian, gay, or straight; married or single. The life of each one of us could be a novel—or a TV soap opera—if the story were disclosed and told right. The sins and sufferings of those of us gathered here right now, this afternoon, are enough to break the heart of God.

And God's heart is broken—and God assures us that where sin and, yes, death abound, there life and grace, yes, and love the *more* abound.[10]

Our sins and our sorrows and the power of death are where either we break into despair or we break into Christ's new life. Our sins and our sorrows are where all our great gifts are hidden—above all, the gift of our compassion, the gift of our love.

So I am coming on in now. Catch the points again: thanks for everybody here this afternoon—and for those who are not here and . . . yet who are.

Compassion—that's the *main* point, isn't it? To learn compassion—how . . . to be . . . compassionate.

So tame your tongues. Together, let us give up gossip.

Instead—pray . . . your own real words. The Spirit makes a home in us, intercedes for us and brings us back to life.

---

10. See Romans 5:20.

And now include Michael Granzen in your love even more than ever you have before.

But love one another in the congregation, in the presbytery, in the struggles. Love one another—in joy and in sorrow, in success and in conflicts and failure.

Indeed, your love—"tough love," at times—but your love *for one another* will be as important to Michael Granzen as loving him directly. That will be to make the gospel credible to him, to make a believer of him—and give him joy and power in his ministry—that *we* love one another!

But don't do that with condescension, as if *you* "had it together." Let us learn to love one another as fellow-sinners and sufferers, on our way to die . . . even as we are. Let us love one another as God loves each of you . . . and loves me.

Remember Jesus' haunting question: "When the Son of Man comes, will he find faith?"[11] When Christ comes, will Christ find faith?

When the battle of life is over and our work is done and we are *fully* revealed in the presence of God, will there be found in us faith and hope and love? That is Jesus' question.

Even so, come, Lord Jesus!

---

11. Luke 18:8. For the final seven paragraphs, see John 15:12–17; Revelation 22:20.

27

Words of Welcome Offered at a Wedding Service

THERE IS NO AUDIENCE today—not really. And, finally, no performance is being offered here.

    We are a congregation, a community called together today as people of God. We are the community in which—and before whom—Judith and John know themselves—and know themselves now called into marriage.

    We are the community of their unity and encouragement. This community includes both the living and the dead. We are here not only as individuals, not only as ourselves; we are here on behalf of all those in Judith's and John's past—living and dead—who have loved them and strengthened them, taught them and called them to account. And we are here on behalf of all those who in the future enter into the lives of John and Judith, and into whose lives they enter.

    So, we are not simply an audience but part of a celebration and a service of worship. And this wedding service asks something of us all. Judith and John are counting on us. They count on pledging themselves and listening with our support and strength—both now and in the days to come.

    It takes a lifetime to say and hear, and learn, the important things—and even then we miss and falter (as those of us who are older know best of all). So let us not say, "They shouldn't have . . ." or "They should have . . ." or judge at all. Judge not, that you be not judged.[1] As the Scriptures have it,

---

1. Matthew 7:1 (RSV).

"See to it that . . . no 'root of bitterness' spring up."[2] Instead, let us receive the mystery and wonder of it all.

Learn again even to forgive. For as we forgive, so we experience forgiveness.

Renew your own vows, your own best commitments; renew your hope, your joy, your courage, and your love.

This marriage is not just a private good but for the common good.

Be of good cheer. Be amused. Fear neither your laughter nor your tears.

Begin to see again that the Lord our God is good; has given us food and drink, and life itself. Even one another—God has given us. Even the presence of God among us we have been given.

> O God, Creator of all that is,
> Savior of the lost and Spirit of eternal life,
> we would enter in and celebrate
> and worship in your name.
> Amen.

---

2. Hebrews 12:15a, b (RSV).

28

Coleman Brown on Student Development
The Importance of Humility, Mystery, and a Sense of Reverence

EXCERPTS FROM AN INTERVIEW BY GARY PAVELA[1]

PAVELA: How is spiritual growth related to psychological and moral growth?

BROWN: The psychological and the moral and the spiritual overlap; they're not identical, and each without development in the other spheres is inadequate. If we are to understand these three, I think we must continually reflect on our relation to the social. One of my favorite quotations is from Martin Luther King: "I can never be what I ought to be until you are what you ought to be, and you can never be what you ought to be until I am what I ought to be." I would say with some confidence that we simply don't believe that today—that it's too frustrating for many of us, even those who would be discoverers of spirituality.

If our spirituality simply makes us feel good [and] is used simply to provide perspective, simply to relax us, I think it will not in the long run amount to much. Our spirituality, like our physical exertion, must hurt as well as heal, challenge as well as comfort, and do justice to the hard facts of life as well as the pleasing ones—and disclose our laziness and self-deception, as well as provide us encouragement, and acceptance, and yes, maybe—perspective. The spiritual requires humility, a sense of the precariousness of the present and of the possible in the future; true spirituality recognizes tragedy

---

1. See Brown, "Coleman Brown on Student Development." Originally printed in *Synthesis* magazine (date unknown).

as well as trust and hope and contemplation and love. The spiritual life is an arduous life . . .

PAVELA: I assume you agree with those who have suggested that the concepts of awe, mystery, and reverence are repressed in the modern world, much as sexuality was repressed by the Victorians. What other factors may be involved in promoting such repression?

BROWN: I do agree. You ask about the factors, and that's a dangerous question; I'm not a historian. It seems to me that a doctrine of human innocence that has grown since the eighteenth century is at least as hard to swallow as the doctrine of the original sin. We tend to say today, particularly in educational institutions, that "humanity has problems" but that we ourselves are not the problem; but I'm not so sure.

The repression that you speak of is in part invited by a doctrine of human innocence. Our atomized individualism—and the sources of that are multiple—but certainly our economic system and the need to be able to function as a saleable individual has led to a kind of repression.

The invitation of culture continually is to make the self-interested individual the center, and when the self, in that sense, is the center, it will be under enormous pressure to repress some of the most important things about our existence. Our narcissism requires that we repress matters that disclose our need for humility, for forgiveness, our need for others, let alone the "Other."

The authority of explanatory knowledge has led us to a sense of an empty universe. Explanations tend to empty, don't they? Contemplation needs fullness. When we can see through everything, there's nothing left to see. We are in a situation in which we can't bear either our own finitude and apparent insignificance, or the awe and reverence necessary for the rediscovery of our significance.

Our significance is something with which we're endowed. It's very hard for me to understand how it is self-derived. If we have no awe or reverence for the mystery of why we came into being, I wonder how long we can find significance in our own being. A sense of personal significance for your life in a way that you can't get away from is a powerful anchor in times of terrible uncertainty.

Also, when a sense of personal significance is lost, when I'm only accountable to myself, the question arises, "What is this infinite worth of the individual? I guess we made it up." Then there is a denigration of our humanity that is hard to stop without some kind of recovery of spirituality.

One other thing about repression. It seems to me that we repress these questions of meaning because of the awesome questions of justice that they raise. Jefferson, who never released his slaves, nevertheless during the slavery period said something like "I tremble to think that God is just." Spirituality divorced from the question of justice is still a thing of repression. The awful disparities of our society, or our world, lead to repression of the question of justice, and thus to repression of attention to a human community built on love and justice . . .

PAVELA: It sounds as if you believe *individuals* are a witness to something, not institutions.

BROWN: That's right, I guess, and I'm not anti-institutional. I think that healthy institutions are crucial for protecting and making possible our creative relationships. I just believe we've got to be careful about institutional visions, about our own limits and about our own evil.

Karen Horney said that all neurosis begins with discovery of the hypocrisy of the parenting figures. Of course, we're all hypocrites. I am, and I want to say so and to be on the record. Nothing is more dangerous or almost unavoidably hypocritical than to answer questions on spirituality and matters of spirit. If we are insisting that we are better than others somewhere deep inside ourselves—however much we may hide it from ourselves and from others—then we must wrestle with that insistence fiercely, and certainly if we are dealing with young people. This is a deep psychological, moral, and spiritual matter. But in order to help others, we must, as Jung puts it, face our shadow; we must recognize our evil impulse, acknowledge what some call our sin. In other words, in order to help others, we've got to be able to get to the truth about ourselves. And this we cannot finally do, I think, except by the power of the spirit.

29

Prayer of Confession

For the Colgate University Church

SERVANT LORD AND GOD of Glory:

    We are before you this morning as broken men and women in need of forgiveness—having come from anguished moments in the night, and betrayals in the day; having said cutting words—or no words.

    Often bewildered by the obvious or subtle suffering that we see—or that is our own—we have been uncertain. We have concentrated on defense of ourselves and have found the condemnation of others easy. We have not received others simply as they are, nor met them as ourselves.

    Hear our various inward cries. Forgive us and heal us. Alone we cannot be healed. Therefore, lead us to the discovery of others; free us from our several bondages; cleanse our hearts with honesty; give us courage to accompany our fears; and bring us even to faith, and hope, and love.

    Amen.

30

Blessing

Now go in confidence that God hears your prayers and mine,
 the prayers we sing and speak,
 the prayers wrapped in our sighs too deep for words.
 Discover the healing hidden in secret truths over which you have despaired.
 God grant you a cheerful and a faithful heart, fresh courage, and the love to make it all worthwhile.
 And may the blessing of God dawn on you even in the darkest hours that ever come:
 The peace of God be with you today and even forever.

My Teacher

CHRIS HEDGES

JULY 20, 2015

I DROVE TO HAMILTON, New York, last December to take part in the funeral service for the Reverend Coleman Brown. Coleman, who had taught at Colgate University, had the most profound impact of all my teachers on my education. I took seven courses as an undergraduate in religion. He taught six of them. But his teaching extended far beyond the classroom. The classroom was where he lit the spark.

He was brilliant and slightly eccentric. Concerned one winter day that the heating system in Lawrence Hall was making us students too comfortable and complacent, he opened the windows, sending blasts of snow into the room as we sat huddled in our jackets. He had a habit of repeatedly circling words on the blackboard with chalk, leaving behind series of massive white rings and faint white streaks on his face (he repeatedly ran his index and middle fingers down his cheek as he spoke). His worn tweed coats seemed to always have a soft coating of chalk dust.

He was loved, often adored, by most of his students, whom he looked upon as an extended family. His office hours were packed. He regularly brought groups of students home for meals and evenings with him and his wife, Irene, and their four children. Three decades later, some of the most vivid memories I have of Colgate are of doggedly following him out of the classroom to continue the conversation he had begun in class, of meeting him weekly in his office, of listening to his sermons on Sunday mornings in the chapel, of dinners at his house and, finally, after my graduation, of bursting into tears in front of my parents as I said goodbye to him.

Education is not only about knowledge. It is about inspiration. It is about passion. It is about the belief that what we do in life matters. It is about moral choice. It is about taking nothing for granted. It is about challenging assumptions and suppositions. It is about truth and justice. It is about learning how to think. It is about, as James Baldwin wrote, the ability to drive "to the heart of every answer and expose the question the answer hides."[1] And, as Baldwin further noted, it is about making the world "a more human dwelling place."[2]

I wanted to learn. Coleman wanted to teach. And my education—my real education—is not discernable from my college transcript. Coleman and I met late Friday afternoons each week in his book-lined office. There and in class he introduced me to the theologians Reinhold Niebuhr, Paul Tillich, William Stringfellow, and Daniel Berrigan. I devoured the books he gave me, especially Niebuhr's *Moral Man and Immoral Society*, which I read and reread. He gave me poems by John Donne, W. H. Auden, and T. S. Eliot. He taught me the importance of C. S. Lewis and Fyodor Dostoevsky. I read *The Brothers Karamazov* twice in college because of Coleman, although the novel was never taught in any of my classes.

Coleman would read poems and cherished prose passages out loud as I met with him in his office. It was about the musicality of language. His sonorous voice rose and dipped with intonations and emphasis. To this day I still hear his recitation in pieces of writing and poems. He understood, as Philip Pullman writes, that "the sound is part of the meaning, and that part only comes alive when you speak it," that even if you do not at first understand the poem "you're already far closer to the poem than someone who sits there in silence looking up meanings and references and making assiduous notes."[3] Coleman had open disdain for New Criticism, the evisceration of texts into sterile pieces of pedantry that fled from the mysterious, sacred forces that great writers struggle to articulate. You had to love great writing before you attempted to analyze it. You had to be moved and inspired by it. You had to be captured by the human imagination. He once told me he had just reread *King Lear*. I recited a litany of freshly minted undergraduate criticism, talking about subplots, themes of blindness, and the nature of power. He listened impassively. "Well," he said when I had finished. "I don't know anything about that. I only know it made me a better person

---

1. Baldwin, "Creative Process," 670.
2. Baldwin, "Creative Process," 669.
3. Pullman, "Paradise Lost," 49.

and a better father." I would spend the week memorizing poems he had read to me—Auden's "September 1, 1939" and "Epitaph on a Tyrant," Eliot's "Journey of the Magi," passages of Shakespeare—and return the following Friday to recite them to him.

Poetry, he taught me, is alive. It must be felt. It has a hypnotic power that, as Shakespeare understood, is a kind of witchcraft. And poetry, along with all other writing, is just a spent, dead force if you do not surrender to its spell.

"If you graduate knowing how to read and write, you will be educated," Coleman said.

I was a writer, but the two people who most influenced my life—my father and Coleman—were Presbyterian preachers and social activists. Coleman, before he went to teach at Colgate, had been a minister in an inner-city church in Chicago. As a seminarian at Union Theological Seminary he had worked in East Harlem. He was involved in the Chicago Freedom Movement, which was a tenant action collaboration with the Southern Christian Leadership Conference, and, like my father, he was a member of Clergy and Concerned Laymen, a group of religious leaders who opposed the Vietnam War. Martin Luther King Jr. preached at Coleman's church in Chicago (an event for which Coleman could not be present).

A descendant of the abolitionist John Brown, he placed at the center of his critique of American society the poison of white supremacy and the nightmare of racism that had been and remains part of our body politic. Being educated meant understanding how racism and white supremacy were ingrained in the beliefs, institutions, laws, and systems of power—especially capitalism—that ruled America. And I felt, largely because of the example of Coleman's life, that I should become an inner-city minister. I applied to Harvard Divinity School during my senior year at Colgate, an application for which my Shakespeare professor, Margaret Maurer, as she later told me, ruefully wrote a recommendation that informed the admissions committee that I had probably read more books than any other student she had taught but that "unfortunately most of them were never assigned." This was true in a formal sense. But of course Coleman had informally assigned many of them.

When I was accepted at Harvard, Coleman announced he would teach me how to preach. He was one of the finest preachers I have ever heard. There was and is no course at Colgate University in preaching. But that spring, in the basement of the chapel, there became one, although it would never be noted in the registrar's office. I wrote a weekly sermon. Coleman sat in a chair in front of me and took notes in felt pen on a yellow legal pad. For all his compassion and gentleness, he was possessed of an intellect that was uncompromising and intimidating. My sermons were torn to shreds under his critique. I would be sent back to do them again. And again. And again. At the end of the semester he seemed satisfied.

"Now you know how to preach," he told me. "Don't let anyone change you."

This truth did not escape my homiletics professor at Harvard, Krister Stendahl, who pulled me aside after my first sermon to the class and asked, "Where did you learn to preach?" I won the divinity school's preaching prize.

I lived across the street from the Mission Main and Mission Extension housing project in Roxbury, the inner city in Boston, and ran a small church as a seminarian. It was one of the poorest and most dangerous projects in the city. I commuted to Cambridge for classes and went home to the ghetto. The vast disconnect between Harvard, where students went on about the suffering of people they had never met, and the poor filled me with despair. I went back to Colgate to sit again in Coleman's office. The slants of pale, yellow light fell with a comforting familiarity on the shelves of books and the tweed jacket of my old teacher.

There was a long silence.

"Are we created to suffer?" I finally asked.

"Is there any love that isn't?" he answered. I would leave Harvard, without being ordained, to go off to war as a reporter. I would cover conflicts for twenty years in Central America, the Middle East, Africa, and the Balkans. I would see the worst of human evil. I would come back once or twice a year to the United States. And I would almost always find my way to Hamilton to see Coleman Brown.

I have always thought of myself as a preacher. This is not a vocation one proclaims openly if he or she works for *The New York Times*, as I did. Preachers, like artists, care more about the truth than they do about news. News and truth are not the same thing. The truth can get you into trouble. During the calls to invade Iraq I denounced the looming war, drawing on my seven years in the Middle East and my former position as the Middle East bureau chief for the *Times*. My outspokenness led to my being issued a formal reprimand and leaving the paper. It was then I began to write books. I sent my drafts to Coleman. He sent chapters back with notes and comments. In one proposed chapter of the manuscript that would become *American Fascists: The Christian Right and the War on America*, he drew large X's across four full pages and wrote at the bottom of the fourth page, "Frankly, you are over your head." In a book I was writing on the New Atheists, he sent back the opening page, which I had spent some time putting together. Every sentence with the exception of the first had been meticulously crossed out with his thick black felt pen. "Keep the first sentence and cut the rest," he wrote. He lifted to his level many passages in my books, especially in *War Is a Force That Gives Us Meaning*, which I dedicated to Coleman and my father. My books bear the imprint of his wisdom.

His decline was long and painful. He suffered dementia and neurological damage that left him in a wheelchair. He would, on my periodic visits, rouse himself with herculean effort to connect, to summon from deep inside him the great spirit and intellect that somehow never left him. On my last visit with him before he died at eighty, I came with my friend and one-time classmate from Colgate and Harvard, the Reverend Michael Granzen. We sat at the dinner table with Coleman and Irene Brown. "Now which preacher here will say the grace?" I asked of Coleman and Michael. "You will," Coleman said.

I was ordained last October. The first time I wore a clerical collar was at Coleman's funeral. My hand, and the hands of some of Coleman's other students who had gone on to be preachers, rested, at the end of his service, on his coffin. I too am a teacher. I teach in a prison. My students do not, as I did not, learn in order to further a career or to advance their positions in society. Many of them will never leave prison. They learn because they yearn to be educated, because the life of the mind is the only freedom most will ever know. I love my students. I love them the way Coleman loved his students. I visit their families. I have met at the prison gate the very few who have been released. I have had them to my home. I have pushed books into their hands.

Last semester one of my most dedicated students stayed behind after the final class. This is a man who when I mention a book even in passing will find it, take it to his cell and consume it. He was imprisoned at the age of fourteen and tried as an adult. He will not be eligible to go before a parole board until he is seventy.

"I will die in prison," he said. "But I work as hard as I do so that one day I can be a teacher like you."

In the Christian faith this is called resurrection.

Remembering My Dad, Coleman Brown

Joshua Brown

My father, the Reverend Dr. Coleman Barr Brown, taught philosophy and religion at Colgate University for twenty-nine years—and he loved to recall a moment one September when he was meeting incoming first-year students. An earnest young man approached him and said, "I know what a minister is and a priest. I know what a rabbi is. But what is a Coleman?"

What, indeed? My father, like all people, was a complex creature, with many facets. "We wear many masks," he would say. And part of his deep faith was that we have, under these masks, a true face that we might not even recognize ourselves. But, my dad would say, the God who made each of us sees our true faces—and loves us as we are.

People heard Coleman Brown's sermons from many different places—and part of his power as a preacher was to imagine and understand this. "Come as you are," he would often say. For me and my brother Bradford, more than once that meant hearing our dad in our sweaty hockey jerseys as we'd rush from a Sunday morning peewee game to Colgate University's chapel.

As the youngest of his four children, I was a welcome and active—and mandatory—member of the University Church, a truly ecumenical, and truly amazing, gathering that our father led. Most in the congregation were Colgate students, with a scattering of faculty and community members, who came together, as my father often said, as "believers, seekers, and doubters." Most, I'd guess, were raised in Protestant churches, but I certainly remember a hearty current of students who described themselves as Catholics, Jews,

Buddhists, wanderers, and atheists, and, of course, "spiritual but not really religious."

The students were sometimes joined by revered Colgate professors, including the Peace Studies teacher and decided skeptic of Christianity, my dad's dear friend Huntington Terrell; Jewish philosopher Jerry Balmuth, who would slip in and out just to hear the sermon; and, many Sundays, my father's beloved mentor, the great Kierkegaard scholar and minister Steve Hartshorne and his wife, Ruth—all would come to listen to my dad preach the sermons gathered in this book.

The worship services surrounding these sermons were an almost indescribable mixture of quiet prayer and evangelical testifying complete with full-volume "amens." There were sturdy old hymns belted out on Colgate's grand organ—my father's tenor rising into "God of Our Life, Through All the Circling Years"—and largely improvisational moments as the whole congregation held hands in a warm loop that wound around the altar. There were elements of the stern Presbyterian theology my father adopted as a young inner-city minister in the 1960s; hearing him say John Hunter's communion prayer, "Come to this table not because you must, but because you may . . . not because you have any claim on heaven's reward but because in your frailty and sin you are in constant need of God's mercy and help," comes to me from memory as I write this. And there was a 1970s- and 1980s-infused sense of the personal possibility and psychological drama of religious practice. All glued together by the Spirit—and my dad's preaching.

Like so many people, I loved hearing my dad talk and read. He had a voice and way of putting words into the air that called out from the deep. He would look me—and each member of the congregation—in the eye as he preached, and that made a boy spiritually attentive. I'm not alone in remembering that my dad preached to you, not at you. But sometimes an eight- and ten-year-old have their own ideas about religious exploration. During church one Sunday, Brad and I slinked away from the seats where we were supposed to be sitting behind our mother and into a dark underworld: the crawl space under the platform on which the congregation gathered at the front of the chapel. There, the seams between sections of floor overhead cast thin lines of alluring, bright light. With our service bulletins, we formed a small paper wedge and, very slowly, a yellow shark's fin, one inch high, moved down the aisle in one of the cracks in the floor, through the congregation, toward the lectern where my father was preaching. I don't recall what scripture he was explicating that morning, but I do remember my mother's face peering into the gloom and calling us back to our proper places. And I do remember, in later years, my dad laughing and laughing about the shark that almost reached his cordovan shoes.

The University Church was as close as I ever got to Sunday school. I loved the singing of the Sojourners, a student-led gospel group in the African-American tradition. No mumbling-under-the-breath kind of choir, they could sing praise to the Lord! My religious teachers were a constant stream of smart, seeking, and sometimes soulful college students—polite Episcopalians, unreconstructed hippies, Black Baptists, cheerful frat boys, evangelicals in dangerous territory, magnificent leaders, ministers-in-the-making who didn't yet realize it, broken-hearted kids with dead parents—who would gather in the chapel or on the wooden rocking chairs and shabby couch in my parent's living room. There, in our house, my dad's preaching would, in a sense, continue. He led student committees of the church, gathered his classes for dinner, and hosted a discussion group called "Believers, Seekers, and Doubters." These gatherings, for me as a young child—and on into high school—were a heady and sometimes bewildering amalgam of Jesus' parables, references to Wittgenstein and Reinhold Niebuhr, raw conversations about racism and justice, calls for nuclear disarmament, plans for anti-hunger actions in Madison County, all leavened with my mother's Chinese noodle and spinach casseroles.

(Let me pause on the casseroles. There is another essay to be written about my mother, Irene, and another about my parents together. But suffice it to say that theirs was a decades-long partnership of ministry. My mother spotted a handsome hall monitor in high school at age sixteen and their romance lasted more than sixty years. They came of age in the especially sexist 1950s and my father never learned to cook. My mother went from housewife to founder and director of Madison County's Community Action Program, managing a staff of thirty-five who provided aid to the poor and homeless. "We grew up together," my mother likes to say, and my father adored my mother, depended on her so much.)

My father's role, always, was to make sure that we went around the circle, where everyone got to speak and everyone was heard. Once, when it came to my turn, I remember asking, as a fifth-grader in a sea of undergraduates, this question: "Why were there miracles in the Bible and I've never seen one?"

In the silence that followed, my father said, "That's a good question." My dad deeply believed in questions. Questions as the way to understanding. Questions as an end point of understanding, not just the beginning. Of course, he appreciated education: when he graduated from Evanston Township High School in Illinois in 1952, he'd been president of the national association of student councils; he graduated *magna cum laude* from Princeton University in 1956, taking the top student prize.

"What a waste," my dad overheard one of his history professors say, when he learned that my father was going into the ministry rather than pursue a political career or become an academic historian. He would tell this story in later years, with the conviction that comes from having listened rightly for his calling against louder winds.

He received his MDiv and PhD degrees from Union Theological Seminary in New York, writing his doctoral dissertation on "Grounds for American Loyalty in a Prophetic Christian Social Ethic—with Especial Attention to Martin Luther King, Jr." He loved books and learning and would often go to the *Columbia Encyclopedia* to address a family dinnertime conversation about some fine-grained point of history.

But he did not see ignorance and mystery as cousins at all. Ignorance is the lack of knowledge and education—but mystery, he would say, paraphrasing Marcel, is "the nature of being. It is something in which I am involved." So, to approach the mystery, my dad wanted to know what questions were the right ones to pose. And, more urgently, like Rilke, how to live the questions. In his later years as a professor, he would cheerfully warn students, "It's possible to get all A's and flunk life." My mother and siblings and I all have a copy of a photo of my dad, by one of his former students, that shows him posed and pondering in a classroom. On the chalkboard at his back, he's written, "Audacity and Humility—How to hold them *together*?"

I've spent a lot of my professional life working on conservation of biological diversity, the protection of wildlands. I'm enamored of the Gaia Hypothesis, the notion that our planet is best understood as a single organism. I think deep ecology has a place in our religious conversations, maybe especially in Christian ones. Sometime around the year 2000, I recall waxing enthusiastic about the intricate interrelationship of all species with my dad. He listened with a searing kind of care and attention, as he would when the conversation turned serious. For many long minutes we walked through the dark streets of Hamilton, New York, from one puddle of streetlamp light to the next, as I talked. Finally, he turned to me and said, "What is your deep biology telling you?"

There was something maddening for me, a thirty-something aspiring science journalist, about his question. But it was a good question that took the outer living world that I was trying to love and brought it inside me. My father was troubled and anxious about his inner life, about the inner life of souls. "Our hearts find no peace until they rest in you," he concludes the second sermon in this book. His concern and wisdom about this inner life was a great revelation to many of his students, a source of comfort for those who knocked on his office door in Hascall Hall. For me as his son, his concern was amazingly powerful, both soothing and smothering, confounding and a generous gift. I don't know the answer to his question to this day. But it's a good question.

The sermons in this book, given between 1974 and 1989, correspond to the years of my growing up, elementary school to college. I, of course, did not know my father as he learned to preach in front of congregations as a seminary student in the East Harlem Protestant Parish—my mother recalls that he declined to take any preaching classes at Union. Nor was I yet born when he—a white man from an affluent suburban family—was ordained into the ministry and became pastor, from 1962 to 1968, at the interracial Olivet United Presbyterian Church, surrounded by housing projects on the Near North Side of Chicago. My older brother and sister, Justin and Susan, grew up there, in the midst of the work my mom and dad did for civil rights and protesting against the Vietnam War. In 1965 and '66, my dad joined the rallies of the Chicago Freedom Movement, led by Martin Luther King Jr., to demand open housing, and better education and transportation, for Black people in Cook County. He marched with King in Marquette Park in July 1966, where they were attacked with bricks and bottles.

After King's assassination in 1968, police cordoned off many Black neighborhoods where people were rioting—including the one in Chicago where my family lived near the Olivet Church. My dad and my brother Justin went out to do an errand and were stopped at a police barricade as they returned. "Father, you don't want to go in there," a policeman said, noticing the clerical collar my dad wore in those days. "But I *live* there," my dad replied. "You're on your own," the officer said, and my dad and brother strode hand in hand across the line and went home.

My first memories of my dad preaching were at the Millers Mills Community Church, a tiny Baptist church in the farming community of West Winfield, New York. My dad had recently been hired as an instructor in philosophy and religion at Colgate and took on the extra job of being supply preacher on Sundays. We'd pile in the car early in the morning and drive the thirty miles to church, propelled by the promise of sections of *The Lion, the Witch and Wardrobe* that he'd read as his children's sermon. And then propelled home by smoked cheese and fudge that my father would purchase, each week, at a roadside shop.

My dad became Colgate's chaplain in 1974, teaching and preaching until his retirement from the chaplaincy in 1989 and from the faculty in 1996. (He taught part-time until 1999.) In both roles, he almost always wore a tie, sometimes a tweed jacket with patches (because it actually needed patches), or one of the selection of old Brooks Brothers suits that he'd gotten as an undergraduate or bought at the Salvation Army thrift store. An issue of the student newspaper once ran a spoof edition in which they pilloried prominent members of the faculty. My father was not spared. Among the various goofy faux-Norse deities that were presented, he was described as the "god of timeless fashions and endless qualifiers." My dad loved that and he had a great capacity to laugh at himself. As teenagers, Brad and I convinced him that microwave ovens could heat up to eight thousand degrees Fahrenheit, far beyond the melting point of steel. He loved that one too and would laugh, slapping his knee, every time we retold the story with glee.

For years, he and Hunt Terrell were selected by *The Princeton Review* as the two professors at Colgate whose courses could not be missed. At his funeral, my dad's friend and colleague Chris Vecsey gave the eulogy and recalled, when my dad was retiring, looking at student evaluations of teaching from across my dad's career. "The SET forms, as we call them, were unsurprising in their superlatives," Vecsey said. "However, the intensity of student response was compelling beyond comparison. I have never read SETs like Coleman's. To call them 'excellent' or 'inspirational' does injustice. What students said about Coleman's teacherly impact on their lives, moved me, repeatedly, to tears."

My father moved me to tears too, but to be the child of Coleman Brown is a different proposition than to be one of his students. So many of his students were his admirers, were seekers coming for advice, were swept up by his astounding capacity for listening deeply and responding from the depths of compassion. As his children—I think I can speak for my three siblings—he loved us with a fierce love and we loved him back with an equal ferocity. But we didn't always admire him and he didn't always approve of us. It was a natural parent-child dynamic, he knew—he read Jung, Freud, Horney—but it played out in the roiling waters of a minister who asked, "What are you doing with your life?" And amidst a powerful public narrative about one of Colgate's great minds, a man beloved for his ability to preach out of the realization of his own fallenness. As he says in one of the sermons in this book, "Parents curse as well as bless their children. And each of us must work that out by the grace of God" ("Strong at the Broken Places"). Hearing our dad in church, calling us into new relationship with God, as you might imagine, was complicated for his kids.

My father is buried on a gentle hill above the campus at Colgate, above the gold-domed building where he was chaplain. As I paused there recently, I was recalled to two other times my father was on this hillside. One was a walk he took with Elie Wiesel, just the two of them, when the great Jewish chronicler came to speak at Colgate, and they walked together, talking among the dead. Another was a winter day when I was a young boy. Just yards from his grave, there is a patch of woods. And, on a frigid afternoon in the mid-1970s, my dad drove us—my two brothers and my sister, my mother, our dog, and me—up there in our VW Beetle. To collect kindling. This was not a practical way to keep our fireplace going. My father was not a handy man. He didn't use a saw nearly as well as his black felt pen. But we all followed him, sweeping through the woods, gathering downed branches and twigs until we had a big stack. Then he chopped them with a hatchet and tied a great bundle to the roof of the tiny car. Then he got behind the wheel, my mother arranged my siblings in the rear seat, with me and the beagle tucked into the strange well for luggage behind the rear seat of the car—and we drove back through the town of Hamilton, singing, "Amazing grace, how sweet the sound that saved a wretch like me"—to our home.

In some ways, my dad's ministry was conducted by letter. He wrote hundreds—thousands—of letters to his students, colleagues, and friends over the years. And his intellectual and spiritual life was fed by a rich tissue of these letters, good books he read and shared, daily devotional reading in the Bible, and quiet conversations. So being struck by Lewy body dementia was particularly tragic for him. His once graceful hand became a crabbed scrawl. Then he couldn't write at all. As the disease progressed, he lost his ability to read. He grew more sleepy, and there were periods of great agitation. His vigorous debating and deft conversational skills retreated. Then he even found it hard to speak, to remember the words. We worried that the harder, angry parts of my father might grow more so. But as the disease tore through his brain, my mother took unflagging care of him—"she always believed in his essence," my sister said. And an unexpected peace descended on my father.

At Thanksgiving, in 2014, just weeks before his death, many members of my family were all gathered in my dad's room, getting ready to go home after a weekend visit. My dad had been sleeping, but when he awoke, he joined us in singing Christmas carols. And he sang and sang, in a firm whisper, for more than an hour, all the old tunes coming back intact. "This is our Christmas," he said to my mother.

And several times, all my siblings and I recall, near the end of his life, my father would awake briefly, after days of drifting on the edge of sleep, to share two words. Just as we were packing the minivan to leave, he sat up in his wheelchair and looked me in the eye. The questions had fallen away. Instead, he made one declarative statement: "So grateful." Me too, Dad, me too.

Bibliography

Arnold, Matthew. "Dover Beach." In *New Poems*, 112-14. London: Macmillan, 1867.
Auden, W. H. "September 1, 1939." In *Another Time*, 98-101. New York: Random, 1940.
Baldwin, James. "The Creative Process." In *Collected Essays*, 669-72. New York: Library of America, 1998.
Becker, Ernest. *The Denial of Death*. New York: Free Press, 1975.
Bellah, Robert N., et al. *Habits of the Heart: Individualism and Commitment in American Life*. Berkeley: University of California Press, 1985.
Berger, Peter L. *A Rumor of Angels: Modern Society and the Rediscovery of the Supernatural*. Garden City, NY: Doubleday, 1969.
Bernstein, Leonard, and Stephen Sondheim. "Somewhere." In *West Side Story: A Musical*, by Arthur Laurents, 89. New York : Random, 1958.
Berrigan, Daniel. *No Bars to Manhood*. New York: Bantam, 1971.
Best, S. Payne. *The Venlo Incident*. London: Hutchinson, 1950.
Bethge, Eberhard. "Editor's Foreword." In *Prisoner for God: Letters and Papers from Prison*, by Dietrich Bonhoeffer, 7-12. Edited by Eberhard Bethge. New York: Macmillan, 1960.
Boisen, Anton T. *Out of the Depths: An Autobiographical Study of Mental Disorder and Religious Experience*. New York: Harper, 1960.
Bonhoeffer, Dietrich. *Prisoner for God: Letters and Papers from Prison*. Edited by Eberhard Bethge. New York: Macmillan, 1960.
Boswell, James. *The Life of Samuel Johnson, LLD*. Malone's 6th ed. Everyman's Library. New York: Knopf, 1811.
Brown, Coleman B. "Coleman Brown on Student Development: The Importance of Humility, Mystery, and a Sense of Reverence." Interview by Gary Pavela. *The Pavela Report* 19.14 (2014) n.p.
———. "The Colgate Continuum." *The Colgate Scene On-Line*, May 1996. Online. http://www4.colgate.edu/scene/may1996/brown.html.
———. *Our Hearts Are Restless Till They Find Their Rest in Thee: Selected Sermons to the Colgate University Church, 1974-1989*. Hamilton, NY: Sermon Project, 2003.
Buechner, Frederick. "All's Lost, All's Found." *Christian Century* 97 (1980) 282-85.

———. *Telling the Truth: The Gospel as Tragedy, Comedy & Fairy Tale*. San Francisco: Harper & Row, 1977.

Bultmann, Rudolf. *Jesus Christ and Mythology*. New York: Scribner's, 1958.

Busch, Eberhard. *Karl Barth: His Life from Letters and Autobiographical Text*. Translated by John Bowden. Philadelphia: Fortress, 1976.

Buttrick, George Arthur. "The Gospel according to St. Matthew: Exposition." In vol. 7 of *The Interpreter's Bible*, edited by George Arthur Buttrick, 288–89. New York: Abingdon-Cokesbury, 1951.

Chesterton, G. K. "O God of Earth and Altar." In *Pilgrim Hymnal*, edited by James W. Lenhart, 436. Boston: Pilgrim, 1963.

———. *Orthodoxy*. Westport, CT: Greenwood, 1974.

Coffin, William Sloane, Jr. "Baccalaureate Sermon." Sermon delivered at Colgate University, Hamilton, NY, May 27, 1979.

———. "The Righteousness of Faith." In *Sermons from Riverside Church 1980*, 5. New York: Riverside Church, 1980.

Dante Alighieri. *The Divine Comedy 1.1: Inferno*. Translated by Charles S. Singleton. Bollingen Series 80. Princeton: Princeton University Press, 1970.

DeLamotte, Roy. "Can Blacks Escape the Mainstream?" *Christian Century* 97 (1980) 276–77.

Dutcher, Patricia Nan. "Sojourners in Our Time." Sermon delivered at Colgate University Church, Hamilton, NY, March 21, 1982. Typed copy.

Eliot, T. S. "The Rum Tum Tugger." In *The Complete Poems and Plays*, 153–54. New York: Harcourt, Brace, 1952.

Forsyth, Peter Taylor. "IV. The Preacher and the Age." In *Positive Preaching and Modern Mind: The Lyman Beecher Lectures on Preaching, Yale University, 1907*, 111–57. London: Hodder & Stoughton, 1907.

Freud, Sigmund. *Civilization and Its Discontents*. Translated and edited by James Strachey. New York: Norton, 1962.

Frost, Robert. "The Death of the Hired Man." In *The Poetry of Robert Frost: The Collected Poems; Complete and Unabridged*, edited by Edward Connery Lathem, 34–40. New York: Henry Holt, 1979.

———. "Provide, Provide." In *The Poetry of Robert Frost: The Collected Poems; Complete and Unabridged*, edited by Edward Connery Lathem, 307. New York: Henry Holt, 1979.

———. "The Strong Are Saying Nothing." In *The Poetry of Robert Frost: The Collected Poems; Complete and Unabridged*, edited by Edward Connery Lathem, 299–300. New York: Henry Holt, 1979.

Griffin, Emilie. *Turning: Reflections on the Experience of Conversion*. Garden City, NY: Doubleday, 1980.

Hartshorne, M. Holmes. "Honor Thy Father and Thy Mother." Sermon delivered at Colgate University Church, Hamilton, NY, May 4, 1975 (Parents' Weekend).

Hemingway, Ernest. *A Farewell to Arms*. New York: Scribner's, 1929.

Heschel, Abraham. "Children and Youth." In *The Insecurity of Freedom*, 39–51. New York: Schocken, 1972.

———. "Idols in the Temples." In *The Insecurity of Freedom*, 52–69. New York: Schocken, 1972.

Holmer, Paul L. *The Grammar of Faith*. San Francisco: Harper & Row, 1978.

James, William. *Talks to Teachers on Psychology: And to Students on Some of Life's Ideals.* New York: Norton, 1958.
Kerr, Hugh, and Charles H. Purday. "God of Our Life, Through All the Circling Years." In *Pilgrim Hymnal*, edited by James W. Lenhart, 97. Boston: Pilgrim, 1963.
Kierkegaard, Søren. *Fear and Trembling and The Sickness Unto Death.* Translated by Walter Lowrie. Princeton: Princeton University Press, 1968.
Killian, Michael. "Colgate Students Mourn Yet Another Death." *Syracuse Post-Standard*, March 15, 1989. 89.
King, Martin Luther, Jr. *A Knock at Midnight.* Recorded sermon. Nashville: Creed Records (Nashboro), 1980.
———. "Remaining Awake through a Great Revolution." Sermon delivered at the National Cathedral, Washington, DC, March 31, 1968. Online. https://kinginstitute.stanford.edu/king-papers/publications/knock-midnight-inspiration-great-sermons-reverend-martin-luther-king-jr-10.
Kistler, Jonathan H. "Unpublished Remarks Delivered at Colgate University Commencement." Hamilton, NY, May 28, 1972. Mimeographed copy.
Kunkel, Fritz. *In Search of Maturity: An Inquiry into Psychology, Religion, and Self-Education.* New York: Scribner's, 1943.
Lewis, C. S. *The Screwtape Letters.* New York: Macmillan, 1961.
Love and Death. Directed by Woody Allen. Beverly Hills: MGM, 1975.
Luccock, Halford. "The Gospel according to St. Mark: Exposition." In vol. 7 of *The Interpreter's Bible*, edited by George Arthur Buttrick, 827. New York: Abingdon-Cokesbury, 1951.
Lynch, William F. *Images of Hope: Imagination as Healer of the Hopeless.* New York: New American, 1966.
Marder, Janet. "The Meaning of Life: Thanksgiving 2001." Sermon delivered to Congregation Beth Am, Los Altos Hills, CA, November 23, 2001.
Matheson, George, and Albert L. Peace. "O Love That Wilt Not Let Me Go." In *Pilgrim Hymnal*, edited by James W. Lenhart, 399. Boston: Pilgrim, 1963.
Miller, Arthur. *After the Fall.* New York: Viking, 1964.
Newman, John Henry. *The Heart of Newman: A Synthesis.* Arranged by Erich Przywara. London: Burns and Oates, 1963.
Newton, John. "Amazing Grace." Arranged by Edwin O. Excell. In *Hymns, Psalms, and Spiritual Songs*, edited by the Presbyterian Church, 280. Louisville: Westminster John Knox, 1990.
Niebuhr, H. Richard. *The Responsible Self.* New York: Harper & Row, 1963.
Ordinary People. Directed by Robert Redford. Hollywood: Paramount Pictures, 1980.
Pascal, Blaise. *Pensées.* Everyman's Library. New York: Dutton, 1948.
Pieper, Josef. *The Four Cardinal Virtues.* Notre Dame: University of Notre Dame Press, 1966.
Pullman, Philip. "Paradise Lost: An Introduction." In *Daemon Voices: On Stories and Storytelling*, edited by Simon Mason, 47–67. New York: Knopf, 2018.
Putman, Curly. *Green, Green Grass of Home.* n.p.: 1964.
Raines, Robert A. *Going Home.* San Francisco: Harper & Row, 1979.
Russell, Bertrand. *Mysticism and Logic.* New York: Norton, 1929.
Schweitzer, Albert. *The Quest of the Historical Jesus.* New York: Macmillan, 1957.
Taylor, Gardner C. "At Calvary: Two Words at the End." In *How Shall They Preach?*, 141–48. Elgin, IL: Progressive Baptist, 1977.

———. "Judgment and Mercy at Palm Sunday." In *The Scarlet Thread*, 84–92. Elgin, IL: Progressive Baptist, 1981.

———. "Making a Great Promise Reasonable." In *The Scarlet Thread*, 49–55. Elgin, IL: Progressive Baptist, 1981.

Taylor, Vincent. *The Gospel according to St. Mark*. London: Macmillan, 1955.

Thielicke, Helmut. "The Parable of the Seed and the Soils." In *The Waiting Father: Sermons on the Parable of the Father*, translated by John W. Doberstein, 52–60. New York: Harper & Row, 1959.

———. "The Salt, Not the Honey of the World." In *Life Can Begin Again: Sermons on the Sermon on the Mount*, translated by John W. Doberstein, 24–34. Philadelphia: Fortress, 1963.

Thomas, Dylan. "And Death Shall Have No Dominion." In *The Collected Poems*, 77. New York: New Directions, 1953.

Tillich, Paul. "Knowledge through Love." In *The Shaking of the Foundations*, 108–17. New York: Scribner's, 1955.

Troeger, Thomas H. *Creating Fresh Images for Preaching*. Valley Forge, PA: Judson, 1982.

"We Are Climbing Jacob's Ladder" African-American Spiritual. In *Pilgrim Hymnal*, edited by James W. Lenhart, 495. Boston: Pilgrim, 1963.

Wittgenstein, Ludwig. *Philosophical Grammar*. Edited by Rush Rhees. Translated by Anthony Kenny. Oxford: Blackwell, 1974.

Wordsworth, William. "Poems of the Fancy, XX." In *The Poetical Works of Wordsworth*, edited by Thomas Hutchinson, 130. Revised by Ernest De Selincourt. London: Oxford University Press, 1969.

Zander, Walter. *Is This the Way? A Call to Jews*. London: V. Gollancz, 1948.